Price Waterhouse is a leading worldwide professional organization of accountants and auditors, tax advisers and management consultants. Through a global network of firms practicing in 450 offices within 110 countries and territories, Price Waterhouse professionals provide advisory services to businesses, individuals, government entities, and nonprofit organizations.

The Price Waterhouse U.S. firm frequently consults with the Treasury Department and the Internal Revenue Service on tax issues. The firm also offers seminars and publishes a variety of periodicals and booklets on tax and personal financial planning subjects.

Through its more than 100 U.S. offices and its legislative monitoring service in Washington, D.C., Price Waterhouse advises businesses and individuals nationwide on the planning and compliance implications of the tax law.

Price Waterhouse

If you would like more information on personal tax planning or retirement planning, look for our other publications that are part of **The Advisers Series**—*The Price Waterhouse Personal Tax Adviser* and *The Price Waterhouse Retirement Planning Adviser*.

Distributed by Pocket Books

THE PRICE WATERHOUSE

INVESTORS' TAX ADVISER

1991-1992 EDITION

New York   London   Toronto   Sydney   Tokyo   Singapore

POCKET BOOKS, a division of
Simon & Schuster Inc.,
1230 Avenue of the Americas,
New York, NY 10020.

Copyright © 1991 by Price Waterhouse and
Donna S. Carpenter.

ISBN: 0-671-74731-2

First Pocket Books printing November 1991

10 9 8 7 6 5 4 3 2 1

POCKET and colophon are registered trademarks of
Simon & Schuster Inc.

Printed in the U.S.A.

Contents

As We Went To Press . . .

Congress went on recess, leaving a number of wide-ranging tax proposals on the legislative table. If ultimately enacted later this year, these proposals may have an impact on your tax planning this year and in the future.

The legislators are considering a package of bills designed to simplify a variety of tax law provisions affecting both individuals and businesses. They are also debating separate bills to simplify various pension rules. The fate of the simplification legislation may depend on whether Congress enacts more substantive tax legislation, such as extending certain tax incentives slated to expire at the end of this year. If it does, some simplification provisions would most likely be attached. We cannot, of course, say for sure what the final outcome of any of these proposals will be, but forewarned is forearmed.

That said, here's a summary of some of the items being considered.

Tax simplification. The principal simplification package would include the following provisions for individuals:

- **Gain on the sale of your principal residence.** Effective on the date of enactment, the rules on the deferral of tax on gain realized on the sale of your principal residence would be liberalized. Specifically, you could roll over gain more than once within a two-year period. Also, you could roll over your gain from one home to another in the order the homes are purchased.

- **Due date for payment of estimated taxes.** Beginning with the 1992 tax year, the due date for the second estimated tax payment would be July 15th.

- **Payment of taxes by credit card.** You could pay your taxes using your credit card, subject to certain conditions.

- **Kiddie taxes.** Beginning with returns filed for 1992, the new rules would adjust for inflation the dollar amounts

vii

used in electing to include the unearned income of a child in your (the parent's) return. Also adjusted for inflation would be the amounts used to determine the exemption of a child under age 14 for purposes of alternative minimum tax (AMT).

- **Household employees.** If you employ a domestic worker you would pay the social security and federal unemployment (FUTA) taxes imposed on the worker's wages with your income tax return (and, where required, with quarterly estimated income tax payments). Also, the requirement to withhold and pay social security taxes would be raised from $50 in wages per quarter to $300 in wages per year.

Other tax measures proposed by members of Congress would affect:

- **Individual retirement accounts (IRAs).** Under one proposal, all taxpayers would be eligible to contribute to IRAs within limits. Also, there would be two types of IRAs: one would allow you to deduct fully your contribution. The other would not allow deductible contributions, but you could withdraw your earnings tax-free, provided you meet certain conditions. Both types would allow you to withdraw your money without penalty if you were a first-time home buyer or needed the money to meet education expenses or financially devastating medical expenses.

- **Middle income tax relief/higher tax rates for higher-income taxpayers.** Proposals under consideration would provide increased tax benefits for families with children, raise the top income tax rate, and impose a surtax on higher-income individuals.

- **Capital gains tax.** Various proposals call for reducing the tax on capital gains, particularly for investments made in start-up businesses.

- **Luxury tax.** The luxury tax currently imposed on the purchase of "big ticket" boats, airplanes, automobiles, furs, and jewelry would be repealed.

- **Expiring tax provisions.** Certain tax provisions, currently set to expire by the end of 1991, may be extended. These include allowing self-employed people to deduct 25 percent of their health insurance premiums and allowing employees to exclude from their income certain tuition reimbursements made by employers.

Additional tax proposals include increasing the gasoline excise tax, payroll taxes, and tax rates to pay for tax benefits or other programs including education.

Because the fate of these and other tax proposals was uncertain as we went to press, you should consult with your tax adviser to determine how any of these proposals, if enacted into law, may affect you.

Free Information on the Latest Tax Legislation

If Congress enacts these or any other **significant** tax proposals after publication of the 1991–1992 edition of *The Price Waterhouse Investors' Tax Adviser*, we will provide you— free of charge—with an update on the changes. Write to us with your name and address and ask for a complimentary copy of the Special Edition of *U.S. Taxes, Views & Reviews.*

Send your request to:

TAX UPDATE
PRICE WATERHOUSE
P.O. BOX 30048
TAMPA, FL 33630

This offer expires April 15, 1992.

Introduction

If the wild gyrations of the financial markets in the past few years accomplish nothing else useful, they remind us that uncertainty is every investor's unbidden companion.

We ignore uncertainty at our peril. That's why smart investors seek ways to profit regardless of whether the markets go up or head down. One of those ways is to keep more of the money you make from investing in your pocket—not Uncle Sam's.

That's where *The Price Waterhouse Investors' Tax Adviser* comes in. The purpose of our volume is to provide you with the information you need to keep more of what you make from your investments in *your* pocket—not Uncle Sam's.

Our book explains in plain English how you can legally and honestly slash your federal tax liabilities. And it provides strategies for paring down your tax bill.

What's more, it alerts you to little-known rules and regulations that may—if you aren't careful—cost you hundreds of dollars or more in extra taxes.

Being aware of the tax implications of your investments is even more important than you might think. Why? Because cutting your tax bill to the legal minimum can dramatically affect your after-tax return, particularly over the long haul.

Here's an example: Say you're a taxpayer in the 28 percent tax bracket, you're married and file a joint return, and you have $10,000 to invest. You want to know whether you'll earn more in a tax-free municipal bond fund that currently yields 5 percent or in a fully taxable mutual fund that yields 7 percent.

If you invest in a municipal bond fund, the income from that fund, which you choose to reinvest in the same fund, is exempt from federal income taxes.

During the first year, your investment will grow to $10,500. What about in subsequent years? If the yield remains the same—that is, 5 percent annually—your investment will multiply to $16,289 over 10 years and to $26,533 over 20 years.

Now, say you choose to invest your $10,000 in a fully taxable mutual fund. Assuming that the yield holds at 7 percent, you remain in the 28 percent bracket, and you reinvest your earnings, your investment will grow to $10,504 by the end of year one, after you subtract $196 in taxes. Your after-tax return adds up to 5.04 percent—not the advertised pretax yield of 7 percent.

What if you hold the investment for ten years? It will grow to $16,351—only $62 more than if you'd invested the same amount in the municipal bond fund. And if you hold the investment for 20 years, it will grow to $26,736—only $203 more than if you'd invested your dollars in the municipal bond fund.

So, as a taxpayer in the 28 percent bracket, you're only slightly better off putting your money in the taxable mutual fund than the tax-free municipal bond fund.

But let's change the scenario just slightly. Say you're a taxpayer in the 31 percent bracket, married, and file a joint return.

If you invest $10,000 in a mutual fund earning 7 percent, it will grow to $10,483 by the end of year one, after you subtract $217 in taxes.

By the end of ten years, your investment will grow to

$16,027, and, by the end of 20 years, $25,687—or $846 less than if you'd invested in the municipal bond fund. And, if you're subject to the new itemized deduction limitation and the phaseout of personal exemptions (see Chapter 1 for details) your effective marginal tax rate may be higher than 31 percent, thereby further reducing your after-tax return from a taxable mutual fund.

So, your pretax yield of 7 percent becomes an annual after-tax yield of only 4.83 percent—0.17 percent less than the yield on the municipal bond fund. That means, as a taxpayer in the 31 percent bracket, you're slightly better off putting your money in the municipal bond fund.

Although a discussion of the tax rules of the various states would fill an encyclopedia, one last example illustrates the dramatic difference between investing in a taxable versus tax-free fund if you live in a state, such as California or New York, which levies its own tax on individual income. Let's say you're in the 28 percent bracket for federal income tax and an 8 percent bracket for state income tax. Your net effective tax rate is 34 percent (we'll show you how we reached 34, not 36, percent in Chapter 2).

With a 7 percent taxable fund, your investment is worth $10,462 in year one. Your $700 pretax interest dwindles to $462 as a result of your federal and state tax burdens, effectively leaving you with an annual after-tax yield of 4.62 percent. Compare this yield to the 5 percent tax-free (make sure to check with your tax adviser that those bonds are also tax-free for state tax purposes). After 20 years, your initial $10,000 has grown to $24,677, compared to $26,533 or $1,856 less than if you invested the same $10,000 in the tax-exempt fund.

The moral of these simple examples is clear. You must take the impact of taxes into account in planning your investment strategies and in assessing the return on your investments. Further, there's only one way to really know the impact of taxes on your return from your investments, and that is to know the rules and to run the numbers. Once you know the numbers, you can make informed investment choices based on the economics of the investment as well as other non-tax considerations (for example, your risk tolerance and your long- or short-range investment goals).

Obviously, taxes do make a difference—often a big difference—in the amount of money you'll realize from your investments. So, we hope what you learn from this book will help you become a more astute—and, therefore, more successful—investor.

1

Mastering The Fundamentals

What counts as income when it comes to your investments? Income from every source is subject to taxation. One exception to this rule, however, is income from a municipal bond or municipal bond fund, for example, that's specifically excluded by law.

In this section, we run through the entire menu of *taxable* and *nontaxable* income—from interest and dividends to gains from the sale of stocks and mutual fund shares. A host of specific tax-saving strategies also are provided.

Before beginning, though, we must outline a few definitions because these terms are used frequently in this chapter—and the ones that follow.

Your *taxable income* is the amount on which your federal income tax is calculated. You determine your taxable income by subtracting your allowable deductions from your income from all sources—wages, dividends, interest, and so on.

Your *marginal tax rate* is the rate you pay on your last dollar of taxable income. Let's say you're single, and your taxable income adds up to $43,800 in 1991; your last dollar is

5

taxed at 28 percent. Your marginal tax rate, then, is 28 percent.

Even though there are presently far fewer rates than there were in the past, it's still important to know your marginal rate if you're considering making an investment. That way, you can calculate the tax consequences of your decision.

Your *effective tax rate*, on the other hand, is the overall rate at which your income is taxed. You calculate this rate by dividing your total tax bill by your taxable income. For example, you're married, file jointly, and your taxable income in 1991 comes to $42,113. On that amount, you pay 15 percent on your first $34,000 of income, or $5,100, and 28 percent on the remaining $8,113, or $2,272, for a total tax bill of $7,372.

Divide your total tax bill—$7,372—by your taxable income—$42,113. The result—18 percent—is your effective tax rate.

Tax Rates

The law contains three regular tax brackets, 15 percent, 28 percent and 31 percent. To make it easy for you, we've put together a tax rate schedule for 1991. Here it is:

Single	
$ 0 to $ 20,350	15%
20,351 to 49,300	28
49,301 or more	31

Head of household	
$ 0 to $ 27,300	15%
27,301 to 70,450	28
70,451 or more	31

Married filing jointly and surviving spouse	
$ 0 to $ 34,000	15%
34,001 to 82,150	28
82,151 or more	31

Married filing separately	
$ 0 to $ 17,000	15%
17,001 to 41,075	28
41,076 or more	31

Keep in mind that the income levels at which these rates apply are adjusted each year for inflation. So the scheduled rates we just gave apply only in 1991.

Beginning in 1991, tax rates are also affected by a special 28 percent maximum tax on long-term capital gain income. See Chapter 4 for the lowdown on how this special tax rate may affect the tax you will owe.

HIDDEN TAX INCREASES

You may recall that in previous years a 33 percent *surtax* rate applied to a range of earnings of higher-income taxpayers. This surtax phased out the benefit of the 15 percent tax bracket and the benefit of personal exemptions.

The good news is that this higher 33 percent tax rate has been repealed for years after 1990.

Although the maximum tax rate is now 31 percent, the bad news is that your *effective marginal tax rate* may actually be higher because of two new wrinkles in the tax law—the phase-out of personal exemptions and the floor on certain itemized deductions.

Neither of these items directly increases the tax rate applied to your income. Rather, they both decrease the amounts you may deduct in calculating your taxable income, thereby increasing your *effective* marginal tax rate.

Let's take a look.

Personal exemption phase-out

Beginning in 1991, Congress has changed the way personal exemptions are phased out. Instead of the previous 5 percent surtax, the amount of the personal exemption deduction you can claim is now actually reduced when your adjusted gross income (AGI) exceeds designated trigger levels.

As with many other limits now in effect, these trigger levels are indexed to inflation.

The trigger levels are:

- $150,000 for married couples filing jointly and surviving spouses

- $125,000 for heads of household

- $100,000 for single people

- $75,000 for married couples filing separately

The deduction for personal exemptions is phased-out by 2 percent for each $2,500, or fraction of $2,500, that your AGI tops the trigger point. The phase-out rate is 4 percent for married persons filing separately. Sounds confusing? It's not as bad as it appears.

To calculate the phase-out amount, you first subtract the trigger level from your AGI. Next, you divide the remainder into increments of $2,500. Since the rules say you lose 2 percent for each increment of $2,500 or fraction of $2,500, you must always round the result up to the next whole number. (For example, 10.1 is rounded up to 11.)

Now take that number and multiply by 2 percent (4 percent if married filing separately). This is the percentage of the personal exemption deduction that you lose. Here's an example.

Say your AGI for 1991 totals $201,000. You are married, have 2 children and file a joint return. So you have 4 exemptions, which gives you a total personal exemption deduction before the phase-out of $8,600 (4 times $2,150).

The difference between your AGI ($201,000) and the trigger level for married individuals filing a joint return ($150,000) is $51,000. $51,000 divided by $2,500 comes to 20.4. Now round the 20.4 up to 21 and multiply it by 2 percent, which gives you 42 percent. The result? Your deduction for personal exemptions is reduced by $3,612 ($8,600 times 42 percent). You get to deduct $4,988 ($8,600 minus $3,612).

The phase-out range is in effect for the following levels of income (after the upper limits, you lose entirely the benefit of your personal exemptions):

- $150,001 through $272,501 for married couples filing jointly and surviving spouses

- $125,001 through $247,501 for heads of household

- $100,001 through $222,501 for single people

- $75,001 through $136,251 for married couples filing separately

What do these new rules mean in cold hard cash? The maximum tax savings of one personal exemption is $667 ($2,150 times the maximum tax rate of 31 percent). In the example we just gave, the phase-out of personal exemptions would cost you an additional $1,120 in tax ($667 times 4 exemptions times 42 percent).

If your adjusted gross income falls within the exemption phase-out range, the phase-out has the effect of increasing your effective marginal tax rate by approximately 0.53 percent for each exemption you claim. So the effective marginal tax rate for the couple in our example increases from 31 percent to more than 33 percent.

Itemized deduction floor

Here's the second new wrinkle in the tax law that affects returns for 1991 and beyond: It's a new "floor" on itemized deductions. If your AGI exceeds the threshold amounts designated by Uncle Sam, a portion of your itemized deductions will not be deductible.

The threshold amount is $100,000 ($50,000 for married couples filing seperately).

Uncle Sam imposes the floor on all expenses that would otherwise be deductible—with the exception of medical expenses, casualty and theft losses, investment interest, and gambling losses to the extent of gambling winnings.

The rules require you to reduce these otherwise allowable deductions by an amount equal to 3 percent of the amount of your AGI that tops the treshold. These itemized deductions, however, will never be reduced by more than 80 percent. (You should know that only very high-income taxpayers will be affected by this 80 percent limit.)

In other words, to figure the reduction, you must make two calculations. Confused? Here's an example.

Say you're married, file jointly, and your AGI in 1991 adds up to $200,000. You tally up your itemized deductions and come up with the following totals: $11,000 in state and local taxes, $7,000 in mortgage interest, $1,000 in investment interest, and $2,000 in charitable contributions—or a total of $21,000.

Now, since your AGI of $200,000 tops the threshold of $100,000 set by Uncle Sam, the rules require you to reduce the amount of itemized deductions you claim on your return by either:

- 3 percent of the excess of your AGI over the threshold, or

- 80 percent of the deductions, whichever is less.

So, first you subtract the threshold amount—$100,000—from your AGI of $200,000 and multiply the sum—$100,000—times 3 percent. The result is $3,000.

Now, 80 percent of the sum of your state and local taxes, mortgage interest, and charitable contributions—80 percent of $20,000—equals $16,000. (Keep in mind that you ignore the $1,000 investment interest expense—and any medical expenses, casualty and theft losses, or gambling losses, if you'd deducted those items—when you calculate the 80 percent limitation.)

Since $3,000 is less than $16,000, your floor is $3,000. So you may deduct a total of $18,000 in itemized deductions—that is, the $1,000 in investment interest that's not subject to the floor, plus the $17,000 that remains once you subtract $3,000 from the rest of your deductions.

If you are subject to the 3 percent floor, your marginal tax rate effectively increases by 0.93 percent. That means it jumps from a top rate of 31 percent to nearly 32 percent.

 **CAUTION** When you compute the reduction, you must first apply any other

limitations on itemized deductions. Your miscellaneous itemized deductions, for example, are first subject to a 2 percent
floor, then lumped in with the other itemized deductions and
subject to the new 3 percent floor. We'll see how the 2 percent
floor works in Chapter 7.

OTHER MATTERS

Before we move on, a few more words to the wise.

You—not your tax preparer—are responsible for reporting
all the income you receive on your federal income tax return.
So, you should keep accurate records of all the money you
take in. Otherwise, you may overlook something.

And, if you haven't already, make sure you let any financial institution you do business with know your taxpayer identification number—for most investors, their Social Security
number. You do so by filling out Form W-9, "Request for
Taxpayer Identification Number and Certification," which the
institution will send you.

If you don't? The institution may withhold 20 percent of
your earnings toward taxes. As a result, you may end up making a tax-free loan to Uncle Sam for the amount withheld.
What's worse, you may find yourself subject to a civil penalty
of $50. Not a pleasant prospect.

Here's something else you should know: Investment income
is taxable to you in the year you receive it or—in IRS
jargon—constructively receive it. You constructively receive
income when the amount is either credited to your account or
made available to you.

In other words, you don't have to pocket the money for it to
be taxable. For example, you own stock in XYZ Corp. On
December 27, 1991, XYZ dividend income is credited to your

brokerage account for remittance to you by the broker. However, due to the holiday weekend, your broker does not remit the dividend check to you until January 3, 1992.

Even though you don't receive the check until the new year, you still must report that amount as income in 1991. The reason: In the eyes of the government, you had constructive receipt of the money, since it was available to you on December 27, 1991.

If you'd like more information on how investment income is taxed, ask the IRS to send you a free copy of its Publication 550, *Investment Income and Expenses*. You also may find Publication 564, *Mutual Fund Distributions*, helpful.

Now, let's move on to what's taxable—and what's not—when it comes to your investments, beginning, in the next chapter, with the interest you receive.

2

Get Smart About Interest Income

Uncle Sam wants to make sure you pay federal taxes on *all* your interest income. That's why he requires payers of interest, such as banks and savings and loans, to report to the federal government the amounts of interest they pay and to whom.

He says these institutions must mail you a Form 1099-INT, "Statement for Recipients of Interest Income," by the end of the last day of January of the new tax year.

What if you don't receive your Form 1099-INT within a few weeks of that date, or you do receive your form but disagree with the amount of interest reported? Telephone or write the institution and ask for a duplicate or explain why the number listed is incorrect.

The institution will mail you a copy of your 1099 or, if it agrees that the number is wrong, issue you an entirely new form. When you receive your new 1099, though, make sure it's marked "corrected," so there's no confusion about which form is the right one.

What if you continue to disagree with the amount listed? Report what you think is the correct number on your return and include an explanation of the change. You don't need to attach your 1099 to your return—in this case or any other.

Simply report your total interest income on line 8a of your Form 1040. If, however, your total taxable interest comes to more than $400, make sure to complete Schedule B—Interest and Dividend Income—and attach it to your return. Also, before you sign your tax return, compare the amount on your return with that recorded on all your Forms 1099-INT to make sure that you haven't forgotten anything.

If you fail to report all your interest income, Uncle Sam may slap you with a penalty equal to 20 percent of the additional tax due. Also, you pay interest on the additional tax beginning on the day your income tax return was due.

TAXABLE INVESTMENT INTEREST

Most of us know that interest from bank accounts is taxable. What are other sources of taxable investment interest? Here's our list, in alphabetical order.

Interest on annuities

We know—mention the word *annuity* and your eyes glaze over. But annuities offer you a host of benefits—guaranteed principal, interest that accumulates tax-deferred, and monthly checks for the rest of your life. Now, are you interested in annuities?

Annuities are savings plans that are sponsored by insurance companies. They promise to pay you a regular income, in most cases, starting the day you retire and running for the rest of your life. The size of these payments depends on your life expectancy, the amount of dollars you've contributed, and the interest rate the insurance carrier uses.

When it comes to annuities, Uncle Sam imposes a whole host of complicated rules and regulations that are covered in detail in Chapter 14.

Interest on certificates of deposit

When stocks are on the rise, few investors are entranced by certificates of deposit (CDs), which are issued primarily by banks and savings and loans. But the popularity of CDs rises when the market is down or the economic outlook appears uncertain.

You normally buy certificates of deposit for terms ranging from several days to several years. When you invest in a CD, you let your bank or other institution use your cash for a specified period of time and, in exchange, receive a competitive rate of interest.

What if you cash out of your CD early?

Your bank or savings and loan will likely slap you with an early, or premature, withdrawal penalty that's sometimes as large as the entire amount of interest due you.

The following are some strategies that will help you get the most out of your CDs.

TIP CDs are available not only from banks and thrifts but brokerage firms as well. And, certificates from brokerage houses often pay a higher rate of interest because brokerages buy CDs in bulk from banks and can negotiate a higher rate of interest.

Most brokerages don't slap you with a penalty for early withdrawal. Why? Brokerages make a secondary market in CDs. What does that mean to you? If you want to cash out of your CD early, your broker will sell your certificate to another investor.

TIP So you want to defer interest income on CDs from one year to the next? Then buy a certificate that matures in the following year.

Unless you receive interest—or interest is credited to your account and made available for withdrawal—during the current year, Uncle Sam will tax your earnings when you receive them—that is, when the CD becomes due.

This tax strategy applies *only* to certificates with a maturity of one year or less. With CDs of longer maturities, you report the amount of interest the certificate earns annually—even if you don't actually pocket the cash.

 TIP When you withdraw money before maturity, Uncle Sam treats the early withdrawal penalty as an adjustment to your gross income. That means you reduce your gross income for tax purposes by deducting the early withdrawal penalty.

Here's how to do the calculation: Report the gross amount of interest paid or credited to your account during the year without subtracting the penalty. The interest you receive and the early withdrawal penalty count as two separate transactions—at least as far as Uncle Sam is concerned.

Then, you write off the penalty in full as an adjustment to your income on page one of your Form 1040. You'll find the amount you should deduct on your tax return on Form 1099-INT, in the box labeled ''Early withdrawal penalty.''

Here's something else you should know: Many banks won't allow you to cash in a portion of your CD. When it comes to withdrawing your money, it's all or nothing. However, you may be able to withdraw interest you earn at any time during the term of the CD.

 TIP When it comes to investing in CDs, most banks and savings and loans set a minimum deposit amount, as well as a minimum term of maturity. Sometimes investors even borrow money from the same bank or thrift in order to meet the minimum deposit requirement.

Let's say your bank offers a $10,000, six-month CD that pays an annual yield of 8 percent. You invest in the CD—using $9,000 of your own money and $1,000 you borrowed from the bank that's offering the CD. Your annual interest rate on the loan is 14 percent.

The CD earns you $400 in interest but you receive only $330—that is, your $400 in interest income minus the $70 in interest on your $1,000 loan. The bank mails you a Form 1099-INT reporting $400 in interest income. It also mails you a statement listing your $70 in interest expense.

How are these items treated on your return?

You include the $400 in your interest income for the year. Then you write off the $70 in interest expense as an itemized deduction on Schedule A of your Form 1040. What if you don't itemize? That's bad news; you lose the deduction.

Interest earned by your children

Some parents open savings accounts for their children, then list themselves as custodian of the account. Interest on these accounts is taxable to the child as long as the account legally belongs to the child, and the parents don't use any of the funds to support the child.

However, unearned income—including interest income—of minor children under age 14 may be taxed at the parents' rates if that rate is higher. Once children reach the age of 14, though, it's a different story. Their unearned income is taxed at their own rates.

Your children are required to file tax returns if they receive unearned income greater than $550 or if their gross income exceeds the standard deduction.

In some cases, though, Uncle Sam allows you to report your children's unearned income on your tax return to avoid the hassle of filing separately for your children. You do so by filing Form 8814, "Parent's Election to Report Child's Interest and Dividends," with your Form 1040.

In which cases may you do so?

Uncle Sam says you may report your children's unearned income on your return if a child reports unearned income of no less than $500 but no more than $5,000, and this amount consists only of interest and dividends (including Alaska Permanent Fund dividends).

Another requirement must be met. The child must have no earned income—say, from babysitting or running errands for the local drugstore—to report.

Still another requirement is that the child must be under the age of 14 at the close of the tax year. Also, the child must have made no estimated tax or withholding payments under his or her name and/or under his or her own Social Security number.

If you do elect to include your child's unearned income on your return, Uncle Sam treats your child as if he or she had no gross income for the year. And your child won't have to file a return.

Instead, you add your child's gross unearned income of more than $1,100 to your—the parents'—gross income on your return.

Here's how the IRS taxes this amount: You pay no tax at all on the first $550 of unearned income—thanks to the standard deduction. You pay a flat 15 percent tax on the second $550 of unearned income. Then, you're taxed at your highest marginal rate on any remaining unearned income.

☞ **CAUTION** Reporting your child's unearned income on your return won't increase your combined federal tax liability, but it may boost your combined state tax bill.

Why? Your child's income may be low enough to escape state taxes if he or she filed a separate state tax return. But when you add your child's income to your own, the amount is almost certain to be subject to state income taxes—and at your highest marginal bracket.

 TIP Uncle Sam lets you help your children accumulate money for some future goal—to pay for college, for example. It's easy. You just transfer some of your income-producing assets to your children, and the interest (or other income) on those investments is taxable to them.

You may give up to $10,000 a year to each child—$20,000 if your spouse joins in the giving—with no tax consequences. The money each child earns is taxable at his or her rate, as long as the child is 14 years of age or older.

TIP One of the least complicated ways to give money is under the Uniform Gifts to Minors Act (UGMA) or the Uniform Transfers to Minors Act (UTMA).

What's the difference between the two acts? The UGMA covers gifts of money or intangibles, such as cash, stocks, or bonds. The other—UTMA—includes gifts of "real property," which in IRS jargon is real estate.

These acts allow parents—or anyone for that matter—to give money or other property to a child, keeping it under the control of a custodian. The custodian may be a family member, a legal guardian, or any trusted adult that you may choose.

Banks, mutual-fund companies, and brokerage firms can provide all the necessary forms for setting up a UGMA or

UTMA account, and there are no legal fees involved in establishing one.

Gifts under either act are treated as true gifts for federal gift tax purposes. Accordingly, parents or other donors can't take back any of the money or other property they've given nor use the property for their own benefit. Income from the property is taxable to the child unless, under applicable state laws, it's used to satisfy any person's legal obligation to support the child.

Dividends that are taxed as interest

☞ CAUTION   When is money labeled "dividends" really interest? Uncle Sam says you must report as interest so-called dividends on deposits in money-market certificates, savings certificates, cooperative banks, credit unions, savings-and-loan associations, and mutual savings banks.

☞ CAUTION   Don't make the mistake some taxpayers do and assume that interest you have earned on money-market funds is taxed as interest. It's not; it's taxed as dividends.

You won't go wrong if you report the income on your tax return as your bank or other financial institution reports it to you. Interest income is listed on a Form 1099-INT, while dividend income is listed on a Form 1099-DIV. (Dividends are covered in Chapter 3.)

Interest from foreign accounts

If you earn interest from bank accounts or trusts established outside the United States, here's something you should know. You may be required to pay taxes on the interest you've earned in the foreign country—and sometimes at rates that are much higher than those in the United States.

You're also required to pay taxes in the United States. In fact, as a U.S. citizen or resident, you must pay taxes on all your worldwide income.

But here's where Uncle Sam gives you a break. If you're required to pay taxes in the foreign country, he allows you to either deduct those taxes as "other taxes" on Schedule A of your Form 1040, or claim those taxes as a credit on Form 1116, "Foreign Tax Credit," which you attach to your personal tax return.

The credit is generally limited to the amount of U.S. tax paid that's attributable to foreign income. In other words, you end up paying tax on the income at the higher of the two tax rates. It usually makes sense to claim the credit rather than the deduction, since credits reduce your tax dollar-for-dollar. Deductions, on the other hand, simply reduce the amount of your income subject to tax.

☞ **CAUTION** Calculating the foreign tax credit can be extremely complicated, so you should consult your tax adviser if the need arises.

💵 **TIP** If you earn interest income abroad, you must report it on your U.S. tax return in U.S. dollars. And you should attach a schedule to your return that shows how you converted the foreign interest into U.S. dollars. Generally, you use the exchange rate prevailing at the time the interest was paid to you or credited to your account. If interest was earned ratably throughout the year, you may use the average annual exchange rate.

☞ **CAUTION** If you have any foreign bank or financial accounts, be sure to complete Part III of Schedule B of your Form 1040 by answering the questions relating thereto. In addition, if the combined value of the accounts is more than $10,000 during any entire year, you're required to file Form TD F 90-22.1, "Report of foreign bank and financial accounts," with the Department of the Treasury by June 30 of the following year.

For more information on how Uncle Sam taxes your foreign income, ask the IRS for a free copy of its Publication 514, *Foreign Tax Credit for Individuals*.

Interest on frozen assets

If you deposited money at a savings and loan that went belly up, do you pay taxes on the interest credited to your account—even though you can't withdraw the money?

The good news is that Uncle Sam allows you to exclude from taxes amounts that were credited to your account during the year, but you were unable to withdraw by the end of the year. Any interest you exclude under this rule is treated as credited to your account in the next calendar year and becomes taxable when it's available for withdrawal.

Gifts for making deposits

☞ CAUTION Now, here's something you may not know. If you receive a toaster—or any other gift—for making a long-term deposit, the value of that item is taxed as interest income.

You open a money-market account at a local bank. The account earns you $600 in interest. In addition, you receive a free $10 pocket calculator. What happens if you forget about your gift?

At the end of the year, the bank sends you a Form 1099-INT. It lists interest income of $610—that is, the $600 of interest plus $10 for the calculator.

Interest on investments in an IRA or Keogh

You do not pay taxes on interest earned on investments in an Individual Retirement Account (IRA) until you withdraw the money—usually at retirement. Likewise, you pay no taxes on interest earned on investments in a Keogh plan until you withdraw the money, again, usually at retirement.

☞ CAUTION   Uncle Sam caps your annual contributions to IRAs and Keoghs. What if you inadvertently exceed these limits?

The rules require you to withdraw the excess plus any interest you've earned on the excess amount. This interest is subject to taxes. What's more, the IRS may slap you with a penalty for contributing more than you should. For more information on this topic, turn to Chapter 17.

Interest on installment sales

It used to be that you could give up interest income taxed at ordinary rates and replace it with a larger long-term capital gain taxed at a lower rate.

The strategy worked like this. You'd sell a piece of property—an apartment building, say—for an inflated price in order to receive a larger long-term capital gain and, in turn, agree to accept deferred payments carrying little or no interest.

But Uncle Sam zapped this tactic.

In the case of installment sales with payments due more than one year after the date of sale, he says a portion of payments made six months after the sale contain interest. In other words, if you don't charge interest at the minimum rate he prescribes, then you must treat a portion of the principal payment as interest. You also must pay tax on that interest in the year you receive the related payments.

Calculating the amount of interest is exceedingly complicated. Our advice? If you find yourself in this situation, seek the help of a professional.

TIP These rules don't apply to installment sales of $3,000 or less. For more information on the installment sales rules, see Chapter 5.

If you'd like more information on installment sales, ask the IRS for a free copy of its Publication 537, *Installment Sales*.

Interest from joint accounts

You and a friend are joint owners of a savings account. Who reports the interest income? The answer is both of you. You report the amount of interest attributable to the money you deposited in the account; your friend should do the same.

☞ **CAUTION** Financial institutions usually report interest income under the Social Security number of only one person, even if two or more people own the account. So, you face a potential problem by reporting only your share of income. The IRS may issue a deficiency notice to the person whose Social Security number is listed.

Why? He or she didn't report the full amount.

Here's a way to avoid this problem.

Let's say you and your sister are joint owners of a savings account, and the interest the account earns is reported in your name and under your Social Security number. You should complete a Form 1099-INT no later than January 31 of the following tax year, and give Copy B to your sister.

You must also complete a Form 1096, "Annual Summary and Transmittal of U.S. Information Returns," and file it with Form 1099-INT no later than February 28 of the following tax year. On Form 1099-INT, list yourself as the payer and your sister as the recipient.

Now, on line 1, Schedule B, of your Form 1040, include with your share of interest the amount of interest that is attributed to your sister. Then, several lines above line 2, subtotal the amounts listed on line 1.

Below this subtotal, write "nominee distribution" and list the amount reported to you but belonging to your sister. Then subtract this amount from the subtotal.

List the result—which is your share of the interest income—on line 2.

Interest on market discount bonds

Market discount bonds, which can include both corporate and government bonds, have a coupon interest rate—that is, a stated interest rate—of less than the prevailing market rate of interest on bonds of a similar quality and maturity. Therefore, these bonds usually sell for less than their stated redemption price.

For example, assume that on July 1, 1988, a ten-year bond was issued for $10,000. It pays interest semiannually at an eight percent rate and will be redeemed at maturity for its issue price of $10,000.

On July 1, 1991, the prevailing market rate of interest on similar bonds has increased. So, you may be able to purchase the bond from its original holder for $9,000. The difference between the bond's $10,000 stated redemption price and

$9,000—the price you paid—comes to $1,000, representing the market discount. The discount, in effect, compensates you for the lower interest you'll earn on the bond compared to similar bonds.

☞ **CAUTION**   A bond could be originally issued at a discount—called "original issue discount" (OID). Then, because of rising interest rates, that bond could be subsequently sold with an additional market discount. The amount of market discount in this case is the excess of the original issue price plus the total OID includible in the income of all previous holders of the bond over the subsequent purchase price.

For example, you purchase a bond for $9,500, and the bond has a stated redemption price of $10,000. The previous bondholder—who sold you the bond—acquired it at its original issue price of $9,000. By the time he sold you the bond, he had reported $600 of the total OID of $1,000 as income. Your market discount comes to $100—that is, the issue price of $9,000, plus the $600 of OID reported by the previous bondholder, minus your $9,500 purchase price.

We discuss the treatment of OID later in this chapter. For now, you should simply be aware that OID generally represents the discount offered by the issuer of the bond. Market discount, by contrast, is the discount a subsequent bondholder offers. And the tax treatment Uncle Sam accords to each type of discount differs.

The tax treatment of market discount depends upon the date the bond was originally issued. Also, depending upon when you acquired the bond, you may be able to elect special tax treatment.

As a general rule, for market discount bonds issued before July 19, 1984, Uncle Sam treats any gain you realize when you dispose of the bond—to the extent of the discount—as capital gain. You should know that a disposition includes not only a sale or exchange of the bond, but also a redemption of the bond at its maturity date.

For example, a bond was issued on January 1, 1984, for $5,000. You purchased this bond on July 1, 1988, for $4,500—that is, for a discount of $500. On July 1, 1991, you sell the same bond for $4,700. Uncle Sam treats your profit of $200 as a long-term capital gain.

Different rules apply to market discount bonds issued after July 18, 1984. For these bonds, any gain you realize when you dispose of the bond is treated as interest income—that is, as ordinary income, not capital gain—to the extent of the bond's "accrued market discount" through the sale date. Uncle Sam treats any additional gain as capital gain. (Of course, if you sell any market discount bond for less than its purchase price, you post a capital loss.)

How do you figure accrued market discount? The law gives you two choices. The first is known as the "ratable accrual method." Under this method, you treat the total market discount as accruing in equal daily installments over the period that you hold the bond.

In other words, you divide the total market discount by the number of days after you acquire the bond through the bond's maturity date. Then you multiply that amount—the daily market discount—by the number of days that you actually hold the bond.

The result is the accrued market discount at the date you sell the bond. Of course, if you hold the bond until it matures, the accrued market discount equals the total market discount on the bond.

Here's an example. You purchase a bond on September 2,

1990, for $9,200. The bond matures 800 days later—on November 10, 1992—for $10,000. Your total market discount is, of course, $800.

Now, let's say that you decide to sell the bond on April 24, 1992—600 days after you acquired it. Under the ratable accrual method, your accrued market discount would come to $600—that is, $800 (total market discount) divided by 800 days (total days to maturity) times 600 days (the number of days you held the bond.)

The second way to determine accrued market discount is the "constant interest method." This complex method also applies to certain original issue discount bonds—a subject we'll discuss later in this chapter.

In general, the constant interest method corresponds to the actual economic accrual of interest. You compute accrued market discount for each one-year period—beginning on the date you acquire the bond and each anniversary date thereafter—by multiplying your cost basis (what you paid for the bond) plus any previously accrued market discount, by the bond's yield to maturity. Then you subtract any interest actually paid on the bond during that period. (A discounted bond's yield to maturity—which your broker can calculate for you—will be greater than its stated interest rate because of the discount.)

Repeat this calculation for each subsequent period you hold the bond. When you sell the bond, you allocate accrued market discount for the one-year period that includes the sale date over the number of days you actually hold the bond during that period.

Under this method, accrued market discount for each one-year period will increase each year because of the compounding of the accrued market discount. So at any given disposition date, accrued market discount under the constant interest method will be less than under the ratable accrual method. And—you guessed it—that means that Uncle Sam will tax less of your gain as ordinary income.

Confused? Let's say that on January 1, 1991, you acquired a 10-year, 10 percent bond for $9,500. The bond was issued on January 1, 1986, for its redemption price of $10,000. Your total market discount is, of course, $500. And you'll receive interest payments of $1,000 for each full year you hold the bond. The bond has a yield to maturity of 11.3653 percent.

For 1991, your accrued market discount using the ratable accrual method comes to $100 ($500 times 364 days divided by 1,826 days). Under the constant interest method, however, your accrued market discount would come to only $80 ($9,500 times 11.3653 percent, less $1,000).

Then, in 1992, your accrued market discount would again total $100 under the ratable accrual method. But it would total only $89 under the constant interest method ($9,500 plus $80 equals $9,580; $9,580 times 11.3653 percent minus $1,000 equals $89).

The table that follows compares the accrual of market discount under both methods:

Year	Ratable Accrual	Constant Interest
1991	$100	$80
1992	100	89
1993	100	99
1994	100	110
1995	100	122
TOTAL:	$500	$500

Once you elect to use the constant interest method for a particular bond, you may not change the election for that bond, although you may use the ratable accrual method for other bonds. For more information on this method, see IRS Publication 1212, *List of Original Discount Instruments*, or consult your tax adviser.

As we've seen, Uncle Sam generally recognizes market discount as income when you dispose of the bond—either by selling it or redeeming it at maturity. And, depending upon when the bond was issued, the income counts either as capital gain or as ordinary interest income.

However, a special rule lets you elect to report market discount as current income, rather than waiting until you sell or redeem the bond. That is, you report the accrued market discount—using either the ratable accrual or constant rate method—as interest income on your tax return each year you hold the bond.

Why would you want to recognize the income currently, rather than wait to pay the tax? There aren't a lot of reasons, but one may be that you expect your tax rate to increase in future years and want to take advantage of lower rates now.

Here's another reason: You borrowed money to purchase the bond. In this case, you may want to recognize income currently in order to avoid a special rule that limits the amount of interest expense you may deduct each year on the loan.

What is this special rule? Generally, if your interest expense tops the interest income you earn on the bond during the year, you may deduct an amount equal to the interest income plus the amount, if any, by which the excess interest expense tops your accrued but unreported market discount for the year.

For example, in 1991, you take out a loan to buy a market discount bond. You earn $500 of interest on the bond. In addition, your accrued market discount for the year—which you don't have to report currently—comes to $50.

Let's say that you pay interest of $625 on the loan you took out to buy the bond. You may deduct only $575 of that amount—that is, $500 (the amount of interest income) plus $75 (excess interest expense of $125, less accrued market discount of $50). The $50 you are not allowed to deduct becomes deductible when you dispose of the bond. Or, you can elect to deduct the excess in any other year to the extent that your interest income from the bond tops your interest expense on the loan in that year.

Finally, when you dispose of the bond, you can deduct any remaining disallowed interest expense. Your gain on the disposition of the bond is treated as ordinary income to the extent of such deductible interest plus accrued but unreported market discount. The IRS treats any additional gain as long-term capital gain.

If you elect to report your accrued market discount currently, however, you are not subject to any of these special interest disallowance rules. So, in our example, you could deduct the full amount of interest expense—$625 (subject to the investment interest expense limitations discussed in Chapter 6). Of course, you would also have to report the $50 of accrued market discount.

If you *do* opt to report this income currently, make certain you've thought through the consequences carefully. For instance, in this case, the election gives you $50 more in deductions, but also $50 more in income. The bottom line? Your tax bill may not change.

☞ **CAUTION** The law states that you may not change your mind once you begin reporting your accrued market discount each year unless you get permission from the IRS to revoke the election you made.

You should keep in mind one other special rule when it comes to reporting income from market discount bonds.

You *acquired* the bond after October 22, 1986, and the issuer of the bond makes a partial payment of the bond's principal to you before maturity. In this case, you must report the payment as ordinary interest income to the extent of the accrued but unreported market discount as of the payment date. The amount you report reduces the amount of remaining accrued market discount that you take into account when you dispose of the bond.

Let's return to our example on the constant interest method of accruing market discount. On July 1, 1993, the issuer of the bond pays you $250 of the $10,000 face amount of the bond. If you accrued market discount under the ratable accrual method, the entire $250 would be taxable as ordinary interest income. That's because your accrued market discount at July 1, 1993, would be $250 ($500 times 912 days divided by 1,826 days). If you used the constant interest method, however, you would report only $218 ($80 plus $89 plus [$99 times 182 divided by 365 days]) of the $250 as interest income. The remaining $32 would be tax free in the year received and would reduce your basis in the bond.

As always, of course, Uncle Sam carves out exceptions to the rules. Here is a list of bonds that are not subject to the interest income rules for market discount bonds:

- Bonds issued before July 19, 1984, as we discussed above;

- Short-term bonds—that is, bonds with a fixed maturity date that doesn't exceed one year from the date of issue (see ''Discount on short-term obligations,'' later in this chapter);

- Tax-exempt obligations (see ''Interest on tax-exempt investments,'' later in this chapter);

- U.S. Savings Bonds (see "Interest on savings bonds," later in this chapter); and

- Installment obligations (see "Interest on installment sales," earlier in this chapter).

In addition, if the amount of market discount totals less than one-fourth of one percent of the redemption price of the bond multiplied by the number of full years to maturity, you may disregard the market discount altogether—that is, you may treat it as zero. So any gain you recognize when you dispose of this bond is treated as capital gain rather than ordinary interest income.

You pay $9,900 for a 10-year bond, issued four years ago for its redemption price of $10,000; your market discount is $100, and it is less than one-fourth of one percent of the redemption price ($10,000) multiplied by the number of full years to maturity (six years)—or $150. Therefore, you don't have to worry about calculating accrued market discount when you sell or redeem the bond. Uncle Sam treats any gain you recognize as capital gain.

Interest on money-market bank accounts

You pay taxes on interest you earn from money deposited in money-market accounts at banks and savings and loan institutions.

TIP What should you look for when you shop for such an account? You want an institution that offers competitive rates of return *plus* frequent compounding—that is, how often interest is paid on your interest. Why frequent compounding?

Daily compounding means your interest income adds up faster than with quarterly or annual compounding. Say you deposit $10,000 in a money-market account at a bank that compounds quarterly and pays you an annualized rate of 8.5 percent. At the end of the first quarter, your interest income comes to $212.50—that is, $10,000 times 8.5 percent times one-quarter.

In the second quarter, you earn interest not only on your $10,000 of principal but also on your $212.50 of interest income. So your interest income for the second quarter totals $217.00—that is, $10,212.50 times 8.5 percent times one-quarter.

Continue these calculations for the next two quarters and by the end of the year, your interest income adds up to $877.50.

Now, what if you'd deposited your $10,000 at a bank that also pays you an annualized rate of 8.5 percent but compounds daily?

With daily compounding, you'd earn interest on your interest—plus, of course, your principal—every day of the year. In our example, daily compounding would earn you $887.00 in interest by the end of the year—$9.50 more than you'd have earned with quarterly compounding. And, after five years, daily compounding would earn $5,295 in interest—$67 more than the $5,228 you'd have earned with quarterly compounding.

TIP Look for an institution that compounds interest on a 365-day year, not a 360-day one. You'll earn a slightly higher yield with a 365-day year.

TIP Money-market accounts offer you liquidity; you may withdraw your dollars at any time. So they're a good place to maintain your emergency fund.

TIP If you're a safety-minded investor, you may want to opt for a money-market account from an institution that's a member of the Federal Deposit Insurance Corporation (FDIC) or the National Credit Union Administration (NCUA). That way, your principal and any interest due you are added together and guaranteed (up to the amount of $100,000) if the institution goes bust.

TIP You may not know it, but dollars deposited in Individual Retirement Accounts (IRAs) are insured separately by Uncle Sam up to $100,000.

For example, you deposit $100,000 in a money-market account in your name at the local thrift where you also maintain your IRA. The institution goes belly up. What are the consequences to you?

Uncle Sam gives you back only the $100,000 you deposited in the money-market account—not any interest due you because the amount would exceed $100,000. However, he also returns to you the principal plus any interest due you on your IRA—up to $100,000.

☞ **CAUTION** Dollars you deposit in a bank and at one of its branches aren't insured separately by Uncle Sam. They're treated as deposits at the same bank. The same goes for deposits you make in different accounts in the same bank—they're added together and insured up to a maximum of $100,000. (Exceptions exist to this rule and Congress is considering making some changes, so you may want to ask your banker for clarification.)

To be safe, don't deposit more than $100,000 in all of your accounts at any one bank, including its branches.

Interest on Original Issue Discount bonds

A bond is essentially a contract between an issuer (or borrower) and a bondholder (or lender). Corporations use bonds to raise money for a variety of reasons.

The bonds may sell at *par*—their face value or what the issuer will pay when the bond matures—and pay a market rate of interest each year, which you report annually as investment income. Or, they may sell at a discount or premium to par.

Original Issue Discount (OID) bonds—including zero-coupon bonds—are issued at a discount from the face value of the bond.

Original issue discount is simply the difference between the price paid for the bond when it was originally issued and the amount you receive for the bond at maturity. For example, a bond issued for $9,000 that promises to pay $10,000 in 10 years plus annual interest at eight percent has OID of $1,000.

TIP You may buy OID bonds from a variety of sources—banks, brokerage houses, even the Federal Reserve. You can expect to pay a small sales commission—two percent is typical—when you purchase these bonds from institutions.

If you own OID bonds, Uncle Sam usually requires you to report part of the discount as interest income on your tax return each year you own the bonds, even though you don't actually receive the money until you cash in the bonds at maturity. (Note that this rule differs from the one for market discount bonds. In the case of those bonds, the law generally requires that you recognize the market discount as interest income only when you dispose of the bonds.)

How much of the discount do you report each year? Your bond issuer or brokerage firm will calculate the amount and mail you a Form 1099-OID, "Statement for Recipients of

Original Issue Discount,'' each year—if your discount for the year adds up to $10 or more. Your 1099-OID lists the taxable amount you must report.

There's no need to attach Form 1099-OID to your return, but you should keep a copy for your records in case you're audited.

You may be interested in learning how your broker or bond issuer calculates the taxable portion of your OID each year. The rules depend on the type of bond and when it was issued.

For bonds issued after 1954 and before May 28, 1969 (or before July 2, 1982, for government obligations), no OID is included in taxable income until the year you dispose of the bond by selling, exchanging, or redeeming it. Any gain you realize on the disposition is treated as ordinary interest income to the extent of OID accrued on a monthly basis.

Generally, any additional gain is treated as capital gain. If you dispose of the bond at a loss, Uncle Sam treats the entire loss as a capital loss, and you don't have to report OID.

You compute the amount of gain taxed as ordinary interest income by multiplying the total OID by the number of full months you held the bond. Then you divide the result by the number of full months from the date of original issue to the date of maturity.

For corporate bonds issued after May 27, 1969 and government obligations issued after July 1, 1982, you generally report a portion of the OID as interest income each year that you hold the bond. Your basis in the bond for determining gain or loss when you dispose of it is increased by the amount of OID you report.

For example, you purchased a 10-year, $10,000 bond for $9,200 at original issue on January 1, 1989. Two years later, you decide to sell the bond. You've reported a total of $115 of OID as interest income on your 1989 and 1990 tax returns. So, the basis of your bond for computing your gain or loss on the sale comes to $9,315—that means your issue price of $9,200 plus the $115 of OID you've reported as income.

The method your bond issuer or broker uses for determining the annual taxable portion of OID depends, again, upon when the bond was issued. For instance, the annual taxable portion of OID on corporate bonds issued after May 27, 1969, and before July 2, 1982, is calculated as the ratable monthly portion of OID times the number of complete and partial months you held the bond during the year.

What is the ratable monthly portion of OID? It's simply the total OID divided by the number of complete months from the issue date to the maturity date of the bond.

Let's say you purchased a 10-year bond on July 15, 1981, with total OID of $1,000. The ratable monthly portion of OID is $8.33 ($1,000 OID divided by 120 months—the number of complete months from the issue date to the maturity date). And the annual taxable portion of OID for 1981 would have been $46.00 ($8.33 times 5.5 months).

For corporate and government bonds issued after July 1, 1982, and before January 1, 1985, the annual taxable portion of OID is calculated using the complex "constant interest method," which we discussed under "Interest on Market Discount Bonds," that assumes annual compounding. A similar method is used for bonds issued after 1984, but semiannual compounding is assumed. (For more information on this method, see IRS Publication 1212, *List of Original Discount Instruments*.)

☞ CAUTION As we discussed earlier, your bond issuer or brokerage firm will provide you with a Form 1099-OID that tells you how much OID to report as interest income each year. However, since the amount is calculated on the assumption that you held the bond for the entire year or through its maturity date, the amount may not be correct. For example, if you sell the bond during the year, you should report less OID as interest income.

You may prorate the annual OID to the period you held the bond based on the ratio of days you held the bond to total days during the year. Or, you may use the tables in IRS Publication 1212. These tables show the daily portion of OID based on the constant interest method.

Using the amounts in these tables may mean you end up with a lower taxable OID than if you used the simple daily-proration calculation. See Publication 1212 or consult your tax adviser for more information.

TIP Uncle Sam gives you a break if your discount adds up to less than one quarter of one percent of the stated redemption price of your bond multiplied by the number of years until the bond matures. He says you don't need to currently report this amount as income on your tax return.

Say you buy a 10-year bond with a stated redemption price of $1,000. That is, you get $1,000 when you redeem it 10 years from now.

You pay the issuer $980 for this bond, so the original issue discount is $20. Now, multiply 0.25 percent times the $1,000 stated redemption price times 10—the number of years to redemption—and you get $25.

Your discount—$20—is less than 0.25 percent of the stated redemption price of your bond times the number of years to redemption—$25. So there's no need to report your $20 discount on your returns. Of course, if you hold the bond until you redeem it for $1,000, you will report a capital gain of $20—that is, the $1,000 redemption price less your cost basis in the bond of $980.

What if you'd paid $950 for your bond? Your discount is

$50—more than 0.25 percent of the stated redemption price times the number of years to maturity. Therefore, you'd report the $50 as income ratably on your returns for the years you hold the bond.

Your bond issuer or brokerage firm will make these calculations for you. So, if the bond meets the 0.25 percent *de minimis* test, the issuer or broker will report no OID to you. A word to the wise: Before investing in a bond, ask the issuer or broker whether the bond comes with OID.

TIP Uncle Sam carves out some other exceptions to the OID rules. For example, these rules do not apply to tax-exempt bonds, U.S. Savings Bonds, or to short-term obligations—those are obligations with a fixed maturity date not exceeding one year from the date of issue. Examples include Treasury bills and commercial paper.

Other OID rules

There are a number of other rules you should know about when it comes to investing in OID bonds. For example, what happens when you acquire an OID bond from another holder—perhaps the original holder? Do you still have to worry about reporting OID?

The answer is yes. But how much you report depends on whether you acquired the OID bond with additional market discount, which we discussed earlier in this chapter, or with "acquisition premium," which we'll discuss in a minute.

Say you acquire an OID bond with additional market discount. In this case, you will recognize the remaining OID— the amount of OID not yet reported by the original holder— under the OID rules. And you will report the market discount under the general market discount rules.

For example, you acquire a bond for $9,500. The bond has

a stated redemption price of $10,000 and was originally issued for $9,000. The previous holder reported $600 of the total OID of $1,000. Your market discount comes to $100—the issue price of $9,000 plus the OID already reported of $600, minus your $9,500 purchase price. You must also report $400 of OID over the remaining term of the bond.

However, you may find yourself in a situation where, instead of receiving an additional market discount on an OID bond, you must pay an "acquisition premium" for the bond. This circumstance might crop up, for example, where interest rates on similar bonds are dropping.

Uncle Sam defines acquisition premium as the excess of the price you pay for the bond over the sum of the bond's original issue price plus accumulated OID.

Let's say in the example we just gave, you paid $9,800 for the bond. The acquisition premium would come to $200. And that premium reduces the amount of OID you must report each year.

The rules for determining the amount by which the acquisition premium reduces reportable OID each year depends upon whether you purchased the bond before, on, or after July 19, 1984. (You'll find all the details in IRS Publication 1212.)

 TIP In order to invest in OID bonds and not report a portion of your discount as interest income each year, buy these bonds with dollars deposited in an IRA or Keogh. That way, you're not taxed on the discount until the money is withdrawn from your plan, usually at retirement. (See Chapter 17 for more information on retirement accounts.)

TIP Why invest in zero-coupon and other OID bonds? They offer convenience. The amount you invest today will have grown to a set sum at a set date in the future.

You don't need to worry about reinvesting the interest you earn. In fact, you need only decide whether to buy the bond in the first place—and whether or not to sell.

TIP Sometimes bonds sell for more than their stated redemption price. The excess, or "premium," is generally reported as a capital loss when you redeem the bond at maturity. Similarly, if you sell the bond at a loss, the entire amount of the loss is treated as a capital loss attributable to the premium.

OID bonds may also sell for a market premium—a premium that differs from the "acquisition premium" we just discussed. If you pay more than the redemption price for an OID bond, you do not have to include any of the unreported OID in your income.

TIP If you acquire a bond—whether or not it is an OID bond—at a premium, you may elect to deduct, or amortize, the premium over the life of the bond rather than wait to claim a capital loss when you redeem or sell it. The amount you deduct each year reduces your cost basis in the bond for determining gain or loss when you dispose of it.

How you deduct the premium depends on when you acquired the bond. Generally, for bonds acquired after 1987, you offset your interest income by the amount of the annual amortization deduction. For bonds acquired after October 22,

1986, and before 1988, report your annual deduction as investment interest expense on Schedule A of Form 1040, subject to the limits on investment interest expense we discuss in Chapter 6.

And for bonds acquired before October 22, 1986, you claim your deduction as a miscellaneous itemized deduction that is *not* subject to the two percent of AGI limitation.

☞ CAUTION If you acquire a tax-exempt bond at a premium, you may not deduct the premium currently. However, you must reduce your cost basis in the bond by the annual amortization amount.

TIP As you can see, the tax rules concerning OID are among the most complex and difficult to apply. What is the bottom line? If you have any questions, consult your tax adviser.

Interest on passbook savings accounts

What do you need to know—tax-wise, at least—about passbook savings accounts? You pay taxes on your interest in the year you are able to withdraw it. It's that simple.

TIP Banks currently pay interest on passbook accounts at an annualized rate of 5.25 percent; savings and loans, 5.50 percent. Often you can earn two to three percentage points more in interest by transferring your dollars to a money-market account at the same institution.

Interest on savings bonds

If you think now is no time to take needless chances with your money, you may find United States Savings Bonds a safe and rewarding place to put your dollars. What do you need to know tax-wise about these bonds before you invest? Let's take a look.

TIP Many taxpayers don't know it, but the tax they pay on their interest income varies with the type of savings bond—Series HH or Series EE—they buy.

With Series HH bonds, you pay taxes currently. That's because when you buy Series HH bonds, you pay face value, and your interest is mailed to you twice a year by Uncle Sam. You pay taxes on the interest as you receive it.

TIP Series HH bonds replaced Series H bonds, which were issued through 1979. Any outstanding Series H bonds are treated the same as Series HH bonds.

When you purchase Series EE bonds, you buy them at a discount from their face value. When the bond matures, you collect the face value. The difference between the price you pay when you buy the bond and the amount you pocket when you redeem it is your taxable interest.

TIP Series EE bonds replaced Series E bonds, which were issued through 1979. With Series E or Series EE bonds, you have a choice when it comes to reporting the interest. You may report it in the year you cash the bonds or in the year in which the bonds finally mature—whichever comes first. Or you may report the interest each year, but that tack doesn't make much sense in most situations.

And Uncle Sam allows you to switch from one method of reporting interest to another without his permission. All you need to do is file Form 3115 with your return. On the form, specify the savings bonds for which the change is requested.

And print on the top of page one of Form 3115, "Filed under Rev. Proc. 89-46."

You should know, however, that the year you change to the annual reporting method, you're required to report all the interest that's accrued on the bond to date.

Also, you may not use different methods in the same year to report the interest on different bonds. You must use one method or the other for all the savings bonds you hold in any given year.

TIP Be a savvy taxpayer. Report your interest income from your savings bonds in a year in which you have a low income or a low tax rate. But, only do so if you expect either to increase in a later year.

TIP What if you own Series E bonds, and you trade them for Series H bonds? Or you own Series E or Series EE bonds and trade them for Series HH bonds?

You're entitled to a break. The rules say that you pay taxes only on the accrued but unreported interest you actually receive. If you roll all your interest over into more savings bonds, you pay no taxes on the interest accrued through the trade date.

Say you own Series E bonds with a redemption value of $2,723.35, and you trade them for $2,500 worth of Series HH bonds. What about the remaining $223.35? You pocket that amount. When April 15 rolls around, you're taxed only on the $223.35 you actually received and not on any additional accrued interest that is, in effect, "rolled over" in the trade. Such accrued interest will be taxed when you receive it.

This tax break applies only to Series EE or Series E bonds with a current redemption value of $500 or more.

TIP When you redeem a savings bond at a bank or other institution, that institution must forward to you a Form 1099-INT if your interest is $10 or more.

Printed in box 3 of your Form 1099-INT is your taxable interest income—that is, the difference between the amount you paid for the bond and the amount you received. Often, though, this number is incorrect. That's because the institution assumes that the interest you receive is entirely taxable to you at that time of redemption, even though you—or the original buyer—may have reported interest income from the bond each year.

If you find yourself in this situation, report the full amount of interest on Schedule B of Form 1040, then subtract the amount that's not currently taxable to you and explain why.

CAUTION What happens if you buy a savings bond and list yourself and your child as co-owners? In this case, you, the buyer, must pay taxes on the bond's interest. This rule holds true even if you let your child redeem the bond and pocket the proceeds. However, if you bought the bond in your child's name and did not list yourself as co-owner, the interest is taxable to the child.

TIP If you live in a high-tax state—California, New York, or Massachusetts, let's say—savings bonds may be tax-wise investments for you. The reason is that Federal law specifically excludes interest on these bonds from state and local income taxes.

TIP Uncle Sam gives you a break if you're twenty-four years of age or older, invest in Series

EE bonds issued after December 31, 1989, and use the proceeds to pay for *qualified* education expenses for yourself, your spouse, your child, or other dependent. In this case, you don't need to pay taxes on the interest—as long as the interest and principal of the bonds you redeem don't top your education expenses in any particular year.

What if your interest plus principal adds up to more than your education expenses? Uncle Sam caps the amount of interest you may exclude from taxation.

Here's how to figure the amount of interest you may exclude. First, calculate the amount of interest and principal on the bonds you're redeeming. Then add these two numbers together. Next, tally up your qualified education expenses—tuition or other required fees that you pay a college or vocational school, excluding room and board.

Divide your qualified education expenses by the total amount of interest and principal on the bonds. Then multiply the result times your interest from the bonds to get the amount of interest you may exclude from your gross income.

For example, you're redeeming savings bonds valued at $10,000 and using the proceeds to pay your qualified education expenses. Of that amount, $6,000 is principal, and $4,000 is interest. Your qualified education expenses come to $8,000.

You divide your qualified education expenses—$8,000—by the interest and principal from your bonds—$10,000. Now, you multiply the result—0.80—times your interest from the bonds—$4,000—to get $3,200, the amount of interest that's not taxable to you.

You should know that Uncle Sam requires you to subtract from your qualified education expenses scholarships that aren't taxable to you as income. For more information on this topic, ask the IRS for a free copy of its Publication 520, *Scholarships and Fellowships*.

You're responsible for keeping track of the serial numbers, issue dates, face values, and redemption dates of bonds you use to pay education expenses. You may want to use Form 8818, "Optional Form to Record Redemption of College Savings Bonds," for this purpose.

You should also know that the IRS phases out the benefits of the exclusion for taxpayers within certain ranges of "modified adjusted gross income"—$41,950 to $56,950 for singles and heads of households, and $62,900 to $92,900 for married couples filing jointly. (Married couples filing separately aren't eligible for the exclusion.) These ranges are adjusted annually for inflation.

Modified AGI is simply your regular AGI determined without regard to the interest exclusion and modified by adding back certain exclusions for income from foreign sources and certain U.S. possessions and Puerto Rico. You also take into account taxable social security benefits, your IRA deduction, and the passive-activity loss limitation.

How does the phaseout work? Return to our previous example.

You redeemed Series EE bonds for $10,000—$6,000 in principal and $4,000 in interest. Your qualified education expenses came to $8,000. So, under the rules, you were able to exclude $3,200 of the $4,000 you collected in interest income.

Now, let's say you're married and file a joint return. Your modified AGI comes to $74,900. Since this amount falls within the phase-out range, you must reduce your interest exclusion ratably. That means you reduce it by $12,000 (the amount of your income over the $62,900 floor) divided by

$30,000 (the total dollars within the phase-out range of $62,900 to $92,900) times $3,200 (your pre phase-out exclusion), or $1,280. So your interest exclusion comes to only $1,920—$3,200 minus $1,280.

Our advice? Before you invest in these bonds, estimate your income for the year your child will enter college. If you won't be eligible for the exclusion, you may want to put your money elsewhere—municipal bonds or nondividend-paying growth stocks, for example.

Discount on short-term obligations

Any bond or note that matures in a year or less, including both corporate and government bonds, is considered a short-term obligation. You may purchase these obligations at a discount from their face value, and you realize the interest income when the obligation is paid. You're not subject to either the rules on market discount bonds or original issue discount (OID) bonds.

Here's an example: In March 1991, you paid $940 for a short-term note that carries a face amount of $1,000. In February 1992, you receive payment of $1,000 for your note. Uncle Sam says you must report $60 in interest on your 1992 return.

Assume that you sell the short-term note at a gain before its maturity. In this case, you treat the gain as ordinary interest income to the extent of your ratable share of the discount at that date. Generally, you follow the rules we discussed earlier in the chapter for market discount bonds—that is, use either the ratable accrual method or the constant interest method—for determining your ratable share of the discount. Any gain that tops your ratable share is short-term capital gain. Any loss is treated as a short-term capital loss.

Interest on stripped-coupon bonds

Special rules apply to stripped-coupon bonds—bonds from which the coupons have been stripped. The coupons represent a claim for interest payments and, when stripped, may be sold separately from the bonds. Stripped bonds include so-called zero-coupon instruments sold by brokerage houses under the names CATS or TIGRS. The U.S. Treasury also offers zero-coupon bonds under the name STRIPS.

When you buy a stripped bond, Uncle Sam treats the spread between the amount you pay for the bond and its face amount as original issue discount. Therefore, you must report a part of this spread as interest income each year. When you buy a stripped coupon, you treat as OID the excess of the interest payable on the due date of the coupon over the amount you paid for it.

How do you calculate your reportable OID from these bonds or coupons?

Again, which rules you follow depend upon when the bond or coupon was issued—after July 1, 1982 and before January 1, 1985, or after December 31, 1984. In both cases, you use the complex, constant interest method we discussed previously. In the former case, however, you use annual compounding—that means you calculate OID for each one-year period beginning on the date you acquired the bond or coupon. In the latter case, you use semiannual compounding—calculating OID for each six-month period beginning on the acquisition date and six-month anniversary date. You'll find more details on this topic in IRS Publication 1212.

Interest on tax-exempt investments

Interest you receive from tax-exempt investments such as municipal bonds or municipal bond mutual funds are free from federal income taxes.

Most states exempt bonds that are issued within their borders from taxes, too, so they are doubly tax exempt. Check with your tax adviser to find out how your home state treats these bonds.

If you live in a high-tax state, an investment in doubly tax exempt municipal bonds is more attractive to you, as the following example illustrates. Let's say you live in New York and are taxed at a rate of eight percent. You're also in the 28 percent federal tax bracket and itemize your deductions. That means your combined tax rate—28 percent plus eight percent—is 36 percent.

But wait a minute, here's another wrinkle. Although your combined tax rate is 36 percent, you deduct state income taxes on your federal return. So, your net federal and state marginal tax rate is 34 percent, not 36 percent. How did we get 34 percent?

Your net marginal rate is the sum of your federal tax bracket—in your case, 28 percent—plus your true state tax rate, meaning your state tax rate after you calculate the benefit of deducting your state tax on your federal return.

To figure your true state tax rate, multiply your actual state tax rate (eight percent in your case) times the sum of one minus your federal rate of 28 percent (0.72 percent). The result—6 percent—is your true state tax rate.

Therefore, a New York State municipal bond that pays seven percent is the equivalent of a 10.6 percent taxable yield. How did we arrive at that figure? We divided the yield on the bond—seven percent—by 0.66 (one minus 0.34), your federal and state marginal tax rate.

TIP Just as Uncle Sam allows you to deduct state income taxes on your federal return, some states such as Missouri allow you to deduct federal income taxes on your state return. And that, of course, reduces your true federal tax rate.

TIP Most states levy taxes on the interest from out-of-state municipal bonds purchased by residents. There are a few exceptions to this rule, so to be sure, check with your tax adviser.

What if you invest in a bond fund that purchases issues from a variety of states? Your fund will send you a letter outlining the sources of its income.

Then it's up to you to figure out on which of these bonds you must pay state and local taxes.

TIP Municipal bonds—like corporate bonds— are rated by services, such as Standard & Poor's and Moody's, and the higher the rating, the lower the risk of default and interest rate will be.

TIP Generally, tax-exempt interest isn't recorded on a Form 1099-INT. Rather, you'll receive a letter from your financial institution detailing your earnings. And, for information purposes only, you must report those earnings on line 8b of your Form 1040.

However, if you do receive a Form 1099-INT for tax-exempt interest, be sure to report the interest on line 1 of Schedule B of your Form 1040. Then several lines above line 2, subtotal the amounts on line 1. Below this subtotal, write "tax-exempt interest" and show the amount. Then subtract this amount from the subtotal. List the result, which is your taxable interest income, on lines 2 and 4. You must also list this amount on line 8a of your Form 1040.

TIP The payment of interest and principal of some municipal bonds is insured. You should compare the interest rates and the strength of the entity insuring the obligation to determine whether an insured bond is worth investing in.

☞ **CAUTION** Uncle Sam won't allow you to claim a deduction for any expenses, including interest, associated with producing tax-exempt income. That means that if you borrow money to buy shares in a tax-exempt bond fund, you may not write off the interest you pay.

☞ **CAUTION** Some municipal bond funds invest in so-called economic development bonds or industrial development bonds. These bonds are issued by state and local governments to finance private business activities—construction of a shopping mall or a manufacturing facility, for example.

Some of these bonds pay interest that's exempt from ordinary federal income taxes but that's subject to the alternative minimum tax (AMT).

The AMT, which is imposed at a flat rate of 24 percent, is a completely separate tax system that is designed to ensure that everyone pay his or her fair share of tax. We'll tell you what you need to know about the AMT in Chapter 8.

If your municipal bond fund invests in private-activity bonds, it will notify you by mail each year of the proportion of its income that's derived from these bonds. Then, if you pay the AMT, you'll have to count this as interest income.

☞ CAUTION   Certain state and local obligations may be guaranteed by the federal government. If these obligations were issued after 1983, the interest on them will generally be taxable to you. However, interest isn't taxable on obligations guaranteed by the Federal Housing Administration, the Department of Veterans Affairs, and the Student Loan Marketing Association.

☞ CAUTION   If you receive Social Security benefits, take note of the following. Since 1984, Uncle Sam has required that part of your Social Security benefits be included in your taxable income if your adjusted gross income, plus 50 percent of your benefits and any tax-exempt interest, tops a certain level.

That base is $25,000 for single filers, $32,000 for married couples filing jointly, and zero for married couples filing separately, unless one spouse lived apart from the other for the entire taxable year. In such a case, they're treated as single taxpayers for this purpose.

The taxable part is either one-half of your benefits, or one-half of the excess of the sum of your modified AGI (see the following example), and one-half of your benefits over the base amount, whichever is less.

Let's say you're married and file jointly, and your AGI— before Social Security benefits—is $34,000. Your tax-exempt interest for the year adds up to $6,000, and you received $7,200 in Social Security benefits.

Add your tax-exempt interest—$6,000—to get your modified AGI of $40,000. Then add to your modified AGI— $40,000—one-half of your Social Security benefits, or $3,600. The result—$43,600—is your income for the taxability test.

Next, subtract from $43,600 the *base* of $32,000. The difference is $11,600, and one-half of the difference comes to $5,800. In your case, half your benefits—$3,600—is less than half the difference between your modified AGI and the base amount, which is $5,800.

So, $3,600 of your Social Security benefits is taxable.

For more information on this subject, ask the IRS for a free copy of its Publication 915, *Social Security Benefits and Equivalent Railroad Retirement Benefits*.

☞ CAUTION Income that's exempt from taxation in the United States doesn't necessarily escape taxation abroad. For example, interest from municipal bonds is tax-free here, but if you're living and working in West Germany, you can expect to pay taxes on those earnings.

Interest on Treasury bills, notes, and bonds

You pay federal taxes on the interest you earn from any so-called U.S. debt obligations—including Treasury bills, notes, and bonds.

But here's where Uncle Sam gives you a break. He exempts these earnings from state and local taxes. So, if you live in a high tax state, Treasury securities may be especially attractive to you.

For example, you're married, file jointly, and are in the 28 percent bracket. You make your home in sunny Los Angeles, and you invest $10,000 in a 52-week Treasury bill—or T-bill, as they're called—earning interest at an annualized rate of nine percent.

Your tax bill adds up this way: You pay $252 in federal taxes on the $900 you earned from your T-bill—that is, 28 percent times $900. But, you pay no state and local taxes on your T-bill earnings. Therefore, your after-tax earnings equal $648, for an after-tax yield of 6.5 percent.

What if you'd invested your $10,000 in a certificate of deposit also earning interest at an annualized rate of nine percent?

You'd pay $252 in federal taxes *plus* state and local taxes of $84—a marginal state tax rate of 9.3 percent times $900. You'd get to deduct these state taxes on your federal return, and the benefit to you is $24—that is, $84 times 28 percent.

Your after-tax earnings on the CD would come to $588—$900 of interest income minus $336 of federal and state taxes, plus a tax benefit of $24 from your state tax deduction. The state taxes actually reduced your after-tax yield from 6.5 percent to 5.9 percent.

TIP   Another advantage of buying a T-bill: You can easily defer all the interest you earn to the following tax year just by purchasing a bill that comes due next year.

CAUTION   You generally pay a commission—usually 0.2 percent to one percent of the face amount—when you buy Treasuries from your bank or broker. And these commissions reduce your return.

TIP   Do you want to avoid paying commissions when you purchase Treasury securities? You can if you buy them directly from a Federal Reserve Bank. The Federal Reserve Banks, acting as agents for the Treasury Department, sell U.S. government obligations to the public without sales commissions.

If you'd like a brochure on how to buy Treasury securities from a Federal Reserve Bank, telephone the Federal Reserve Bank nearest you, or write the Bureau of Public Debt, Department F, Washington, D.C. 20239-1200. The brochure is free for the asking.

☞ **CAUTION** A Treasury note or bond is issued for maturities of more than a year. You may buy notes that mature in more than four years for a minimum of $1,000 and notes that mature in four years or less for a minimum of $5,000. (If you buy a Treasury note at a discount, the rules for OID bonds, discussed earlier in this chapter, apply.)

By contrast, a T-bill is a short-term obligation issued in denominations of $10,000, and in multiples of $5,000 thereafter. They mature in 90 days, 180 days, or 52 weeks. You should be aware that Treasury bonds, notes, and T-bills are also generally available after issuance by the U.S. government in a secondary market. For example, an investor may purchase, in September of 1991, a Treasury note of $1,000 at 8.5% due to mature in August of 1992. The investor can sell the note at any time prior to its maturity date. Therefore, through a secondary market, investors have an endless array of maturity dates and denominations to choose from for Treasury bonds and notes.

In addition, Treasury bills are issued at a discount. The interest equals the difference between the discounted price you pay for the bills and the face value you receive at maturity. You report this interest income when you redeem the bill at maturity.

What if you sell a Treasury bill before it matures? The selling price may be part interest and part short-term capital gain or loss.

Here's an example: On July 1, 1991, you buy a 180-day, $10,000 T-bill issued at $9,500. If you hold the bill until it matures on December 27, you will report $500 of interest income—that is, the $10,000 you collect when you redeem the bill less the $9,500 you paid when the bill was issued.

Let's assume, however, that you sell the T-bill on August 29, 1991, for $9,800. Your total gain, of course comes to $300 ($9,800 minus $9,500). Of that amount, $167 is ordinary interest income, and the remaining $133 is short-term capital gain.

How do you calculate the interest portion? You allocate your total discount—$500—over the number of days you hold the bond during its maturity period. So, in our example, you divide $500 by 180 days—the total maturity period—to calculate the amount of interest the bill earns each day—in this case, $2.77. Then, you multiply that amount times 60 days, the number of days you actually held the bill, to get $167.

What if you sold the T-bill for only $9,600? In this case, your gain would come to $100, and Uncle Sam would treat the entire amount as ordinary interest income.

Treasury securities are backed by the full faith and credit of the United States government, so they're among the safest investments around.

However, Treasuries aren't for everyone.

Why? You've got to have the cash to meet the minimum investment requirements, and you must be able to afford to tie up your money for a period of time. Also, because they're such safe investments, their interest rates are generally lower than other types of investments such as corporate bonds. But that's the trade-off—safety vs. a higher rate.

3

All The News
About Dividends

You know what dividends are; they're distributions of money, stock, or other property paid by a corporation, partnership, or trust from its earnings.

But, did you know that not all dividends are taxed? In this chapter, we take a look at what counts as dividend income—in the eyes of the IRS—plus we provide you with some tax-wise strategies for deferring dividend income. We start, though, with a few basics.

Uncle Sam requires any person or company that pays you $10 or more a year in dividends to send you a Form 1099-DIV, "Statement for Recipients of Dividends and Distributions." This form must be mailed by the end of the last day of January of the next tax year.

What if you don't receive your Form 1099-DIV within a few weeks of that date? Contact the payor and ask for a duplicate. Now, suppose that you receive a Form 1099-DIV but don't agree with the amount of dividend income listed. You should telephone or write the payor and explain why the number is wrong and ask to be issued a corrected form. Once this new Form 1099-DIV is in hand, make sure it's marked "corrected." That way, neither you nor the IRS will get confused about which form is the right one.

What if you're unable to resolve your dispute with the payor that issued the Form 1099-DIV? Report what you think is the correct amount on your tax return and include with your return an explanation of why you think the amount you're reporting is correct.

There's no need to attach Form 1099-DIV to your return. You report the amount of dividends you received on line 9 of Form 1040.

In box 1a of your Form 1099-DIV is printed the total amount of dividends and other distributions you received during the year. In box 1b is the amount of your ordinary dividends (this figure is included in the total in box 1a).

In box 1e are your investment expenses. You write these off as miscellaneous itemized deductions on Schedule A of your Form 1040. (See Chapter 7 for more information.)

If your dividends total more than $400, you must list the amounts you receive—and from whom—on Schedule B of your Form 1040.

Here's something else you should know. If your brokerage firm collects your dividends for you, you receive a Form 1099-DIV from your broker at the end of the year. You don't receive the form from the corporations that paid the dividends. So, on your Schedule B, you should list your dividends as coming from Brokerage A, not from XYZ Corp.

Don't sign your return until you compare the total dividend income you recorded with all your Forms 1099-DIV to make sure that you haven't forgotten anything. What if you fail to report all your dividend income? Uncle Sam may hit you with a penalty.

The penalty equals 20 percent of the additional tax due.

You also pay interest on the dividend income you fail to report—beginning on the day your tax return was due.

DIVIDEND INCOME

Now, what counts as dividend income? Our list follows.

Dividends earned by your children

Uncle Sam says you may report dividend income your children receive on your tax return but only if certain requirements are met.

What requirements? A child must be under the age of 14 at the end of the tax year. Also, his or her unearned income must total no less than $550 but no more than $5,000, and it must consist of interest and dividends only.

How do you report a child's dividend income on your return? File Form 8814, "Parent's Election to Report Child's Interest and Dividends," with your Form 1040.

☞ **CAUTION** By law, your children must file their own returns if they make estimated tax payments or you make estimated tax payments in their names.

☞ **CAUTION** Likewise, your children must, by law, file their own returns if they're subject to backup withholding.

☞ **CAUTION** When it comes to reporting your children's income on your tax return, there are a host of pluses and minuses to consider.

On the plus side is less paperwork. When you include your

children's income on your return, you file only one return—not two, three, four, or more.

You also may benefit, tax-wise at least, by reporting your children's investment income on your federal return.

Let's say your investment expenses add up to more than your investment income. Uncle Sam says you may write off investment expenses only to the extent of your investment income. In your case, that means you may not write off all your expenses on your current return.

What do you do? You carry forward any investment expenses you aren't able to deduct currently to offset investment income in future years. Now, add your children's investment income to your own and report it on your tax return. Your children's income boosts your total investment income and allows you to offset more of your investment expenses on your current return.

On the minus side, reporting your children's investment income on your return boosts your AGI, which, in turn, may make it more difficult to claim some deductions.

For example, the rules allow you to deduct medical expenses only to the extent that they top 7.5 percent of your AGI. Say your AGI adds up to $40,000, you may write off only those medical expenses that exceed 7.5 percent times $40,000—or $3,000. For example, if you add your children's income to your own, and your AGI climbs to $45,000, your medical expenses must top $3,375 before they're deductible.

Another downside of reporting your children's income on your return is that doing so may make their income subject to state income taxes. Often the income children receive is so small that it isn't subject to state taxes, or if it is, it is subject to state taxes at a low rate. Adding the income your children receive to your own makes it subject to state taxes or subject to state taxes at a higher rate.

Dividends from estates, trusts, or partnerships

If you're the sole beneficiary of a trust or estate that earns dividend income, in most cases you pay taxes on the amount of income the trust or estate receives. However, in certain cases the trust or estate will pay the taxes. What if you're not the sole beneficiary or you're a partner in a partnership? You pay taxes only on the portion that belongs to you.

Your fiduciary or partnership will report your dividend income to you each year on Schedule K-1. Your copy of Schedule K-1 and its instructions will tell you where to report items from it on your Form 1040.

Dividends from foreign corporations

Some foreign governments—but not all—withhold taxes from dividends paid by companies in their countries. And the taxes in these foreign countries can be as much as double what they are here. For example, the top rate in Japan is 50 percent, while the top rate in France is 56.8 percent and Spain, 56 percent. These days, it seems, the U.S. is somewhat of a tax haven.

Now, let's say you own 100 shares of stock in a Japanese corporation, and it declares a dividend of 50 cents a share. When you receive your check, it totals $42.50—not $50—because the Japanese government, under a treaty with the United States, withholds taxes at a rate of 15 percent from the amount due you.

Box 3 of your Form 1099-DIV lists the amount of foreign taxes withheld on your dividends, and box 4 identifies the country that withheld these taxes.

If you receive a Form 1099-DIV with entries in these boxes, Uncle Sam gives you a choice. He says you may deduct the amount of foreign taxes withheld as an itemized deduction under "other taxes" on Schedule A of your Form 1040.

Or you may file a Form 1116, "Foreign Tax Credit," with your Form 1040 and claim a foreign tax credit for the taxes you've paid.

This tax credit reduces the amount you owe Uncle Sam by taking into account the taxes you've paid to other governments.

Most people are better off—tax-wise, at least—claiming a foreign tax credit rather than taking an itemized deduction. That's because a credit reduces your tax liability dollar for dollar. A deduction, meanwhile, simply cuts the amount of your income subject to tax.

Calculating your foreign tax credit is exceedingly complicated and not something most taxpayers want to tackle alone. If you receive investment income from abroad, you may want to seek help from your tax adviser when it comes time to file your return.

TIP The rules that govern dividends paid by foreign corporations also apply to dividends from mutual funds that invest in foreign securities.

Let's say that more than 50 percent of your mutual fund's assets are invested in foreign securities. In this case, it may pass on to you the right to claim a deduction or foreign tax credit for the taxes the fund has paid. You'll find this amount listed in box 3 of your Form 1099-DIV.

TIP Here's something else you should know. Uncle Sam doesn't require all foreign corporations to provide you with a Form 1099-DIV.

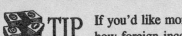

TIP If you'd like more information on how foreign income is taxed, ask the IRS for a free copy of its Publication 514, *Foreign Tax Credit for Individuals*.

Loans taxable as dividends

If you're a stockholder in a corporation and receive a low-interest or no-interest loan from that company, Uncle Sam "imputes" (tax jargon for attributes) income to you. This income equals the interest you would have paid if the loan were made as an arm's length transaction. However, you report the imputed income as dividend, not interest, income.

How do you calculate your imputed dividend income? It equals the amount of the outstanding loan times the applicable federal rate (determined by the IRS and based on an average rate the federal government pays on its borrowings).

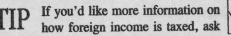

TIP Note that Uncle Sam allows you an offsetting imputed interest deduction subject to the limitations on the deductibility of interest. (See Chapter 6 for the details.)

CAUTION The rules governing low-interest and no-interest loans are complicated. It's wise to consult your tax adviser if you're party to such a loan.

Mutual fund dividends

If you invest in a stock mutual fund, and it pays you dividends on the stocks you own, these dividends are taxable to you. (See Chapter 13 for more on mutual funds.)

Patronage dividends

Patronage dividends, those you receive from a cooperative, are usually taxable. These amounts are tax-free *if* they're a return of some of the money you spent at the cooperative. A farm cooperative is a case in point.

For example, you purchase $5,000 worth of livestock feed from your local farm cooperative and don't use this feed in your trade or business or as part of an investment. At year's end, the farm cooperative mails you patronage dividends totalling $50. This amount isn't taxable to you as long as the amounts you spent were for personal items.

Why? It's actually a rebate of some of the amount you spent at the cooperative during the year.

Short-term gains that are taxed as dividends

Say that you own shares in a stock mutual fund, which earns short-term capital gains by selling shares it's held for one year or less. If any net short-term gains are passed along to you in the form of dividends, how is the money taxed? As short-term capital gains or dividends? The answer is as dividends. Since the money is paid to you as dividends, Uncle Sam says, it's taxed as dividends.

You may not use short-term capital gains passed through to you by a fund to offset any capital losses you may have. (As you no doubt know, long-term capital gains are taxed as capital gains. For the details, see Chapters 4 and 5.)

Spill-over dividends

Spill-over dividends are those dividends declared in October, November, or December by a regulated investment company (that is, a mutual fund) or real estate investment trust (REIT) but not paid to you until after the end of the year.

☞ **CAUTION** A special rule applies to spillover dividends. The regulation says that you must pay taxes on these amounts in the current tax year, as long as the company pays you your dividends in January of the following year.

For example, you own 100 shares of a mutual fund. On December 15, 1991, the fund declares a quarterly dividend of 50 cents a share. You receive a check for the amount due you—$50 or 50 cents times 100 shares—on January 13, 1992. Under the rules, you must report the $50 you received as income on your 1991 tax return, even though you didn't pocket the money until 1992.

Dividends paid in stock or cash

Usually, dividends paid in the form of stock aren't taxable as ordinary income. What about dividends that are paid in cash? You report them on your Form 1040.

💰 **TIP** If you buy a stock on or near the date a dividend is declared, make sure that you receive all the money due you. Sometimes, sales aren't recorded in time by the corporation paying the dividend, and it forwards the payment to the former owner.

If you don't receive a dividend that you know is due, check with your stockbroker. He or she will help you straighten out the situation.

Dividend reinvestment plans

Dividends are taxed as ordinary income to you even if you choose—as lots of us do—to reinvest these dollars in additional shares of stock.

Uncle Sam allows you to deduct fees you pay to participate in dividend reinvestment plans. Don't make the mistake some taxpayers do, and subtract these fees from your dividend income. Report your dividends in full, then write off these fees on Schedule A of your Form 1040.

Dividends from restricted stock

Have you ever heard of restricted stock? It's stock you get from your employer for services you perform and that's not transferable to someone else.

Uncle Sam doesn't require you to add to your taxable income the value of the stock when it's awarded to you. However, you must pay taxes on any dividends you receive. These dividends, though, are taxed as *wages*, not dividends.

Your employer includes these amounts with your wages and reports them on your Form W-2. What if you also receive a Form 1099-DIV reporting the same dividends?

List the dividends from your restricted stock on Schedule B of your Form 1040 along with all your other dividends. Then subtotal the amount. Beneath the subtotal, write "dividends on restricted stock reported as wages on line 7, Form 1040," and subtract the amount of these dividends.

Dividends from stock held jointly

Let's say you and a friend own 100 shares of stock in XYZ Corp. You purchased the shares in 1989 for $1,000, and each of you contributed $500 toward the purchase price. Now, XYZ pays you $50 in dividends.

Who reports that amount as income? You or your friend? The answer is both of you. Each of you contributed 50 percent of the purchase price of the stock, so each of you is entitled to 50 percent of the dividends. You both report $25 in income on your returns.

What if you contributed 80 percent of the purchase price and your friend 20 percent? You'd be entitled to 80 percent of the dividends and he, 20 percent. And each of you would report the amount you'd receive on your personal tax return.

☞ **CAUTION** You should know that a corporation paying dividends will record the amount only to the Social Security number of one person on Form 1099-DIV. And that's a problem when it comes to joint ownership.

If the total is reported to your Social Security number and you list only a portion of the income on your return, the IRS will probably send you a deficiency notice.

What do we advise? When you file your return, report the full amount of dividends paid on Schedule B of your Form 1040. Write "amount attributable to others" or "nominee distribution" in the dividend section of your Schedule B.

Then, subtract the portion that went to the other person. Also list on Schedule B the Social Security number of the person who jointly owns the stock.

Dividends from taxable money-market funds

When you invest in a money-market mutual fund, you buy shares in that fund. In most cases, you receive one share for every dollar you invest. What's more, your dividends are paid in shares.

Let's say you invest $2,000 in a money-market fund that earns interest at an annualized rate of nine percent. Your $2,000 buys you 2,000 shares. By the end of the year, your 2,000 shares, or $2,000, grows to 2,180 shares, or $2,180— that is, your principal plus $2,000 times nine percent.

How do money-market funds work? They pool the dollars people deposit to invest in short-term obligations of federal, state, and local governments, as well as corporations and banks. The interest net of allowable expenses they receive is passed along to you in the form of dividends.

These dividends are taxed as *dividends*, not as interest income. (By contrast, interest on a money-market account at a bank is taxed as interest.)

What if you make the mistake of reporting these amounts as interest income? You're likely to receive a letter from the IRS asking for an explanation. So make sure to list your income from money-market funds in the *dividend* section of Schedule B of your Form 1040.

TIP You may not know it, but money-market funds pay a rate of return that's typically higher than most money-market bank accounts. And that's their primary advantage.

How do you find the account with the highest yield? You may want to subscribe to a publication that tracks the performance of money-market mutual funds.

TIP Money-market funds also offer you liquidity—that is, you may withdraw your money at any time and without penalty. So they're a good place for your emergency fund or temporary excess funds.

How do you take money out? All you need to do is write a

check or, in some cases, visit an automated teller ma-
chine. You also may transfer or wire money to your
checking account.

Another plus of money-market funds is protection from inflation. Short-term interest rates usually rise with inflation,
and so do your earnings from a fund.

☞ **CAUTION** Money-market funds—unlike
money-market bank accounts—
aren't insured by the federal government. So you may want to
evaluate the credentials of the mutual fund company or brokerage firm and identify what types of securities it holds.

How do you know what types of securities your fund holds?
Look at its prospectus. It lists the types of obligations in which
the fund invests.

Dividends from tax-exempt money-market funds

Do you want to reduce your taxable income? Consider investing in a tax-exempt money-market fund. The interest you
receive—in the form of dividends—isn't taxable on your federal tax return.

TIP Is a tax-exempt fund right for you? There's
only one way to know, and that's to run the
numbers. Compare the return you'd earn on a tax-exempt fund
with the return from one that's taxable. How? Here's a simple
formula to help you compare returns.

Divide the interest you expect to collect from your tax-exempt fund by one minus your marginal tax bracket expressed
as a decimal—0.31, let's say.

Here's another way to look at it: You're in a 31 percent
federal tax bracket and an 8 percent state bracket, and you're
faced with a choice—invest $1,000 in a taxable

money-market fund yielding 7 percent or in a money-market fund that's exempt from both federal and state income taxes yielding 5 percent.

Which investment makes the most sense for you?

If you invest in the taxable fund, you'll pocket $70 in dividends each year. But from that amount you'll have to subtract $25.56 in federal and state taxes (taking into account the tax benefit of deducting the state taxes on your federal return; see Chaper 2 for details). So, from your $70 of dividend income, you'll net only $44.44, for an after-tax yield of 4.4 percent (compared to the pretax yield of 7 percent). If you invest in the tax-exempt fund instead, you'll pocket $50 in dividend income each year—all of it tax free.

4

The Right Way to Calculate Your Gains and Losses

What's a capital gain? It's the profit you make when you sell a capital asset. Almost everything you own and use for investment is a capital asset. Stocks, bonds, mutual fund investments, gold, silver, antiques, your personal residence, gemstones, and oriental rugs all fall into the capital assets category.

A long-term capital gain is the profit you make when you sell a capital asset that you've held for more than a year. A short-term capital gain, on the other hand, is the profit you make when you sell a capital asset that you've held for a year or less.

Long-term capital gains are currently taxed the same as ordinary income, such as salaries, interest, and dividends—with one exception. For upper-middle and upper income taxpayers in the 31 percent tax bracket, the rules say that your long-term capital gains will not be taxed at more than 28 percent. Short-term capital gains are taxed at the same rate as ordinary income.

The Bush administration has been pressuring Congress to further lower long-term capital gains rates, but until it does, most people are stuck. So, depending on your income, you're taxed on your capital gains at the rate of 15 percent or 28 percent.

Even though long-term capital gains receive little favorable tax treatment, Uncle Sam requires investors to keep track of them and categorize them on their tax returns. He also requires you to keep track of your short-term capital gains.

In this chapter, we run through the rules governing capital gains. Before we begin, though, here are a few basics.

How do you calculate your holding period? Uncle Sam says you start counting from the day *after* you purchase an investment, and you include in the holding period the day you sold that investment.

It works like this: Say you purchased 100 shares of ABC Corp. on January 30, 1991. As the rules require, you start counting your holding period on January 31. Now, say, you sell your shares for a profit on January 30, 1992. Your gain is short-term because you did not hold the stock for more than a year.

Here's something else you should know: For securities traded on a public exchange, your holding period for tax purposes begins on, and your gain is taxable as of, the respective trading dates, not the settlement dates.

For example, say you sell some stock on the New York Stock Exchange on December 27, 1991. The rules of the stock exchange say that the trade closes with delivery of the stock five trading days after the sale—in your case, January 6, 1992. That's the same day you receive payment from the stock you sold.

Now, you want to know—when do you report the gain? In 1991, the year the stock traded? Or in 1992 when you pocketed your gain? The answer is in 1991.

Your brokerage firm will send you a Form 1099-B that lists the proceeds from all your sales for the year based on the trade date. It's best to rely on this document for information when tax filing time rolls around, rather than on your brokerage statements.

Why? If you buy or sell stock near the end of the year, these trades may not appear on your December statement, and, as a result, you may overlook them.

But you should reconcile the information in your records with what's reported on your Form 1099-B.

What if your Form 1099-B is incorrect? Contact your brokerage firm or other financial services institution, and ask that it issue a corrected form. It is important that amounts shown on Form 1099-B are included in the proceeds reported on your Schedule D of Form 1040. If they don't match, Uncle Sam will likely send you a notice and may assess a penalty for negligence.

What else should you know about capital gains?

The concept of netting. Uncle Sam requires you to net your capital gains and losses. That is, you calculate your net capital gain or loss by first subtracting your short-term capital losses from your short-term capital gains, then subtracting your long-term capital losses from your long-term capital gains. Next, you combine your net long-term capital gains or losses with your net short-term capital gains or losses. The result is your net capital gain or loss.

CALCULATING YOUR BASIS

You also need to master the concept of basis. Basis is generally the amount you pay for an asset plus certain expenses such as sales commissions.

You use basis to figure your gain or loss on the sale or exchange of an asset. In other words, you subtract your basis from your sales proceeds.

The result is your gain or loss.

For each investment you sold or exchanged during the year, you must know:

- The number of shares you bought

- The amount you paid per share

- The date of each purchase

- The total dollar amount of the purchase, including items such as commissions and fees

- The number of shares you sold or exchanged

- The price you received per share from the sale or exchange

- The date of each sale or exchange

- The total dollar amount you received from each sale or exchange

Now, you ask, where do I get all this information? The answer is, from your personal records, and monthly statements, and Form 1099-Bs that your brokerage firm or financial institution mails you.

If you sold less than all of your investment in a particular stock, bond, or other security, you must also know how to identify which shares were sold so you can determine the proper basis to use. Uncle Sam provides two different methods to identify the shares sold.

Selling specific shares

You've kept good records. You know how many shares you bought, when you purchased them, and how much you paid. If you can identify which shares were sold, Uncle Sam requires you to use the specific share method. Sometimes this method gives you a choice about whether to realize a gain or a loss.

Say you own 565 shares of stock in XYZ Corp. You purchased 250 shares at $10 a share in February 1989 , 15 shares at $15 a share in January 1990, 200 shares at $14 a share in July 1990, and 100 shares at $12 a share in August 1990.

Now, say you tell your broker on June 1, 1991, to sell the 200 shares you purchased in July 1990 at $14 a share. Because you specified the shares to sell, figuring your basis is easy. In this case, it's $14 a share—the price you paid for them.

So, if you sell the 200 shares for $11 per share, you report a short-term capital loss of $3 per share—that is, your $11 selling price less your $14 basis. Your total loss comes to $600—$3 times 200 shares. Since you owned the shares less than a year, your loss is a short-term one.

You may use your $600 loss to offset some capital gains you may have had from other transactions. If you had no capital gains, the rules say you can subtract the $600 from your ordinary income. There's a limit on how much capital loss you may deduct each year from your ordinary income. (More on this topic later in the chapter.)

 TIP   It's important that you have a record of your instructions to sell specific shares. So make sure to keep a copy of your dated letter to your broker or fund. But such instructions are only effective if the stock is held in "street name"—that is, the stock is held for you in the name of the broker or fund. If the shares that are sold are held in your name, it does not matter what the instructions were—the actual certificates delivered are the ones that are considered sold.

First in, first out

You say you haven't kept good records? You may have to use the first in, first out (FIFO) method. Let's go back to our previous example.

You sell 200 shares of XYZ for $11 a share. Under the FIFO method, the shares you sell are considered the first ones you purchased—meaning in February 1989.

You paid $10 a share for that stock, so that's your basis. Your gain, then, is $1 a share—your selling price of $11 minus your $10 basis—or $200.

You can see what a difference FIFO makes—and not necessarily for the better. With FIFO, you must post a $200 capital gain, while with the specific-share method, you're able to claim a $600 capital loss.

Exceptions

Uncle Sam carves out a few exceptions to the rules governing basis. For example, if you receive stock as a gift, your basis is the basis of the donor at the time of the gift. In other words, the donor's basis becomes your basis.

What if you sell the stock at a loss? Then your basis is the lesser of the donor's basis or the fair market value of the stock on the date the gift was made.

A wash sale is a sale of stock at a loss either 30 days before or after you make another purchase of the same (or substantially identical) stock. Your basis in the new stock is what you paid for it; however, it's increased for any loss that is disallowed. See Chapter 5 for more on wash sales.

With Original Issue Discount securities, your basis is the amount you paid for the securities plus the interest income that accrues annually. (For more information on Original Issue Discount, see Chapter 2.)

Finally, if you inherit stock or some other capital asset, your basis is either the fair market value of the asset on the day the person died or its value six months after the person's death if the executor of the estate chooses that date to value the estate.

Your stock basis can also be affected if the corporation issues stock dividends, declares a stock split, makes a capital distribution, or undergoes a reorganization. If you find yourself in one of these situations, you may want to consult your tax advisor. The rules are complicated, and you may need professional help.

DISPOSING OF YOUR MUTUAL FUND INVESTMENT

As with your other investments, the sale, exchange, or redemption of your mutual fund shares usually results in a capital gain or loss. Your gain or loss is the difference between your proceeds or the value of what you receive and your basis in the shares given up.

Holding period

Except in certain circumstances, the determination of whether a gain or loss is long-term or short-term follows the general rule for determination of holding periods. But Uncle Sam provides two little-known exceptions for mutual fund shareholders.

If you held shares of a mutual fund for 6 months or less and you sold the shares for a loss, your loss will be treated as long-term to the extent of capital gains dividends you received on those shares and undistributed capital gains which the fund allocated to your shares. If your loss exceeds the distributed and undistributed capital gains, the excess will be considered short term. (See Chapter 5 for more on capital gain dividends and undistributed capital gains.)

A similar exception exists for exempt-interest dividends to prevent investors from buying shares of a mutual fund just prior to the declaration of an exempt-interest dividend and then selling the shares shortly thereafter. Such a scheme would allow an investor to receive tax-exempt income in exchange for a short-term capital loss since the value of the shares would decrease by the approximate amount of the dividend immediately after the distribution. Uncle Sam says you may not deduct any losses from the sales of shares in a mutual fund to the extent of exempt-interest dividends if the holding period is less than 6 months.

☞ CAUTION For these two rules, the definition of "holding period" is slightly different from the general rule. So if you think you may be disposing of your shares in a mutual fund and the holding period is close to 6 months, and you have had options to sell the shares, you have granted options to buy the shares, or you acquired the shares in a wash sale, you should consult your tax adviser.

Basis

The general rules for figuring the basis of capital assets discussed above apply to your mutual fund shares. But the record keeping for the basis in your mutual fund shares may be more complicated than with other investments.

The reason? Often mutual fund investing results in more transactions that affect your basis—for example, dividend reinvestment, undistributed capital gains, periodic redemptions or sales, and nontaxable distributions.

When you buy shares in a mutual fund, the amount you pay is your initial basis. This price includes the cost of the shares plus any load or other costs of acquisition.

If you exchange shares in one mutual fund for shares in another mutual fund, add any service charge or fee paid in connection with the exchange to the basis of the new shares. If, however, the mutual fund deducts the service charge from your proceeds rather than requiring separate payment, Uncle Sam lets you use the net proceeds when you calculate the gain on your old shares rather than adding the charge to the basis of your new shares.

You should know if you acquire additional mutual fund shares by having your dividends reinvested, your cost basis in those shares equals the amount of the dividend.

After you have acquired shares in a mutual fund, you might have to make certain adjustments to the basis of your investment.

You increase the basis if there are any undistributed capital gains allocated to you. You reduce the basis by any so-called "nontaxable distributions" which are a return of capital. See

Chapter 5 for a discussion of how the basis adjustment is de-termined if your fund has undistributed capital gains or non-taxable distributions.

Identification of shares sold

Perhaps one of the most complex tasks of mutual fund in-vesting is the determination of the basis of the shares that you sell. If you maintain adequate records and you liquidate your entire investment in one transaction, the determination of the basis is relatively simple. But what happens if you sell only a portion of the shares you hold? If you have any combination of nontaxable distributions, undistributed capital gains, rein-vested dividends, and past sales, the determination of the basis of individual shares may be quite difficult.

As with other investments, the general rules of share identi-fication apply. If you can specifically identify the shares sold, you can use the basis of those shares to determine the amount of the gain or loss.

To accomplish this specific identification, you must have the cooperation of the fund's transfer agent. Sometimes, par-ticularly, with some no-load funds, the transfer agent will not identify the shares for you. In that situation, you must use one of the other techniques for share identification.

TIP If you already have a net capital loss for the current year, you may want to sell the shares with the lowest basis. You may be able to reduce the capital loss that is carried forward without incurring additional tax in the current year. See the discussion of the rules for limitation of capital loss deductions later in this chapter.

Like sales of other stocks, if you can't specifically identify the shares you sell, the general rule is that you use the first-in, first-out (FIFO) approach.

If specific identification of shares is impracticable and the FIFO method would result in large capital gains, Uncle Sam provides two averaging methods for determination of the basis of shares sold. Only mutual fund shareholders may use the averaging methods.

The two methods are called the single-category method and the double-category method. Under both of these methods, you use the average basis of the shares you hold when you sell to determine the cost basis of the shares sold to be used for the calculation of gain or loss.

☞ CAUTION To use either of the averaging methods, Uncle Sam says you must maintain your shares in the custody of a custodian or agent in an account maintained for the acquisition or redemption of shares of the mutual fund.

Single-category method. If you elect the single-category method, all the shares you own in a given mutual fund are grouped into one category, and the average basis per share is calculated. Your average basis per share is determined by taking your total basis of all shares of that fund at the time of the sale and dividing that amount by the total number of shares you hold at that time.

Under the single-category method, the determination of whether the gain or loss is long-term or short-term is based upon the FIFO method. Thus, the shares you sell will always be considered to be the ones you have held the longest.

Double-category method. The double-category method, as the name implies, divides your holdings at the time of sale into two categories—those shares held for more than 1 year and those shares held 1 year or less. So your shares are divided into long-term and short-term categories. You then determine the average basis for the shares in each category in the same manner as you do for the single-category method.

When using the double-category method, you specify to the transfer agent from which category the shares will be sold. The shares will be deemed to have been sold from this category without regard to any stock certificates actually delivered.

But Uncle Sam says you must receive, within a reasonable period of time after the sale, a written confirmation of your specification from the custodian or agent. If you do not receive a confirmation or if you do not make a specification, the FIFO method will be assumed. That is, you will be deemed to have sold the shares from the long-term category first.

TIP The double-category may present savings opportunities over the single-category method because of the flexibility to use the basis which allows the smaller current tax bill.

In practice, however, the double-category method may be much more difficult to work with. And since long-term capital gains currently receive little preferential tax treatment, you may not feel like the extra burden from this method is worth the added flexibility.

☞ **CAUTION** Once you elect either of the averaging methods for a fund, you must continue to use that method with respect to all sales from that fund until you have completely liquidated your interest.

Capital losses

What's a capital loss? It's the opposite of a capital gain. Here's the good news when it comes to capital losses: Uncle

Sam allows you to use your capital losses to offset your capital gains plus $3,000 of ordinary income. Also, the rules let you carry forward any capital losses you aren't able to deduct currently to future tax years.

Say your capital losses for the year come to $8,000, and your capital gains total $1,000. The difference between the two—$7,000—is your net capital loss.

You may use up to $3,000 of this amount to offset your ordinary income. So, if your taxable income is $50,000, you could reduce it by $3,000. As for the remaining $4,000, you may carry forward this amount to offset income in future years.

Capital losses that you carry forward retain their "character"; that is, short-term capital losses remain short-term capital losses, and long-term capital losses remain long-term capital losses.

☞ **CAUTION** Don't make a common mistake and lump your capital losses from passive investments, such as limited partnerships, with your other capital gains and losses.

The law says your capital losses from passive activities are subject to the $3,000 cap on capital losses. What's more, the law imposes special restrictions on the deductibility of passive losses. In most cases, you may deduct your capital losses from passive activities only from your passive income. We provide the details in Chapter 9.

Capital losses on bonds bought at a premium

Here's something else you should know. Sometimes you pay a premium for a bond; that is, you pay more for it than its face value at maturity. This situation normally crops up when market interest rates fall below the interest rate of the bond.

How is this premium handled? See the discussion in Chapter 2.

Capital losses on collectibles

☞ CAUTION If you're an investor in jewelry, coins, stamps, antiques, or the like, you may not be able to write off your capital losses on these items. Why?

Uncle Sam says you're entitled to a deduction only if you're able to prove that your primary purpose in purchasing the item was to make a profit. You're also required to show that you didn't purchase these items purely as a hobby or for your personal enjoyment.

Capital losses when your income is zero

TIP You say you had zero or negative taxable income before you deducted your capital losses? You may be able to carry forward all or a portion of your losses to next year.

Here's an example.

Say you're single, and your taxable income—before you subtract your capital losses but after you claim your personal exemption—adds up to a $250 loss.

Now, how do you calculate how much of your capital losses you may carry forward to next year? Add back to your taxable income—in your case, a $250 loss—your personal exemption of $2,150. The result is taxable income of $1,900.

Your net capital loss for the year adds up to $3,000. You subtract $1,900 from $3,000 and the result—$1,100—is the amount you may carry forward to next year.

5

How to Get the Most from Your Capital Gains

What else do you need to know about capital gains? Let's take a look at some lesser-known facts about capital gains and, more important, some tax-saving strategies.

Gains and losses from sale of business property

If you invest in a business—a partnership or S corporation, for example—you are likely to have "§ 1231 gains and losses" reported to you on your Form K-1.

Although property used in a trade or business is not considered a capital asset, Uncle Sam provides a tax break for § 1231 property—that is, real estate or depreciable property used in a business that has been held for more than one year. A portion of the net gain during a taxable year from the sale of § 1231 property may be treated as a long-term capital gain. Some of the gain may be considered ordinary if it relates to prior depreciation expense. The partnership or S corporation will perform these calculations for you. So the amount that shows up on your K-1 as § 1231 gain or loss will be the amount eligible for § 1231 treatment.

On the other hand, a net § 1231 loss is deductible as an ordinary deduction without regard to the limitations on long-term capital losses. There may, however, be other limitations on deducting a § 1231 loss—see, for example, the discussions on passive activities in Chapter 9 and at-risk rules in Chapter 19.

In order to determine whether you have a net § 1231 gain or a net § 1231 loss, you must add up all your § 1231 gains for the year and then subtract all your § 1231 losses. If the result is positive, you have a net § 1231 gain. If the result is negative, you have a net § 1231 loss.

☞ **CAUTION** If you deducted no § 1231 losses in the previous 5 years, all of the current-year § 1231 gain will be treated as a long-term capital gain. But if you were able to deduct § 1231 losses in that time period, Uncle Sam allows only the portion of the gain which exceeds the prior year losses to be treated as a long-term capital gain and the balance is treated as ordinary income.

But once a prior year § 1231 loss is applied against a later § 1231 gain—also known as being "recaptured"—causing that § 1231 gain to be treated as ordinary income, it does not need to be recaptured again when additional § 1231 gains are realized in subsequent years.

Say in 1990 you had a § 1231 gain of $400 reported on your K-1 from XYZ Partnership. You had no other § 1231 gains or losses during the year. When you look back at your income tax returns for 1985 through 1989, you discover that the only net § 1231 gain or loss was in 1987. In that year, you reported a § 1231 loss of $500. Since your 1990 § 1231 gain was less than that amount, it will all be treated as ordinary income.

Now, it's 1991 and you have a § 1231 gain of $300. Since only $400 of the 1987 § 1231 loss was recaptured in 1990, you must still recapture an additional $100 in 1991. So in 1991, you would have $100 of ordinary income and $200 of long-term capital gain.

Capital gains and installment sales

An installment sale occurs when you sell an asset in one year and at least one payment is to be received in another year.

Say you purchased unimproved land in 1980 for $60,000 and sell it in 1991 for $100,000. The new owners agree to pay you over a two-year period; that is, they make payments to you of $50,000 in 1991 and 1992.

Under the installment sale rules, the taxable income you report in any year is based upon the amount of cash received during the year.

So, in 1991, your gain from the sale adds up to $20,000—that is, one half of the gain since you received one half of the selling price in 1991. You report your profit as long-term capital gain and, as the current law requires, pay taxes at your ordinary rate—not to exceed 28 percent.

☞ CAUTION Uncle Sam won't let you report gain from the sale of stocks, bonds, or other securities that are publicly traded using the installment sale method. Also, the installment sale rules don't apply to sales of inventory, or if a sale results in a capital loss. For other installment sales, however, Uncle Sam requires you to use the installment sale rules unless you make an election on your tax return to report all of your income in the year you make the sale.

TIP Say you expect to report a net capital loss for the year. And you've sold an asset—a painting, for example, on an installment basis. In addition to interest, the buyer agrees to pay you $1,000 a year for five years. Your profit adds up to $3,500—$700 a year for five years.

You may want to report your entire $3,500 gain from the sale now, rather than as the payments are made to you, because you can use this gain to offset your net capital loss. Or you may claim a net capital loss of up to $3,000 for the year, then carry forward any net capital losses that top the $3,000 limit.

CAUTION If you sell an asset on the installment method, the sales price is more than $150,000 and total installment obligations arising during the year exceed $5 million, you should consult your tax adviser. In this case, Uncle Sam may require you to pay interest on the amount of tax which is postponed under the installment sale rules.

Capital gains and like-kind exchanges

A like-kind exchange is, as its name suggests, an exchange of one item for another that's similar. Like-kind exchanges are tax-free if the property exchanged is used in your business or held for investment. A sale followed by a reinvestment in like-kind property does not qualify for this special treatment.

Say, for example, that you trade gold bullion for Canadian Maple Leaf gold coins. Since you're exchanging gold for gold, your trade qualifies as a like-kind exchange and isn't taxable. Or, say you exchange one piece of rental real estate for another. That transaction also qualifies as a like-kind exchange.

It seems inconsistent, but Uncle Sam says that when you convert U.S. currency into foreign currency, you pay tax on any profit you make. In other words, exchanges of currency don't qualify as like-kind exchanges.

And this same rule applies to exchanges of partnership interests. When you trade an interest in one partnership for an interest in another, your gain is taxable.

Likewise, exchanges of inventory, stocks, bonds, notes, certificates of trust, securities, and choses in action don't qualify as like-kind exchanges and are taxable.

Never heard of choses in action?

You're not alone. The term refers to a right or claim to personal property that you don't have in your possession.

For example, you loan $2,000 to your brother-in-law and he gives you a promissory note representing the loan. This note is a choses in action.

What else doesn't qualify as a like-kind exchange? Exchanges of gold bullion for silver bullion and—believe it or not—of male livestock for female livestock.

Under the rules, you don't have to complete the exchange all in one day. You have 45 days from the date you dispose of one asset to *identify* another one to receive in exchange, in a signed document sent to the other party. Otherwise, the trade is taxable. And Uncle Sam isn't kidding. He doesn't allow one more day.

Here's another restriction on like-kind exchanges: You must complete your exchange through the receipt of replacement property by the earlier of 180 days from the date you transfer ownership of your property or of the due date, including extensions, of your tax return for the year in which the exchange takes place.

Say it's July 13, 1991, and you transfer a parcel of farm land. Uncle Sam gives you until August 27 to properly identify a new piece of property to receive in exchange. Then, you have until January 10, 1992, to actually receive the property and acquire title. If you meet these deadlines, the exchange is tax-free.

☞ **CAUTION**   If you participate in a like-kind exchange, you should consult your tax adviser to make sure you abide by Uncle Sam's rules.

Capital gains that your mutual fund passes along

You're subject to tax on net long-term gains that your mutual fund earns and distributes to you. Say the manager of your mutual fund sells some bonds at a profit and distributes this long-term capital gain to you and other shareholders. These capital gains are taxable to you. See Chapter 3 for a discussion on the taxation of short-term capital gains your mutual fund generates.

You report this amount as a long-term gain regardless of how long you've owned shares in the fund. (You'll find this amount listed on your Form 1099-DIV.)

TIP   When you're considering investing in a mutual fund, you should read what the prospectus says about the amount of unrealized appreciation in that fund.

What's unrealized appreciation? It's the amount the securities in the fund have appreciated over the amount the fund paid for them.

If a fund has significant unrealized appreciation, you may get back a portion of your original investment as a long-term capital gain distribution—something you probably don't want to happen. Here's how it works.

Let's say you invest $10,000 in a fund. Say, too, that $2,000 of the $10,000 is the value of the fund's stocks that tops their original cost to the fund—in other words, unrealized appreciation. As the fund manager sells these stocks, he or she triggers capital gains. If these capital gains are distributed to you, you must pay tax on them. Assuming the fund earns no other income, if the fund manager sells all the stocks that have appreciated and distributes the capital gains, you end up with an investment worth $8,000 and cash of $2,000, less federal and state capital gains tax.

However, a mutual fund may also have capital loss carryforwards or unrealized losses. These carryforwards or losses may prove advantageous because they may reduce the amount of capital gain income you're required to report.

☞ **CAUTION** After making complex calculations, your mutual fund may determine that a portion of the distributions that you received during the year is actually a return of part of your investment. A distribution that is a return of capital (also known as a "tax-free dividend" or "nontaxable distribution") usually does not represent taxable income. Instead, these distributions reduce the basis in the shares you hold.

However, say the nontaxable distribution tops your basis. In this case, it results in a taxable capital gain. Whether the gain is long-term or short-term depends on how long you've held shares in the fund.

TIP If you'd like more information on how income from mutual funds is taxed, ask the IRS for a free copy of its Publication 564, *Mutual Fund Distributions*.

Capital gains that your mutual fund retains

Sometimes a mutual fund retains—rather than distributes to investors—its long-term capital gains. The bad news is, the law requires you to report as long-term capital-gains income your portion of that amount even if the fund doesn't actually hand the money over to you. It also doesn't matter how long you've owned the shares.

The good news? The fund has already paid taxes on the gains it retained, so you're entitled to a tax credit for the amount of tax that was paid on your share of the income.

Your fund will send you Form 2439, "Notice to Shareholder of Undistributed Long-Term Capital Gains," listing the amount of the long-term capital gain you must report and the tax paid by the fund on that amount. You may claim a credit for that tax on your Form 1040.

How? Enter the amount of tax eligible for the credit shown on Form 2439 on line 59 of your Form 1040. Then attach Copy B of your Form 2439 to your return.

You also increase your basis in your mutual fund investment by the difference between the amount of undistributed gains you report and the amount of tax the fund paid for you.

What all this means is that you're in essentially the same tax and economic position as if you'd actually received the capital gain, paid tax on it, and then reinvested the difference in the fund.

☞ **CAUTION** You should know that capital gains your mutual fund retains and reports to you on Form 2439 aren't recorded on your Form 1099-DIV but are in addition to those listed on your 1099-DIV.

☞ **CAUTION** You should hold onto Copy C of your Form 2439. That way, if you're audited—either in the current year or in the year you sell your mutual fund shares—you can substantiate amounts claimed on your return, including increases in the basis of your mutual fund stock.

As we saw in the previous chapter, an increase in basis can either decrease your capital gain or increase your capital loss when you subsequently sell the mutual fund stock.

Capital gains and property settlements

You and your spouse decide to call it quits. You get the title to the apartment building the two of you own, and he gets all the stocks and bonds in your joint brokerage account. What are the tax consequences of your settlement?

When you transfer ownership of capital assets from one spouse to another in cases of divorce, the transaction isn't taxable—as long as neither spouse is a nonresident alien. Another requirement is that the transfer occur within one year from the date the marriage ends.

If you'd like more information on this topic, ask the IRS for a copy of its free Publication 504, *Tax Information for Divorced or Separated Individuals*.

Capital gains from real-estate investment trusts

Report your capital gains distributions from real-estate investment trusts (REITs) as long-term capital gains no matter how long you've owned stock in the trust. Your REIT will mail you a 1099-DIV listing this amount soon after the close of the tax year.

Capital gains and short sales

Short sales. A short sale occurs when someone sells stock which he or she either does not own or does not want to transfer. The seller borrows identical stock—from a broker, say—to deliver to the buyer. At a later date, the seller "covers" the short sale by either delivering the stock owned or acquiring identical stock and delivering it to the lender. The seller recognizes a capital gain or loss measured by the difference between the basis of the stock delivered and the proceeds received from its sale.

TIP Did you know it's possible to nail down a 1991 paper profit on your stocks and have it taxed in 1992? In effect, you freeze a profit (or loss) and postpone the tax by using a technique known as a "short sale against the box."

For example, to fix the current paper profit in a block of stock, you go to your broker and tell him or her you want to arrange a short sale.

It works something like this. On December 1, 1991, you own 100 shares of stock in XYZ Corporation with a basis of $1,000 and a current value of $3,000. The stockbroker allows you to borrow another 100 shares, using your existing shares as collateral. You then sell the borrowed shares, thus fixing your profit.

Sometime in 1992, you cover the short sale by delivering your original shares to the broker in repayment.

The result? The profit on the 1991 short sale becomes next year's taxable income. The maneuver can work beautifully purely as a tax move, but if the stock value increases after the short sale, you lose the benefit of that appreciation. This is also true, of course, of any stock you sell.

CAUTION If you sell stock short which you do not own, you have the potential for unlimited losses if the price of the stock goes through the roof before you acquire the shares to close the sale.

TIP If the price of XYZ stock drops before you close the short sale by delivering the stock, you can "buy in" the short position and retain your low basis stock.

For example, say on January 12, when your short position is still "open,"—that is, you haven't delivered stock to the lender—the value of 100 shares of XYZ drops to $2,000. You may want to buy in the short position by acquiring 100 new shares to cover the short position.

In this case you would recognize a capital gain of $1,000 ($3,000 sales price—$2,000 cost of new XYZ shares), rather than the $2,000 gain you would have recognized if you had delivered the original shares. And the original shares would keep their basis of $1,000 and their long-term holding period.

Stock options

The buyer or the "holder" of an option has the right within a stated time period to buy or sell a specified amount of the underlying property at a stated price. The amount paid for a put or call (defined below) is called the "premium." The seller or "writer" of an option is obligated to sell or buy the underlying property at the stated price if the option holder exercises the option. Options are available on a multitude of assets.

Although the tax rules are generally the same for all options other than "§ 1256 contracts," this discussion will cover only the tax aspects of noncompensatory put and call options on stock. (A § 1256 contract is any regulated futures contract, any foreign currency contract, any nonequity option including options on commodities, commodity futures contracts, debt instruments and broad-based stock indexes. If you invest in § 1256 contracts, you should consult your tax adviser regarding the special rules which apply.)

A put is an option to sell. As the holder of a put, you have the right to require the writer to purchase the underlying stock from you at the stated price. A call is an option to buy. If you are the holder of a call, you may require the writer to sell stock to you at the stated price.

If you buy a put and later exercise it, the premium you paid for the put reduces your proceeds from the sale of the underlying stock when you calculate your gain or loss on the sale of the stock. If your put expires before it is exercised, you generally recognize a short-term or long-term capital loss depending on how long you held the put before it expired.

If you are the writer of a put, you don't recognize income when you sell it. If the holder of a put you wrote allows it to expire, you generally recognize a *short-term* capital gain at the date it expires. The gain equals the premium received.

If the put is exercised and you—the writer of the put—have to buy the underlying stock, the premium you received for the put reduces your basis in the stock you buy. In this case, your holding period for the stock begins on the day the stock is bought—not on the day you sold the put.

If you write a put and want to cancel the put before it expires or is exercised, you may buy an identical put—that is, "buy in" the put. In this case, you would have a *short-term* capital gain or loss equal to the difference between the premium paid for the buy-in and the premium received on the sale.

TIP Rather than selling stock short against the box, you may choose to buy a put. Similar to a short sale against the box, you are able to lock in a gain, but the tax on the gain is deferred until you exercise the put.

The disadvantage of buying a put is the option price in a put is usually less than the current market value of the underlying stock. And you have to pay for the put. But if you buy a put, rather than a short sale against the box, you may take advantage of future increase in the stock value.

For example, you own 100 shares of APJ Corporation which you bought several years ago for $800. On December 3, 1991, 100 shares of APJ is worth $2,500 so you buy a put to lock in your gain. If the value of 100 shares of APJ soars to $4,000 on January 21, 1992, you may choose not to exercise the put and sell your APJ stock on the market. Had you sold

short APJ on December 3, you couldn't avail yourself of its subsequent price rise.

If you exercise a call you hold, the premium you paid for
the call is added to the price you pay for the stock to determine
your basis in the stock used to calculate the gain or loss when
you later sell the stock.

If a call you hold expires, the premium you paid is generally a short-term or long-term capital loss depending on how
long you held the call.

You could sell a put or call you hold before it expires. If
you do, you generally recognize a capital gain or loss. The
amount of the gain or loss depends on what you paid for the
put or call and how much you sold it for. And the general
rules for the determination of holding periods apply to the
sale.

If you write a call, you don't recognize income when you
sell it. If the holder of the call lets it to expire, you generally
recognize a *short-term* capital gain at the date it expires equal
to the premium received.

If a call you write is exercised and you must sell the underlying stock to the holder, the premium you received for the
call increases your proceeds when you calculate the gain or
loss on the sale of the stock. In this case, the gain or loss is
long-term or short-term depending how long you held the
stock—not when the call was sold.

You may also buy in a call you write if you want to cancel
it before it expires or is exercised. You do this by buying an
identical call. In this case, you would have a *short-term* capital gain or loss equal to the difference between the premium
paid for the buy-in and the premium received on the sale.

Capital gains on tax-exempt investments

Tax-exempt investments aren't always tax-free. When you sell or exchange tax-exempt bonds or shares in a tax-exempt fund and post a profit, you're taxed on your gain.

Likewise, when you shift money between municipal bond funds, it's the same—in the eyes of Uncle Sam—as selling shares in one fund and buying shares in another. If you earn a profit on the transaction, that profit is taxable to you as a capital gain.

Capital losses and involuntary exchanges

An involuntary exchange—or involuntary conversion, as it's sometimes called—is the sudden loss of an asset that doesn't occur in the ordinary course of business.

Rental property destroyed by fire qualifies as an involuntary conversion, as well as land seized by a state highway department for use in the construction of a road.

What if you lose an asset through an involuntary conversion and are compensated for it? The law says you must report the excess of the compensation over your basis as income on your tax return, unless you reinvest the money in similar property within 2 years after the year you are compensated.

Here's an example. Say you and your partners invest in an Ohio wheat farm. The U.S. Army Corps of Engineers announces plans to build a dam, and your farm is needed for the project.

You and your partners ask the Corps to pay you $100,000, and—to your surprise—it agrees. Now, you must decide whether to use the money to purchase another farm or invest the $100,000 elsewhere. What are the tax consequences of both moves?

If you and your partners reinvest the $100,000 in another

farm in a timely way, none of you has to report that amount as income on your tax returns.

But if you and your partners decide to sink the money in stocks or bonds, you'd better watch out. Uncle Sam says you must report the excess of the $100,000 over your basis as income on your tax return and pay taxes on it.

Losses on small business stock

Congress wants you to invest in small companies, and it's willing to share the risk with you. It says that you may deduct from your ordinary income—wages, salaries, and so on—losses of up to $50,000 ($100,000 if you're married and file jointly) on so-called small business stock. So if your stock qualifies as small business stock, losses aren't subject to the annual $3,000 capital loss limitation.

What qualifies as small business or—as the IRS calls it—Section 1244 stock? It's the stock of a small business corporation with total capital of less than $1 million. The stock must be acquired directly from the corporation. Also, small business stock isn't convertible into other securities of the corporation.

A company must meet all sorts of other requirements for its stock to qualify as Section 1244 securities. So our advice is to ask a company whose securities you're considering purchasing if its stock qualifies under these rules.

TIP You should also know that the $50,000 ceiling on losses is per taxpayer per year. So if you're considering selling Section 1244 stock that will produce a loss of more than $50,000 in one year, it's smart to stagger the sale of these shares over more than one year.

Say you're married, file jointly, and you've invested $200,000 in 1,000 shares of Section 1244 stock. You plan to sell the stock at a loss of $150,000.

If you sell all your shares in 1991, you deduct only $100,000 from your ordinary income. The remaining $50,000 is treated as a long-term capital loss; that is, you may use it to offset your capital gains but the excess may be written off only at the rate of $3,000 a year.

A better idea is to sell enough of your stock in 1991 to generate a $100,000 loss, then sell the remaining stock in 1992. That way, the entire loss is deductible from your ordinary income much sooner. (You file Form 4797 with your tax return to report your loss from Section 1244 stock.)

Capital losses and the wash-sale rules

☞ **CAUTION** You could be in for a large and unexpected tax bite if you plan to offset your capital gains with losses the IRS classifies in the wash-sale category.

What are the wash-sale rules? They're Uncle Sam's way of preventing you from selling stock, including stock in a mutual fund, at a loss, writing off the loss on your tax return, then immediately buying the stock back.

These rules say that you may not take a loss if, within a period beginning 30 days before you sell your security and ending 30 days after that date (a period of 61 days), you have acquired or entered into a contract or option to acquire "substantially identical stock or securities."

Moreover, the Supreme Court has ruled that you may not take a loss if your spouse purchases identical shares. The rules don't apply, incidentally, if you received your new stock or security through a gift, bequest, inheritance, or tax-free exchange.

Let's say on September 15, 1990, you bought 100 shares of XYZ stock for $1,000. On March 22, 1991, you bought an additional 100 shares of XYZ for $975. On April 15, 1991, you sold the 100 shares you purchased on September 15 for $900.

Since you bought 100 shares of the same stock within the period beginning 30 days before the date of the sale and ending 30 days after that date, you may not claim a $100 loss on your return.

However, the basis of the shares you retained is increased by the amount of the loss. Also, the holding period of the shares you sold is added to the shares you retained. Thus, the shares purchased on March 22 would have a basis $1,075 ($975 plus $100) and the holding period would be increased by seven months.

Capital losses on worthless securities

You're entitled to claim a capital loss in the year securities you own—stocks, bonds, and so on—become worthless. What's a worthless security? It's one that is valued at zero or, in some cases, one that is selling for only a nominal amount—less than one cent a share, let's say.

State taxes on capital gains

TIP You may not know it, but some states tax long-term gains differently than short-term capital gains. Your tax adviser will know the rules in your state.

6

The Right Way To Write Off Interest

Interest—the cost of borrowing money—is probably the most complicated of all deductible expenses. That's because some interest costs are deductible, some are not, some are only partly so, and the situation changes from year to year.

Interest charges fall into a number of categories—personal interest, business interest, and so on. But in this chapter, we look at the ones that investors are most likely to claim and provide tax-saving strategies for each. Let's start, though, with a few words about leverage.

LEVERAGED INVESTMENTS

What's leverage? It's when you use some of your own money and some borrowed money to make an investment. You deduct your interest, and you enhance your return because total return is measured only on the amount of your own money invested.

Confused? Here's an example.

Let's say you shell out $2,000 to buy 200 shares of a stock selling for $10 a share. If the price of the stock rises to $15, the value of your holdings climbs to $3,000. Your gain is $1,000—that is, the market price of $3,000 minus your $2,000 purchase price. Therefore, your return is 50 percent ($1,000 divided by $2,000).

Now, what if you'd bought 400 shares of stock at $10 a share for $2,000 in cash and $2,000 in credit. You'd have $4,000 worth of the same stock. Then, if the stock price shoots up to $15 a share, the value of your holdings would equal $6,000. You pay back the loan, and what have you got? $2,000 more than your original investment of $2,000. And your gain is 100 percent—not 50 percent.

That's how leverage—in a best-case scenario—works; but leverage carries risk, too. Let's say—as in the example above—that you bought 200 shares of XYZ stock at $10 a share. Instead of the stock rising to $15 a share, it plunges to $5 a share.

If you sell your shares, you post a $1,000 loss—that is, your original investment of $2,000 minus the $1,000 you received for your shares.

Now, what if you'd bought 200 shares with your own money and 200 shares on credit and, again, the stock plummets to $5 a share? Your loss adds up to $2,000. You sell the shares and pocket $2,000—just enough to repay the loan. Thus, your entire original cash of $2,000 is lost.

So, you ask, does it make sense for you to leverage—in other words, borrow to make an investment? The answer may be yes if your after-tax rate of return on the leveraged investment tops the after-tax cost of borrowing. But you should know that it's not a tax decision alone.

You also must weigh the risks of investment.

KNOW THE BASIC RULES

Now, for a few more basics. Interest is deductible in the year it's paid. If you pay by check, the day you mail or deliver the check is the date of the payment.

If you pay by telephone or wire transfer, the day the money is transferred is the date of payment. How do you know the date of payment? You'll find it listed on the statement that your bank or other financial institution mails you each month.

Prepaying interest is a no-no—tax-wise, at least. For example, you borrow $5,000 on June 1, 1991, to purchase 500 shares of stock in a high technology company. In December, you pay eleven months of interest. What's your deduction for the year?

Under the rules, you may write off interest payments for seven months—meaning those you made for June through December of 1991. Interest you prepaid for January, February, March, and April of 1992 isn't deductible until you file your 1992 return.

If you're thinking about deducting interest on money you borrowed on your life insurance policy, it also pays to know the rules.

Uncle Sam says that if you file your return using the cash basis of accounting—as almost all of us do—you may only write off interest on these loans when payment is actually made. For example, you're not entitled to a current deduction for interest if the insurance company deducted the interest in advance from the amount of the loan, or you didn't make interest payments when due and the insurance carrier added the interest due to the loan.

Now, what if you borrow money to make interest payments? The IRS says you may not deduct any interest that you pay with borrowed funds unless you borrow from a different lender. Take out a loan from the same lender, and you pocket no deduction until the loan is repaid.

You may not write off interest on a debt unless you're legally liable for it—that is, you're a party to the loan. In other words, the interest payments you make on your brother-in-law's loan aren't deductible on your return, unless you're personally liable for these amounts.

It would be a better idea to give your brother-in-law the cash to make the interest payment, so he, at least, can write off the interest; otherwise, the deduction is lost.

You also may not write off interest on a debt unless—in the words of Uncle Sam—a "true debtor-creditor relationship" exists.

Let's say you loan your son $5,000 to help him make the downpayment on his first house. "Thanks, Dad," he says and promises to repay you someday. Meanwhile, you aren't holding your breath until that day comes. The two of you put nothing in writing and adopted no set schedule for repayment. He may not deduct any interest payments he makes to you because no true debtor-creditor relationship exists.

Now, let's change this scenario slightly. Say your son borrows $5,000 from a local bank to purchase some stock, and you cosign the note. Both of you are legally liable for the loan, so whoever makes the interest payments is entitled to an interest deduction.

RULES FOR DEDUCTING INTEREST EXPENSE

As you read the pages that follow, keep in mind that there are only two ways to reduce the cost of borrowing. One is to share the cost with Uncle Sam.

The other is to pay a lower rate of interest.

So when it comes time for you to borrow, shop around. Interest rates vary from one institution to the another, and so do the fees— such as points—that institutions charge to lend you money.

Mortgage interest

If you borrowed money to purchase a home, the mortgage interest is 100 percent deductible on your Form 1040—as long as you incurred the debt on or before October 13, 1987. What if you signed your mortgage after that date? Then, some restrictions apply.

For example, you may deduct mortgage interest only on principal amounts of up to $1 million. Interest on principal in excess of $1 million isn't deductible.

Also, interest on home-equity loans is deductible only up to $100,000 of principal. However, this interest is deductible regardless of how the money is used—unless the loan proceeds are used to purchase a tax-exempt investment.

Say, for example, that you borrow money on your home-equity line to make an investment. The interest is still deductible as mortgage interest.

The rules require that the mortgage be secured by the property—be it a house, a cooperative apartment, a condominium, a house trailer, or a boat. Trailers and boats, though, must include basic living accommodations—for example, space for sleeping and cooking and bathroom facilities.

TIP For more information on mortgage interest, ask the IRS to send you a free copy of its Publication 545, *Interest Expense*.

Business interest

Business interest is, as a general rule, 100 percent deductible. So, if you're faced with a choice of borrowing to make an investment or for capital for your business, borrow for your business. That way, you're guaranteed to get a deduction for the entire amount of interest paid.

Investment interest

Interest on money you borrow to make an investment is probably tax-deductible. But different rules apply, depending on the type of investment.

The general rule, though, is that your deduction of investment interest in any one year is limited to the amount of your investment income. In other words, if you don't make money on your investments in any specific year, you may not deduct the interest on your investment loans.

Let's say you're an active investor and earn $1,500 in taxable dividends and interest from various stocks and bonds during one year. If you borrowed money to purchase some of those investments, you may write off up to $1,500 in interest expenses.

What if your investment-interest expenses for the year add up to more than $1,500? Uncle Sam says you may carry forward indefinitely the amount not deducted.

Here's another example. Suppose your investment interest expense for the year totals more than $1,500—$2,000, say. You may write off $1,500 of the interest against your current year's investment income, and you may carry forward the $500 balance into next year or beyond. That means, you may carry forward the $500 until you generate enough investment income—from dividends, interest, and capital gains—to offset the deduction.

TIP Did you know that you can convert investment interest to deductible home-equity interest by borrowing against your first or second home? Interest on the loan is totally deductible as long as your home-equity debt doesn't top $100,000.

CAUTION Sorry, but the rules won't allow you to deduct interest on money you borrow to invest in tax-exempt municipal bonds or tax-exempt municipal bond funds. And it doesn't matter if the loan qualifies as home-equity debt. The interest still isn't deductible.

What if you borrow money and use, let's say, half of it to invest in tax-exempt bonds and the other half to purchase stock? You may write off the interest on the part that goes to purchase stock, but not the interest on the part that you use to buy the tax-exempt bonds.

CAUTION Uncle Sam also won't allow you to deduct interest on money you borrow to buy single-premium life insurance policies, endowments, or annuities.

This restriction includes contracts on which you pay almost all the premiums within four years of the date you purchase the policy, as well as contracts on which you deposit an amount with the insurance carrier to cover future premium payments.

☞ **CAUTION** If you're a partner in a partnership, and your partnership purchases some stock on margin, how is the interest treated for tax purposes? Your portion of the interest is passed along to you on a Schedule K-1, and you deduct the interest as investment interest.

Now, suppose you're a shareholder in an S corporation, and your S corporation purchases stock on margin. The interest—as in the case of a partnership—is passed along to you and deducted on your personal return as investment interest.

☞ **CAUTION** Don't let the tracing rules trip you up. These rules require you to deduct interest based on how the proceeds from the loan were used.

Say, for example, that you borrow $25,000 and deposit the money in your NOW account. You use the proceeds to buy some stock, a car for your son, and a computer for your business. This loan—in the eyes of Uncle Sam—produces three kinds of interest.

The interest on the money you use to purchase stock is investment interest. The interest on the dollars used to purchase the car for your son is personal interest, and the interest on the money that goes to purchase a computer for your business is business interest.

Usually, when you take out a loan, you either use the proceeds at once for a particular purpose, or you deposit them in your checking or savings account for a time.

What happens if you deposit the proceeds in an account that contains some of your other funds? Under the rules, the interest on the loan is classified as investment interest. And it remains investment interest until you take the money out of your account and use it.

What's more, if you want the interest classified by how you use the loan proceeds, you must spend the money you borrow within 30 days before or after the money you borrow is actually deposited into your account. You're asking for trouble if you wait longer than 30 days. If you wait more than 30 days, Uncle Sam bases your interest deduction on the first purchase you make from your account.

For example, suppose you borrow $2,000 on January 2 to buy some stock in a high-technology company. You deposit the money in your NOW account, which already has a balance of $4,000.

On February 6, your refrigerator goes kaput. So you buy a new one for $2,000. On February 10—40 days after you took out the loan—you buy the stock. You fork over $2,000 for 200 shares of XYZ Corp. How is the interest treated for tax purposes?

Interest on the entire $2,000 loan is treated as investment interest until February 6, when you buy a new refrigerator. Then the interest on the $2,000 you borrowed is treated as personal interest—in other words, as if you'd borrowed the money to purchase the refrigerator.

Now, here's another scenario. Your balance in your personal savings account is $6,000. You then borrow money to invest in an interest-bearing bond. Six months later, you sell the bond and use the proceeds to pay off all your credit cards.

How does Uncle Sam treat the interest on the loan? He treats it as investment interest for the six months you owned the bond. Then it's personal interest because you used the money to repay your credit cards.

TIP An easy way to have kept your deduction as investment interest—and fully deductible from your investment income—was to have used the money in your savings account to pay off your credit card bills.

TIP For more information on interest, ask the IRS for free copies of its Publication 545, *Interest Expense*, and Publication 550, *Investment Income and Expenses*.

Personal interest

The interest on charge accounts and loans that you take out strictly for personal reasons—car loans, let's say—are not deductible after 1990.

What is the bottom line? You may be better off using some of your dollars to pay off your consumer debts rather than investing them.

How do you know which makes the most sense for you? We've included on page 116 a chart that illustrates how much you need to earn on an investment—given your tax bracket and the interest you're paying on your loan—before that investment makes financial sense for you.

TIP Here's an idea for writing off consumer interest: Borrow the money from yourself—from your own savings. Then, pay back the principal plus interest just as you would a bank. You're effectively getting a deduction on your loan interest because you're not reporting interest income on the amount you took out of the account.

Passive activity interest

Passive activities, which we cover in detail in Chapter 9, are businesses in which you don't materially participate in the management. Passive activity interest is deductible only from passive activity income. You may not write it off from wages, salaries, or any other income.

What if you report no passive activity income? Uncle Sam says you're not entitled to a deduction. But—here's the good news—you may carry forward passive interest that you're unable to deduct to offset passive activity income in future years.

What's more, in the year you sell or dispose of a passive investment, you may deduct the interest related to that activity that you weren't previously able to write off.

Pretax Cost of Borrowing*

Rate of Interest		8%	9%	10%	11%	12%	13%	14%	15%	16%	17%	18%	19%	20%	21%
		Equivalent Pretax Return on Investment													
1991 & Beyond	Tax Bracket 15%	9.4	10.6	11.8	12.9	14.1	15.3	16.5	17.6	18.8	20.0	21.2	22.4	23.5	24.7
	28%	11.1	12.5	13.9	15.3	16.7	18.1	19.4	20.8	22.2	23.6	25.0	26.4	27.8	29.2
	31%	11.6	13.0	14.5	15.9	17.4	18.8	20.3	21.7	23.2	24.6	26.1	27.5	29.0	30.4

*Ignores any potential impact of itemized deduction limitation and personal exemption phase-out (discussed in Chapter 1).

7

How To Make Your Deductions Work For You

You can often save yourself a nice bit of change by itemizing deductions on your tax return. The rule of thumb for any taxpayer is, if you can itemize, you should.

ITEMIZE YOUR DEDUCTIONS

In this chapter, we cover investment-related miscellaneous itemized deductions—expenses subject to the two percent floor. Two percent floor?

That's right. Take your AGI. Multiply by two percent. This number is the floor. Add up your miscellaneous deductible expenses. If their sum is greater than two percent of your AGI—and you itemize—you may deduct the difference.

For example, the year is 1991, and your AGI totals $46,000. Two percent of this sum equals $920. Your miscellaneous deductible expenses come to $1,564. If you itemize on your return, you may deduct $644—that is, $1,564 minus $920.

Don't confuse this 2 percent floor with the 3 percent floor on all itemized deductions (see Chapter 1). To calculate your allowable deductions, you first determine the amount of miscellaneous deductions you can take by applying the 2 percent floor. Then you add in this result with other itemized deductions that are subject to the 3 percent floor we discussed earlier.

You also may want to know that Uncle Sam allows you to write off as miscellaneous itemized deductions expenses that you rack up in association with your investments—as long as those investments produce taxable income.

What if all your money is in tax-exempt bonds? That's easy. You're not entitled to a deduction.

What if your money is in taxable *and* tax-exempt bonds, and you can't identify the expenses associated with each type of investment? You're required to perform this simple calculation. You add up your income from taxable investments and your income from tax-exempt ones. Then, you add these two numbers together. Next, divide your taxable investment income by your total investment income. The result is the percentage of investment expenses you may deduct, subject—of course—to the two percent floor.

Confused? This example illustrates how to figure this amount. Say your taxable interest for the year adds up to $4,800, and your tax-exempt interest comes to $1,200; your expenses total $500. You aren't able to match your expenses with the type of income your investments produced, so the rules require you to perform the following calculation.

Add up your interest income—that is, your taxable interest of $4,800 plus your tax-exempt interest of $1,200—to get $6,000. Next, divide your taxable interest—$4,800—by your total interest income—$6,000—to get 80 percent. That's the amount of your expenses attributable to your taxable bonds.

The 20 percent remaining is attributable to your tax-exempt bonds and not deductible.

HOW TO LOWER YOUR TAX BILL

Now, here's our alphabetical checklist to help you make sure you aren't forgetting investment-related deductions that could lower your tax bill.

Accounting fees

Do you use an accountant to keep track of your investments or help you with your tax matters or investment planning? The fees charged by the accountant are deductible.

Administration fees for an IRA

You may write off fees you pay a trustee for managing assets in your trust. You also may deduct trustee fees you pay in connection with your Individual Retirement Account (IRA)—as long as the fees are billed separately and not paid with dollars deposited in the account.

Write off these expenses on line 20 of Schedule A of your Form 1040—*not* on line 24 of your 1040 where you claim your IRA contribution.

☞ **CAUTION** Don't make the mistake some taxpayers do and deduct capital expenses, such as the commissions you may pay a broker, as IRA administration fees.

Commissions you pay when you buy and sell, let's say, stock in your IRA account are capital costs, and the rules require you to add them to your basis when it comes time to calculate your gain or loss. (See Chapter 4 for the details on figuring your basis.)

☞ CAUTION You also may want to think twice before you allow trustees to take their fees out of dollars you contributed to your IRA. Why? You then have less money accumulating in your IRA.

💵 TIP If you'd like more information on this topic, ask the IRS to send you a free copy of Publication 590, *Individual Retirement Arrangements*.

Bank fees

Fees that banks charge you to service your investment-related account are deductible, but you may not write off check-writing expenses, even if you have an interest-bearing account.

Likewise, you may write off fees that banks or brokers charge you to collect interest and dividends on the taxable bonds and stocks you own.

Clerical help and office rent

You may deduct office expenses, such as rent and clerical help, that you rack up in connection with managing your taxable investments.

☞ CAUTION Uncle Sam says you may not deduct home office expenses if you use your home office to monitor your investments. Why? Although you have a profit motive, investment activities on your own behalf are not considered a trade or business.

You also may not write off the cost of a security system

installed to protect investments—for example, art objects—from theft.

Computers

Uncle Sam allows you to deduct through depreciation the cost of a computer you use to keep track of your investments; but, you may write off *only* that portion attributable to investments.

Let's say you pay $5,000 for a computer and use it 60 percent of the time for managing your investments. The law allows you to depreciate 60 percent of the cost of the computer. That means that you can write it off gradually over five years or more.

TIP If you'd like more information on deducting the cost of your computer, ask the IRS for a free copy of Publication 534, *Depreciation*.

Custodial fees for dividend reinvestment plans

Some companies charge custodial fees when you ask that your dividends automatically be reinvested in additional shares. Fees you pay for holding shares acquired through a plan and collecting and reinvesting cash dividends are deductible.

You may also write off fees that companies charge for keeping individual records and providing detailed statements of accounts. And, you may deduct monthly service charges you pay to a bank or other financial institution to participate in an automatic investment plan.

Investment adviser fees

Fees you pay for investment advice are deductible. But what if you pay for investment advice and aren't able to itemize? You lose the deduction.

TIP Here's an idea to consider: Bunch your deductions in one year by accelerating or deferring payments that are due early the following year. This way, you may exceed the standard deduction—and itemize—at least every other year. For example, you might pay in December investor adviser fees that are due in January.

TIP Here's another strategy to keep in mind.
Say you receive $2,000 a year for an investment that costs you $500 a year to maintain. You give the $1,500 annual profit to your son to help pay his college expenses. You don't write off the $500, because your miscellaneous expenses don't exceed two percent of your AGI.

Consider transferring ownership of the investment to your son. He gets the money to cover his college costs and, since his AGI is less than yours, he may be able to deduct the $500 of investment expenses. Remember, though, when you give away the investment, you give it away forever.

Investment club expenses

You say you belong to an investment club? And it's organized as a partnership? Expenses your club incurs in producing investment income and managing its investments are passed along to you on a Schedule K-1. You report your portion of these amounts on line 21 of Schedule A of your Form 1040.

Legal fees

Fees paid to attorneys for assistance with your investments are deductible *only* if they aren't part of the cost of acquiring or defending title to an investment.

If, for instance, you use an attorney to help you buy stock in a company, the fee isn't deductible. Rather, it's part of the capital cost of purchasing the stock.

You add the fee to your basis in the property when you sell the stock and calculate your gain or loss. (See Chapter 4 for more on basis.)

You also may not write off attorney fees related to your tax-exempt investments.

Mutual fund fees

Uncle Sam provides a break for people who invest in publicly-traded mutual funds. Shareholder expenses incurred by the fund aren't subject to the two percent floor.

Postage, supplies, and safe deposit box rental

You may deduct the cost of postage and supplies that are related to managing your investments. You may also write off the cost of renting a safe-deposit box, provided the box is actually used to store taxable investments or papers related to these investments.

If you use the box only to store jewelry and other personal items or tax-exempt securities, the safe-deposit box fee isn't deductible.

Proxy fights

If you wage a proxy fight opposing management of a company in which you are a stockholder, the IRS allows you to deduct your expenses.

Proxy fights you wage for personal reasons are one exception to this rule. Say, for example, you're a shareholder in a pharmaceutical company, and you wage a proxy fight to halt its practice of testing drugs on animals. Your expenses aren't deductible because you're waging the fight for personal reasons.

Seminars and conventions

Don't expect much help from the IRS in paying for investment-related seminars and conventions. The travel and meal expenses of attending such gatherings aren't deductible. Nor may you claim a write-off for the attendance fee.

Service fees

Service fees that you pay a broker, a bank, a trustee, or other agent to collect your taxable interest or dividends on shares of stock are deductible. Remember, though, that the fee paid to a broker to buy investment property, such as stocks or bonds, isn't a service fee but a capital expense—and isn't deductible.

Stockholder meetings

The IRS says you may not deduct transportation and other costs of attending stockholder meetings of companies in which you are only a shareholder. However, you may write off these expenses if you're a shareholder and an officer of the company and the company isn't reimbursing you.

Subscriptions

Subscriptions to investment-related publications are deductible, but the tax law won't allow you to write off multiple-year subscriptions in a single year.

Let's say you subscribe to an investment newsletter; you pay for a three-year subscription—a hefty $900—in 1991. Under the rules, you may not deduct $900 on your 1991 return. Rather, you write off $300 a year for the next three years.

Tax-related expenses

Your labors in preparing your tax return are free. But, if you engage and pay someone for help, those fees are deductible.

For example, you may write off appraisal fees, as long as they're paid to determine the fair market value of property donated to charity. You may also deduct legal or accounting fees for tax advice, as well as tax planning and preparation fees.

Also deductible are fees you pay for determining, collecting, or refunding a tax—including income tax, estate tax, gift tax, sales tax, or property tax. And the cost of tax preparation and planning books, including this one, is also deductible.

You may also write off the cost of contesting a tax assessment—even if you lose—and of obtaining a federal tax ruling from the IRS.

TIP You write off tax preparation fees in the year that you pay them. So, you claim a deduction on your 1991 return for fees you pay in 1991 for preparing your 1990 return, as well as any fees you paid for an early start on your 1991 return.

Telephone expenses

The law allows you to deduct the cost of investment-related telephone calls. These expenses include long-distance and cellular telephone charges. Uncle Sam says you may not write off any portion of your basic monthly charge for the first telephone in your home.

Transportation

You like to do business in person, not on the telephone. Hop in your car and drive to your stockbroker's office. Uncle Sam says your transportation costs—including parking fees—are a deductible investment expense.

8

Understanding The Alternative Minimum Tax

You may consider yourself lucky. Through a judicious use of deductions, deferrals, and credits, you've slashed the tax you owe on your income to a very small amount.

Congratulations. But before you go out and celebrate, consider this tax fact: There's a separate tax system, called the alternative minimum tax (AMT) that's designed to ensure that you pay your fair share to Uncle Sam. It works like this.

You figure out how much tax you owe under the regular system and calculate the amount you owe under the AMT system. Then you compare the two results and pay the higher amount.

Everyone, of course, isn't liable for the AMT. Might you be? You may if you've taken lots of deductions in the following categories:

- State and local real-estate taxes, income taxes, and personal property taxes

- Passive investments such as oil and gas limited partnerships and real estate

127

- Interest on a refinanced mortgage if the amount you've refinanced is greater than your original mortgage (that is, interest on the excess amount over your original debt)

- Donations of certain types of appreciated property you give to charity

- Home equity interest (if you don't use the loan proceeds to improve your home)

- Miscellaneous deductions

Maybe you're uncertain whether or not you're subject to the AMT. Perhaps, too, you don't want to take the time to do the AMT calculations. If this is the case, you should see your tax adviser.

However, if you think you probably will have to ante up the AMT, read on. We'll help you pay no more tax than is absolutely necessary.

Who pays the AMT?

As we just noted, if you claimed many deductions—particularly in the categories we mentioned—you may be in trouble. Chances are good that you'll have to pay the AMT.

Other circumstances may also make you liable for the AMT. For example, you may have exercised incentive stock options (ISOs) or invested in what are known as private-activity bonds. (State and local governments issue these bonds, so they can raise money for private purposes. For instance, a state may issue industrial bonds, which small businesses then use to build factories.)

☞ CAUTION If you just can't tell whether you'll be subject to the AMT, there's only one way to know for sure. You must "run the numbers."

In this chapter, we tell you what you need to know in four steps. The first step: We tell you how to figure out how much of your income is subject to the AMT. Second, we explain about an exemption that may help you offset some of this AMT taxable income. Third, we show you how to figure out what Uncle Sam calls your tentative minimum tax and minimum tax credit. The fourth step is to provide strategies to enable you to keep your AMT to an absolute minimum.

Okay, first things first. Before you can save any money, you must calculate exactly how much of your income may be subject to the AMT. This amount is called, appropriately enough, alternative minimum taxable income, or AMTI. To get started, take your regular taxable income and make the following adjustments.

Standard deduction and personal exemptions

The AMT rules don't let you claim the standard deduction—the one people take who don't itemize. Nor may you take the deduction for personal exemptions. So you must add these items back.

Itemized deductions

Alas, the regular tax system allows for many itemized deductions that the AMT prohibits. So when you figure your AMTI, you must add most of these deductions back to your regular taxable income.

Which deductions specifically? The items you must add back are: real estate and personal property taxes, state and local income taxes, and medical expenses that total less than 10 percent of your AGI. (As you may recall, for regular tax purposes, you may deduct medical expenses that come to more than 7.5 percent of your AGI.)

In addition to these items, you must add back those other

miscellaneous deductions—professional dues and tax preparation fees, for instance—that you deducted under the regular tax system.

The law does allow some itemized deductions. You may continue to deduct under the AMT: investment interest that doesn't exceed your investment income; home mortgage interest (unless you refinanced after July 1, 1982, for more than the outstanding balance on your mortgage, in which case interest on the excess is not deductible; also interest on home equity loans is usually not deductible unless the loan proceeds are used to improve your home); charitable contributions of certain types of property; and casualty losses.

You should also keep in mind that, although you may not deduct any investment interest in excess of investment income, you may still get a break when it comes to investment interest expense. You may carry forward indefinitely—until you use it up—any of this expense that you're unable to use for AMT purposes in the current tax year.

Also, the rules are different when it comes to interest you pile up when you refinance your home mortgage or take out a home-equity loan. Under the AMT, you may deduct interest only on that part of the refinanced mortgage that doesn't top your outstanding mortgage before you refinance.

And, if you take out a home-equity loan in order to duck the rules on deducting personal interest, the AMT rules could foul up your plans. You usually may not collect an interest deduction on home-equity loans for AMT purposes. (See Chapter 6 for the rules on deducting interest.)

However, as we pointed out earlier, the law does allow for an exception to this rule. Say you use the money you get from the home-equity loan to pay for major home improvements or renovations. In this case, the interest is deductible for AMT purposes.

What if you have interest expense on a loan—home equity

or otherwise—where you used the money for a trade or business or investments? In these cases, Uncle Sam says you may still write off for AMT purposes the interest on the loan. When it comes to investments, though, you may write off only as much interest as you have investment income.

Here's another rule that you should keep in mind. Say you buy a luxury boat, and it qualifies as a second home. There's a good chance that the interest on the money you borrow to purchase the boat is deductible under the regular tax system. But you may not deduct this amount under the AMT system. That's because, according to the AMT rules, a boat doesn't qualify as a dwelling unit.

TIP Remember the 3 percent floor on itemized deductions we discussed in Chapter 1? This limitation does not apply for AMT purposes, so all itemized deductions allowable for AMT purposes—for example, cash contributions to charity—are fully deductible.

Passive activities

You recall from Chapter 9 that passive activities are essentially tax shelters. And they come in many forms, including an investment in a limited partnership or rental property.

What's the precise definition of a passive investment? The IRS considers any investment passive if it constitutes a trade or business in which you do not materially participate in managing. Moreover, all rental activity, by definition, is a passive investment. It makes no difference whether you materially participate.

Under the passive activity rules (which are the same for both regular tax purposes and AMT purposes) you can deduct losses from passive activities only to the extent you have income from other passive activities. You can carry any nondeductible losses forward to future years and use them to offset future years' passive income.

Only in the year you sell or otherwise dispose of your interest in the passive activity will these losses that you've carried forward be deductible against other income (for example, wages, interest, and dividends). And, any loss you may incur when you dispose of the interest is similarly deductible in the year of the disposition.

It's important to realize that the loss you may have from a passive activity that is deductible for regular tax purposes is not necessarily the same as the loss that is deductible for AMT purposes.

The reason? You may write off some items, such as depreciation deductions, faster for regular tax purposes than for AMT purposes. (We'll have more to say on this topic shortly.)

Here's an example: You invested in a real estate limited partnership which produces a regular tax loss of $800 in 1991. Because you have no other passive income, you won't be able to deduct the passive loss for regular tax purposes.

Some of the $800 loss occurred because the property owned by the partnership was depreciated using an accelerated method. The AMT rules say that you may depreciate property only using the straight-line method, which gives you a lower depreciation deduction in the early years that the property is owned.

Now, let's say the partnership recalculates its depreciation deductions for AMT purposes. Instead of the $800 loss reported to you for regular tax purposes, it reports $200 of income for AMT purposes. This means, of course, that for AMT purposes, you realized $200 of income on the same investment that produced no income or deductible loss for regular tax purposes.

You would also have an $800 passive loss carry-over from 1991 for regular tax purposes, but no AMT passive loss carryover.

Stock options

The big advantage of incentive stock options (ISOs)? When you exercise them, you usually pay less for the stock—sometimes much less—than the stock's fair market value. According to the tax code, this difference between the price you pay and the stock's fair market value is the "bargain element," which isn't subject to the regular tax.

☞ **CAUTION** That's usually good news. The bad news? As you may have guessed, the difference counts as an "adjustment" when it comes to the AMT.

What's an adjustment? It's similar to an AMT "preference." Both are items that receive favorable tax treatment under the regular tax rules, but not under the AMT rules. Both adjustments and preferences are commonly grouped together and called AMT preferences.

In the year you exercise your options, you're generally required to add back the bargain element to your AMT income. All is not lost, though. The difference becomes part of your stock's cost basis for AMT purposes. And that means when you finally sell the stock, your gain—for AMT purposes—totals less than it does for regular tax purposes.

Say, in 1986, your company grants you 1,000 ISOs at an option price of $11. You exercise the options early in 1991. The fair market value of the stock when you buy it comes to $61 a share. So you have a tax "preference" of $50,000—the difference between the option price ($11,000) and the fair market value ($61,000). By late 1992, you're ready to sell the 1,000 shares, which you do for $71 a share. Your gain for regular tax purposes totals $60,000, an amount equal to $71,000 less your option price of $11,000.

You face a different situation for AMT purposes. Here your gain totals only $10,000—$71,000 less your AMT basis for the shares, or $61,000 (the $11,000 option price plus the $50,000 bargain element you had to add to your AMT income in 1991).

When you calculate your AMT income in 1992, you subtract the $50,000 difference in the gain.

☞ CAUTION   If you receive ISOs and you're an insider—meaning an officer or director of a corporation under the jurisdiction of the Securities and Exchange Commission (usually any public company)—special rules apply. These rules vary depending on when you exercise the options; the SEC changed the rules effective May 1, 1991, so options exercised before and after this date are subject to different rules and different AMT consequences. See Chapter 15 for a discussion of these special corporate insider rules.

💵 TIP   You should never put tax considerations front and center when it comes to investment decisions. And that bit of advice applies as well to the AMT. If it makes economic sense to exercise your options now, then go right ahead.

Depreciation

You must add back or subtract from your regular taxable income the difference between the depreciation you claimed for regular tax purposes and depreciation you figured using alternative depreciation. What do we mean? Consider this example.

Let's say that in December 1990, you bought the land and building where you have an office. The price came to $125,000. You allocate $100,000 to the cost of the building and $25,000 to the cost of the land.

Now it's time to file your 1991 return, and you write off depreciation for the building. You use the straight-line method over 31.5 years to calculate this deduction. In 1991, then, you may deduct $3,175 in depreciation.

What happens when you figure out your AMT liability? Under the alternative method, you depreciate real property—the building—using the straight-line method over 40, not 31.5 years. So your depreciation deduction would have come to $2,500. That means the difference between the two methods, the amount you must add back to your income for AMT purposes, totals $675.

We'll now project your situation way into the future and imagine that 32 years have gone by. You're still the owner of the building, and you've fully depreciated it by now for regular tax purposes.

Congratulations. After all this time, you get a break. Under the AMT rules, you may still collect a $2,500 deduction each year in years 33 through 40. You no longer must add back dollars; instead, you get to take an additional deduction from your AMT income.

Uncle Sam makes one exception to this rule. The exception applies to real property and leased personal property, which is placed in service—that is, put in use—before 1987.

If this is the case, you must, in calculating your AMT, add back to your regular taxable income the excess of the depreciation you claimed using the accelerated method over the old straight-line depreciation. However, you don't later get to subtract the difference between the straight-line method and accelerated depreciation.

Other preference and adjustment items

A number of other preference and adjustment items apply to the AMT. Let's review them.

The excess of percentage depletion over the tax basis of property that generates the mineral deposit. What does this bit of tax jargon actually mean?

We can explain it best by providing an example. Say you own a 10 percent partnership interest in an oil and gas operation. In 1991, your proportionate share of the percentage depletion, which is simply a deduction that reflects the fact that the value of the operation has fallen, is allocated to you.

Your share of the percentage depletion on the gross income of the oil and gas operation totals $20,000. Your share of the adjusted basis of the land that produces the oil and gas comes to $15,000. That means the tax preference comes to the $5,000 difference, the amount you must add back to your AMT income.

Interest on tax-exempt "private-activity" bonds issued after August 7, 1986. You pay no tax on the income you collect from these bonds under the regular tax system. But—you guessed it—you do pay tax under the AMT. However, the AMT rules let you write off interest expense you incur to buy these bonds, to the extent of your tax-exempt income. The regular tax rules, by contrast, do not let you deduct this interest.

The difference between (1) the fair market value of real or intangible property you contribute to a charitable organization and write off—as an itemized deduction—for regular tax purposes, and (2) the cost of the property. Here's an example. A loyal supporter of your local symphony, you decide to donate 100 shares of stock to this venerable institution. The stock cost you $2,000 two years ago, but it now commands a fair market value of $5,000. Under the regular tax rules, you write off the $5,000 as an itemized deduction. However, the AMT rules let you write off only the price you paid for the stock. So when you calculate your AMT income, you add back to your regular taxable income the $3,000 difference.

TIP There is a new wrinkle in the tax law affecting the donation of *tangible* personal property to qualified charities—say, the donation of a painting to a museum. If you make this donation in 1991, the entire fair market value of the painting is allowed as an AMT deduction, so there is no AMT add-back.

But be careful. This special rule applies only to tangible personal property donated in 1991.

Excess intangible drilling costs that total more than 65 percent of the net income from productive oil and gas wells. As you probably can tell by now, the adjustments you must make when you own shares in oil and gas partnerships are quite complicated. Moreover, in 1990 Congress enacted certain AMT relief provisions related to oil and gas investments that are equally as complicated. So we strongly advise you to consult with your tax adviser if these form part of your investment portfolio.

Research and development costs. For purposes of the regular tax system, you may write off these expenses in the year you incur them. The AMT rules, however, require you to capitalize the R&D expenses—that is, write them off over several years. In this case, you must write them off over 10 years.

You deduct 10 percent of the R&D costs each year of the 10-year period. And this holds true, even though you already deducted them in full for regular tax purposes.

TIP The law does provide a loophole of sorts when it comes to R&D expenses. You may avoid treating them as a preference item by amortizing all or a portion of them for regular tax purposes and deducting them over 10 years.

This strategy, of course, is far from perfect. When you employ it, you get a much smaller deduction each year for regular tax purposes. Therefore, you should run the numbers to see which method of treating these costs saves you the most tax.

Now you've made all the adjustments to your regular taxable income and accounted for all tax preference items. What's left is your AMT income, or AMTI.

Fortunately, the law lets you cut your AMTI by these exemptions: $40,000 for married taxpayers filing a joint return;

$20,000 for married taxpayers filing separate returns; and $30,000 for single taxpayers. But there's bad news, too. If by Uncle Sam's standards your AMTI remains high, you have to cut your exemption. You reduce it by 25 percent of the amount by which your AMT income tops: $150,000 for married taxpayers filing jointly; $75,000 for married taxpayers filing separately; and $112,500 for single filers.

What this rule means, in effect, is that you'll collect no exemption at all if you and your spouse file jointly and your AMT income exceeds $310,000. As a single taxpayer, your ceiling comes to $232,500.

Here's an example. Say you and your spouse file jointly and your AMTI comes to $213,725. So your exemption falls from $40,000 to $24,069.

How did we arrive at that figure? We took your AMTI of $213,725 and subtracted $150,000; the answer: $63,725. Then we multiplied this amount by 25 percent. The result comes to $15,931. Next, we subtracted $15,931 from the $40,000 AMT exemption to get $24,069.

We're almost finished with all the AMT calculations. So far, you've figured out your AMT income and adjusted it by the appropriate exemption amount. We're almost ready to help you compute your alternative minimum tax. You simply take your adjusted AMT income and multiply it by the AMT tax rate of 24 percent. The result you obtain—after you have subtracted any foreign tax credits, recomputed for AMT purposes, the law allows—is your tentative minimum tax (TMT).

Now, compare your TMT to your regular income tax. (Again, first take any allowable foreign tax credits.) If your TMT comes to more than your regular tax, you must pay the difference—the alternative minimum tax—in addition to your regular tax.

But wait. There's more. You still must calculate what's known as the minimum tax credit (MTC). What's that? Think of it as a credit for taxes you paid earlier under the AMT system that you wouldn't have paid under the regular tax system.

Why this benefit? Uncle Sam recognizes that some of your AMT liability may come from the fact that the AMT sometimes speeds up your income. In other words, the AMT rules sometimes require you to report income before you would have to for regular tax purposes.

One example is paper profits you "realize" when you exercise ISOs.

Since, under the AMT system, you pay taxes on this income earlier than you otherwise would under the regular system, you've already paid a portion of your regular tax liability. In a later year, the MTC can reduce your regular tax liability by the amount of AMT taxes you paid in prior years.

So far, in computing your AMT income, you've made adjustments to your regular taxable income that fall into one of two categories. These adjustments are either "deferral items" or "exclusion items." What's the difference? We'll tell you in a minute. But first you should know that the difference affects the amount of your MTC.

Deferral items, as the name suggests, won't reduce the amount of tax you owe permanently. They only defer your tax liability until later.

Exclusion preference and adjustment items are another story. Unless you're subject to the AMT, you never have to ante up the taxes that you attribute to these items. And that's good news.

There are only four exclusion preference items: all itemized deduction adjustments, the appreciated-property charitable-contribution preference item, the percentage-depletion preference, and the tax-exempt bond preference item. Everything else counts as a deferral preference item.

That's nice you say, but how does knowing the difference between these two items help me cut my taxes in the future?

Here's how: Once you've finished calculating your AMT as we described, calculate it again. This time, however, use only the exclusion preferences. Your minimum tax credit (MTC) equals the difference between this adjusted AMT and the AMT you first calculated (limited, of course, to the total AMT you paid for the year). In other words, your MTC is the amount of AMT attributable to deferral items only.

Uncle Sam says that you may carry this credit forward indefinitely (although you may not carry it back) to offset your regular tax liabilities in the future. You may reduce your regular tax, however, only to an amount that equals the TMT in the year you carry forward this amount.

Confused? Here's an example.

Say in 1991, you pay $16,000 in AMT. The entire amount you pay results from your exercising incentive stock options, which count as a deferral tax preference item. So the $16,000 now qualifies as your MTC carryover.

In 1992, you rack up a regular tax liability of $61,000 and a TMT of $59,000. So you may use $2,000 of that $16,000 MTC carryover from 1991 to reduce your 1992 tax payment to Uncle Sam.

However, say that you must pay the AMT year after year. Or say your AMT liability and your regular tax bill are similar. In these situations, the minimum tax credit doesn't help you much at all.

It's important to think about both short-term and long-term strategies when you plan for the AMT. Your short-term strategies should involve accelerating or deferring income and deductions. But you must also consider the impact of the minimum tax credit. For your long-range planning, you must focus on the kinds of investments you make.

Here's an example. Say over the last five years, you've invested heavily in real estate or oil and gas limited partnerships. In fact, these are practically your only investments.

You suspect you may have to pay the AMT either this year or in future years. What should you do? It may make sense for you to shift your money into corporate bonds, say, or stocks or mutual funds. The reason? These investments don't have any effect on the AMT.

Also in the realm of long-range planning: focus on the kind of tax treatment you elect for rental property and other depreciable assets.

TIP One tack you might take would be to choose, for regular tax purposes, the longer alternative method of depreciation. If you do, you won't be required to add to your AMT income the difference between accelerated depreciation and alternative depreciation.

Of course, you may be out of luck when it comes to preferences from limited partnership investments. With these investments, you don't have much influence over decisions.

TIP You should always assume that you will be liable for the AMT. Then run the numbers each and every year.

You should also project your tax situation two years out. That's because the actions you take this year affect your AMT situation next year. Obviously, making these calculations can be burdensome.

Remember, you can't wait to worry about the AMT until you're ready to send in your tax return. The rules say that you must pay 90 percent of the tax you'll owe for any one year in withholding and estimated tax payments. And that means you may have to fork over more in estimated taxes if you're subject to the AMT.

9

Making Sense of the Passive Loss Rules

Did you know that it is only since Congress adopted the 1986 Tax Reform Act that the terms passive activity, passive income, and passive loss have become part of our tax vocabulary. These concepts aren't always easy to grasp—nor are the regulations governing them.

Here, we detail the strict rules governing passive investments. First, though, a few words on who is affected by the passive activity rules. When our national legislators passed the law governing passive activities, their intent was to discourage tax shelters, but the rules went far beyond that simple goal.

Instead, they ended up affecting nearly every person engaged in business. If you're a shareholder in an S corporation, a shareholder in a closely-held corporation, a self-employed person, or a partner in a partnership, you're potentially affected by these rules.

You're also affected if you own rental real estate or rent out other types of property such as video tapes, hotel rooms, or tools. And, as a result, you may face burdensome restrictions and paperwork requirements.

Defining the terms

What's a passive activity? In the eyes of the IRS, a passive activity, subject to the rules we're about to discuss, is either a trade or business activity in which you invest but aren't a material participant, or a rental activity.

☞ CAUTION You should know also that limited partnership investments are almost always passive. Here's why: Limited partners almost never materially participate in managing the trade or business of the partnership.

Here's something else you need to know. Passive activities are investments that can generate two kinds of income.

One is passive income, meaning income from a trade or business or rental activity. The other is portfolio income, which includes interest, dividends, royalties, and so on. The law also says that income from personal services—that is, payments you receive for services rendered—and retirement plans is nonpassive income.

If all this seems a bit confusing at first, it is nonetheless important to master. That is because, as a general rule, only likes may offset likes.

Passive activity losses, for instance, may offset only passive activity income. Or, put another way, your passive losses may not reduce taxable income from nonpassive sources—salary or portfolio income, for instance. Here's an example to show what we mean.

Say you're a doctor in private practice, and you invest in a real estate limited partnership in 1990. In 1991, the partnership produces a $10,000 loss. Meanwhile, income from your medical practice adds up to $120,000, and your interest income from other investments is $5,000.

Because your real estate partnership is a passive investment, the losses it generates can't offset your nonpassive or portfolio income.

So under the law, your AGI comes to $125,000.

What's a passive rental activity?

What's passive when it comes to rental activities?

The IRS considers all rental investments, with several exceptions listed below, to be passive regardless of whether you materially participate. And rental activities include any investment that generates income from payments for the use of tangible property, rather than for services.

Included, then, are real estate rentals, equipment leasing, and rentals of airplanes or boats—as long as no significant services (flying or fishing lessons, say) are provided in making the property available to your customers.

Passive activity exceptions for rental activities

Also, Uncle Sam carves out several narrow exceptions to the passive activity rules for businesses whose main activity is renting either personal or real property.

What are these exceptions? Let's take a look.

• *Exception 1—The average rental period of your property is seven days or less.* You usually determine the average rental period by dividing the total number of days you have rented the property by the number of rental periods. (But the calculation becomes more complicated if you charge more rent for some units in the same complex; for example, you pocket more for the handful of chalets nearest the slopes of your ski resort. You should see your tax adviser if your property falls into this category.)

Uncle Sam defines a rental period as a period during which a customer has a continuous or recurring right to use the property.

This exception exempts most hotels, motels, and bed and breakfasts from the rental property rules, as well as such businesses as short-term auto rentals, tuxedo rentals, and video cassette rentals.

Exception 2—The property isn't rental property if the average rental period is 30 days or less and if you or someone you hire provides significant personal services to your rental customers. Examples of rentals of this type include resort accommodations.

☞ CAUTION In the eyes of the IRS, significant personal service doesn't include routine repair, maintenance, security, and trash collection nor services required for the lawful use of the property. In addition, significant personal services must be performed by individuals, so telephone and cable services don't apply.

The IRS has stated that in determining what services are significant, all relevant facts and circumstances are taken into account. These include the frequency of services provided, the type and amount of labor required to perform the services, and the value of the services relative to the amount charged for the use of the property.

Exception 3—Extraordinary personal services are provided by the owner of the property without regard to the average period of customer use. The IRS included this exception so that operations such as hospitals wouldn't be subject to the rental activity limitations.

What are extraordinary personal services? They're services provided in connection with a customer's use of the property, but the "rental" is incidental to the receipt of the services. For example, a patient in the hospital is renting the bed, but the bed rental is merely incidental to the major service of the visit, which is hospital care.

Exception 4—The rental of the property is treated as incidental to a nonrental activity of the taxpayer. Take, for example, a developer who has constructed a condominium. During the marketing period, some of the units are temporarily rented. Under these circumstances, the rental won't be considered a rental activity.

Exception 5—Property is customarily made available during defined business hours for the nonexclusive use of various customers. A golf course, for example, might qualify under this exception. While golfers pay a fee to use the course, the course is available during defined business hours and for the nonexclusive use of various customers.

Exception 6—Property you provide free of charge to a partnership or S corporation isn't rental property if you're a material participant in that partnership or S corporation. This rule applies to any property that you may own that you provide free of charge to your business. And it can include buildings and equipment.

☞ CAUTION   When your rental investment meets one of the exceptions, your income isn't automatically deemed passive. Instead, you determine whether you must treat your business as a passive activity by running through the material participation rules (which we describe in the next section).

PASSIVE TRADE OR BUSINESS

Now you know what's automatically passive when it comes to rental activities. But what's passive when it comes to a trade or a business, or when it comes to a rental activity that meets one of the above exceptions?

Let's start with the activity rules. Under these rules, you must first determine whether your involvement with many trades or businesses constitutes a single undertaking or multiple ones. What's a single undertaking? It's a trade or business that's conducted at the same location and owned directly—that is, not through a partnership or S corporation—by the same person.

Say you're the sole owner of an auto dealership, and your company both sells and repairs cars on the same lot. Your dealership qualifies as a single undertaking even though you're engaged in two businesses; that is, you both sell and repair automobiles.

What if you sell cars on one lot and repair them in a building two miles away? In this case, your auto dealership no longer qualifies as a single undertaking because you failed the location test. Instead, you have two undertakings.

Here are a few more twists.

Say you're the sole owner of a company that sells and installs electric garage door openers. The location requirement doesn't apply to you. Why not? The IRS says you have no fixed place of business, since your operations (the installation of garage door openers) are conducted at the customer's place of business.

Or say you're a partner in a partnership that owns a neighborhood convenience store. And you also own—by yourself—a convenience store in a nearby town.

Each store qualifies—by itself—as a single undertaking. That is, you may not lump them together and treat them as a single undertaking. Each qualifies as a single undertaking because—when they're combined—they fail the location test and the ownership test.

Now, you ask, why should I care whether my trade or business is a single undertaking or more than one separate undertakings? Here's the reason: Uncle Sam may require you to combine your multiple undertakings into a single activity. So what, you say.

You must pass the material participation test for each *activity*, not each *undertaking*.

What's a single activity? The rule is a single activity is a single undertaking. But Uncle Sam doesn't stop there. He also says that multiple undertakings that are similar and controlled by the same people fall as well into the single activity category.

One undertaking is similar to another if more than half their operations are in the same line of business; that is, they fall into the same IRS business classification, which are based on the Standard Industrial Classification (SIC) codes. (Your tax adviser will have a copy.)

Two undertakings meet the second test if they're controlled by the same people—that is, the same five or fewer people own 50 percent or more of it and the other undertaking.

Here's another test, and it applies to businesses that are vertically integrated. Under the test, an undertaking is similar to another if either undertaking supplies or obtains more than 50 percent of its products or services from the other.

TIP You say you want to treat your numerous rental real estate properties as separate activities? The IRS allows you to do so by electing to report them separately on your return.

But you should know that once you make this election, you may not break your properties into any additional activities. For example, if you combined two apartment complexes into a single activity, you may not later divide those two complexes into two separate activities.

TIP Since rental real estate is always passive (subject to the exceptions we outlined previously), it usually pays to treat them as separate activities. The reason? It may help you when it comes time to dispose of or sell the units, because you can use any suspended losses you've incurred at that time. The same is true, of course, with nonrental real estate activities. (We discuss the treatment of suspended losses later in this chapter.)

MATERIAL PARTICIPATION RULES

Now, on to the material participation rules. If you pass the material participation test, your trade or business (or your rental activity that fell into one of the exceptions) will not be classified as passive.

In Uncle Sam's eyes, you materially participate in a rental or trade or business if you're involved in its operations on a "regular, substantial, and continuous basis." But what does that phrase really mean?

Tests

Not surprisingly, the IRS has devised some tests—seven in this case—to help you tell whether you're a material participant in an activity. If your involvement satisfies just one of these, you're a material participant. If you don't satisfy any, Uncle Sam considers your investment passive.

And note: You may be a material participant one year and a passive investor the next. It's not enough, that is, to satisfy one of the tests in just any one year. The IRS requires you to reevaluate your participation annually.

Test 1—more than 500 hours of material participation. If

you spend more than 500 hours in an activity during the year, you're a material participant for the year. When applying this test, you may count any work that you do in connection with the activity as long as it is the type of work normally done by owners.

Moreover, say your spouse also performs the work of an owner. In this case, you may add his or her participation to your own for purposes of this rule—and the other tests outlined in this chapter.

TIP It doesn't matter that your spouse isn't a part owner of the business or whether the two of you file a joint return for the year.

If the total hours the two of you worked tops 500, you meet the requirements of the first test, and your investment isn't subject to passive activity rules.

Let's say, for instance, that Patrick and Meghan, a married couple, together put in more than 500 hours of work managing a restaurant that Meghan owns.

They meet the requirements of test one. But if Patrick's work had consisted of dish washing, a job that owners don't usually perform and the purpose of his taking on this task was to avoid the passive loss rules, his hours wouldn't count toward the 500-hour threshold.

CAUTION For purposes of this test and the ones that follow, Uncle Sam won't allow you to count the number of hours you spend in your capacity as an investor, unless you're directly involved in the day-to-day management of the business.

What's the role of investor? The IRS says it includes studying and reviewing financial statements, preparing or compiling summaries or analyses or monitoring the finances or operations of the business in a nonmanagerial capacity.

Test 2—substantially all participation. If your participation, or the participation of you and your spouse, represents substantially all of the participation by anyone in an activity for the year, you're a material participant.

Test 3—more than 100 hours of participation and not less than anyone else. This test has two parts.

First, you must spend more than 100 hours during the year operating the business. Second, you must spend more time than anyone else, including nonowners, working in the business. Meet both conditions of this rule in nonrental activities, and the business isn't a passive activity.

Test 4—more than 500 hours worked in several activities with more than 100 hours in each. This test itself isn't tricky, but the consequences can surprise you. The test says that if you spend more than 100 hours on each of two or more activities and a total of more than 500 on all of them, you're a material participant in each of those business ventures.

But that could be bad news. Maybe you wanted one of the activities to give you passive income or losses. Why? Consider this example.

Assume that Joseph, a full-time attorney, invested in several real estate limited partnerships. He expects these investments to lose money for several years.

Joseph is also a general partner in two other, very profitable activities—an auto parts store and a dry cleaning business.

He spends about 300 hours per year in the auto parts store and about 250 hours per year in the dry cleaning business. Both businesses have several full-time employees.

Joseph hopes to write off the passive losses from his real estate investments against the income from the dry cleaning and auto parts businesses.

After all, he figures, he isn't involved in either of the businesses for more than 500 hours, and others spend more time than he does working there.

But Joseph has a problem. Since his participation in each of these businesses comes to more than 100 hours and his total participation tops 500 hours, he meets the requirements of the fourth test.

So, as far as Uncle Sam is concerned, he's a material participant in both the auto parts store and the dry cleaning business. And the income from these businesses isn't passive. The result: Joseph can't use his passive real estate losses to offset the income from his two part-time businesses.

What if you invested in two businesses and both are posting a profit and your hours spent on both of these activities doesn't exceed 500 hours? A special rule applies. Let's take an example where you participate 140 hours in one business and 160 hours in the other.

Under test four, you aren't a material participant, but your profits aren't passive either. The IRS treats them as nonpassive income, and you may not use these earnings to offset any of your passive losses.

Now, let's change the scenario. Say the two businesses are operating in the red. You lose again because of the special rule we outlined above. Uncle Sam now treats the losses as passive losses.

Test 5—material participation in any five of the last 10 years. If you've been a material participant in a business for any five of the most recent 10 years, the IRS considers you a material participant in the business for the current year, no matter how small your actual involvement.

What's the point of this test? Uncle Sam wants to prevent people from shifting income from the passive to nonpassive category—or vice-versa—just to reduce their tax liability. Here's an example to show how that tactic might work.

We'll assume that Joe is the sole owner of Joe's Tool and Die, a very profitable sole proprietorship. He's also an investor in several real estate limited partnerships.

These limited partnerships produce sizable losses, which Joe wants to offset against the profits from his business.

Joe worked full time in his business since he started it in 1982. But he has decided to reduce the amount of time he spends at the tool and die company beginning in 1991, so he can pursue other opportunities.

Since Joe reduced his involvement, he thought his income from the business would be passive. Unfortunately, he's been tripped up by the fifth test.

He has been a material participant in the business since 1982, or nine out of the last ten years. Consequently, even though he doesn't participate in the business currently, the IRS treats him as a material participant for purposes of the passive loss rule.

Test 6—for personal service businesses, material participation in any three previous years. Say you have materially participated in a personal service business—law, engineering, accounting, architecture, health, consulting, performing arts, actuarial science, and so on—in any three preceding years. What are the tax consequences?

In the eyes of Uncle Sam, you're considered a material participant for the current year and into the future.

This test means that once you've been a material participant in, for instance, an architectural firm for any three years, any income you receive from the firm in the future is nonpassive no matter how few hours you toil for the firm.

The IRS considers residual fees, for instance, that inactive partners might receive from a personal service firm as nonpassive income.

Test 7—facts and circumstances. This test is easy to state, but difficult to apply.

It says simply that the facts and circumstances in any specific case will be the final determinant of whether you are or aren't a material participant.

Unfortunately, the IRS hasn't issued much guidance on

how it will look at facts and circumstances. Still, we do have a few guidelines.

First, you may not automatically add, as time spent in the business, the number of hours you devote to management. You may include your management hours only if no one else performs and gets paid for managing the business, and no one else spends more time than you managing the business.

Second, you must devote at least 100 hours to the business during the year to qualify under the facts and circumstances test.

If your participation comes to fewer than 100 hours, you're out of luck. Uncle Sam says you aren't a material participant in the business under this test regardless of any other facts and circumstances.

What about limited partners? Can they materially participate in a business? Generally they can't because state laws normally prohibit limited partners from being active in a business. And limited partners who do become active risk losing their limited liability.

Since limited partners do not normally participate in limited partnerships, the material participation tests we just discussed don't apply.

Exceptions exist, though. The first exception deals with the first test, the 500 hour test. Even limited partners are material participants if they put 500 hours or more into the business.

The second exception relates to tests five and six. If a limited partner meets either the 5-of-10 year test or the any-three-previous year test, he or she is a material participant regardless of the limited partner designation.

A third exception applies to people who are both general and limited partners in the same activity. The IRS considers them, on balance, to be general partners who must go back through test one through six above to determine whether they are material participants.

One final note: Although the law doesn't require it, anyone who anticipates that material participation could be an issue would be smart to keep a daily log of the hours he or she puts into a business. If the decision is a close call, the log could tip the balance.

LOSSES

Losses you rack up in 1991 from passive activities are good for offsetting your profits from other passive activities.

But what if you don't have profits from passive activities? All isn't lost. You may carry your passive losses forward and use them to offset passive income in future years. The passive losses that you carry forward are called suspended losses. And you must keep track of losses from each of your passive activities from year to year.

Here's an example to illustrate how suspended losses work. Say that the year is 1991, and you have invested in three limited partnerships—A, B, and C. All these partnerships are passive investments and, under the tests, are considered separate activities.

Partnerships A and B each generate $10,000 in losses this year. But partnership C rewards you with a $5,000 profit. In total, you lost $15,000 on passive investments—that is, $10,000 plus $10,000 (or $20,000) minus the $5,000 profit.

The passive loss rules won't allow you to deduct your $15,000 on your current tax return. So you carry forward the suspended loss to future years.

The losses from partnerships A and B are used *pro rata*—meaning in proportion—against C's $5,000 passive income, resulting in $7,500 of suspended loss you can carry forward for each partnership, A and B.

Here's how we do the calculation: Multiply the suspended

loss of $15,000 by the ratio of each partnership's loss to your total losses.

For example, partnership A's suspended loss is $7,500—that is, $10,000 (A's loss) divided by $20,000 (A's loss plus B's loss) or 0.5 times $15,000.

Now, say the year is 1992. Partnership A earns a $20,000 profit. Partnership B once again generates a $10,000 loss, and partnership C posts another $5,000 profit. You have a net $15,000 profit for the year ($20,000 from A plus $5,000 from C minus $10,000 from B).

And here's the good news. You carry forward your total $15,000 loss for 1991 from partnerships A and B and apply it against 1992's $15,000 profit. The result: You've reduced your income from passive investments in 1992 to zero.

Remember, the law says you may carry forward these suspended passive investment losses indefinitely. But that isn't all.

When you sell a passive investment, the law allows you to use all suspended losses from the activity you sold right away. And you may use these losses to offset not only your passive income but any other income, including earned income, or wages, and portfolio income as well.

You add suspended losses from an activity you dispose of this year to any current losses from the same activity and any losses you recognize at the time you dispose of the activity. If these losses come to more than your net income or gain from all your passive activities during the current year, calculate the difference. You may use the result to offset any other income or gains, including wages.

To illustrate this rule, let's return to our previous example. Now, say the year is 1992, and you decide to unload Partnership A. On June 30, you sell your entire interest to your neighbor, Lisa.

For the first six months of 1992, partnership A produces

income of $2,000. And, when you sell, you realize a gain of $1,500. Partnerships B and C don't produce any income or loss during 1992. Your only other source of income is your $120,000 salary.

You would obviously like to use at least some of your suspended losses to reduce your hefty income. And you may. In fact, you may use all your suspended loss from partnership A in 1992. But you must determine the suspended losses you're allowed as follows:

- Start by adding the following: the amount of your suspended loss from the previous year (in your case, $7,500); the amount of your loss from the current year (none); and the amount of loss you realize when you dispose of or sell the activity (none).

- Now, subtract from the result your net income from all your passive activities (in your case, $3,500).

- You may use the resulting amount—$4,000—to offset your salary.

What about the $7,500 suspended loss from partnership B? It's still suspended and will carry forward to 1993. You may not deduct it in 1992. The reason: You didn't dispose of your interest in B.

☞ CAUTION What if selling your passive activity results in a loss and the passive activity was a capital asset? In this case, the loss on the sale is treated both as a passive loss and as a capital loss subject to the capital loss rules (see Chapters 4 and 5 for more information on capital losses).

What can you do, you may wonder, if you're faced with substantial excess passive losses? Perhaps you should consider a Passive Income Generator (PIG). Or what if your investment yielded substantial deductions in the early years you owned it but now is generating only paper profits—known in tax lingo as phantom income? We explore some of these issues, and others, in Chapter 10.

Phase-in rules

The rules we've described so far apply to investments you made after October 22, 1986—that is, the date the 1986 Tax Reform Act was enacted. But the law provided a four-year phase-in period for investments you made on or before that date.

This phase-in period allowed taxpayers to offset their nonpassive income—that is, portfolio or earned income—with a portion of their passive losses.

After 1990, the passive loss limitation rules are fully phased in. So in 1991 and beyond, the law makes no distinction between "preenactment" or "postenactment" interests (those acquired before and after October 22, 1986, respectively). Now, passive losses are deductible only to the extent of your passive income until you dispose of your interest in the activity, under the rules we just gave.

Gifts

When you give away an interest in a passive activity to a friend or relative, you lose your right to claim suspended losses. In this case, the recipient of your generosity must add these suspended losses to his or her basis in the investment.

What if, later on, the recipient sells the investment at a loss? Then, for purposes of determining the donee's loss, his or her basis is limited to the fair market value of the interest on the date you made the gift.

Moreover, sales you make to related parties—relatives, your closely-held corporation, and so on—will also not let you immediately use your suspended losses. In this instance, you carry forward the losses until the related party disposes of the investment in a taxable transaction.

For example, say you sell your limited partnership interest to your dad in 1991. You won't be able to use 1990's suspended losses from the partnership when you make the sale. Instead, you continue to carry these losses forward as suspended losses until your dad sells the investment to an unrelated party, at which time you may deduct the losses.

Interest expenses

The law says that if an investment is a passive activity, interest expense on loans associated with that investment isn't subject to the personal or investment interest limits.

The rules say you may write off such passive activity interest only to the extent of passive activity income. If you report no passive activity income, you may not pocket a deduction.

But you may carry forward your passive activity interest indefinitely. In other words, you may use the interest you carry forward to offset passive income in future years. And in the year you dispose of a passive activity, you may deduct all passive activity interest that you hadn't been able to deduct before. In essence, this passive activity interest is treated just like it was a passive loss.

And it makes no difference whether the interest expense is "inside interest"—that is, incurred by the limited partnership itself—or "outside interest," interest on money you borrow to invest in the limited partnership.

What does this rule mean? When you borrow money to purchase a passive activity investment, the interest is combined with your income or loss from the investment to determine your overall passive income or loss from the activity. What if you loan money to the partnership or it loans money to you?

Recent proposed regulations permit you to treat a portion of the interest income generated by such lending transactions as passive, rather than portfolio income.

The one exception to this rule: passive investments that report portfolio income such as a real estate partnership that earns interest income on its excess cash reserves. In these cases, you must classify a portion of your interest expense as investment interest, and it is subject to the investment interest limits.

Here's an example. You're a new limited partner in ABC Partnership in 1991. And, for 1991, you have a passive loss before interest expense of $10,000. In addition, the ABC partnership itself racks up $2,000 in interest expense allocable to you. ABC reports no portfolio income.

The partnership isn't required to treat any of its interest as investment interest. The entire $2,000 is added to your passive loss for the year. You don't need to treat this amount separately as investment interest on your return.

What if ABC did have portfolio income? In this case, the partnership must allocate some of the $2,000 of interest expense to the portfolio income. ABC would then report this amount separately to you. And you would have to treat it as investment interest expense on your return.

Usually, losses you take from your passive investments won't have an impact on your investment interest limitations. (See Chapter 6 for more information about interest deductions.)

Credits

The same rules that apply to losses apply to credits. You may use tax credits passed along to you by shelters only to offset the tax on the net income from these investments.

Consider this example. Let's say you would owe Uncle

Sam $50,000 in tax if you disregarded your net passive income. But you would have to shell out $80,000 if you took into account both your net passive income and your other taxable income.

So the amount of tax that you attribute to your passive income comes to $30,000. And you're allowed to take any credits from your passive investments that don't top $30,000.

This provision applies mostly to a tax shelter that passes along such tax credits as energy credits, rehabilitation credits, and research and development credits.

Like losses, you may carry forward suspended and unused credits to a future tax year. However—unlike losses—you can't use credits to offset tax on earned income and portfolio income when you sell your shelter.

In these cases, however, you may increase your basis by the amount of the suspended credit (limited to the original basis adjustment) before you sell. This provision gives you a lower gain or higher loss when you sell your property. If you go this route, you may no longer carry forward the suspended credit to offset other passive income.

SPECIAL CIRCUMSTANCES

Following are some special circumstances you may face when it comes to the passive activity rules:

Abandoning property

Say last year you invested in a building. This year you lose your only tenant, and it is virtually impossible for you to sell the building or convert it for use by someone else. Is there some way you can dispose of it, so you don't have to treat your loss for the year as passive?

The answer is yes, you can abandon the property. The law

also considers so-called abandonments as dispositions that let you escape the passive loss limitations. So you may claim your entire loss in the current year. The law can be tricky, though, when it comes to abandoning property. If you plan to go this route, consult your tax adviser beforehand.

Also, if you abandon your building after 1987, the suspended loss rules let you take all the losses you have been carrying forward in the year the abandonment occurs.

How do you abandon an investment?

Uncle Sam considers your building abandoned if you can prove that you originally had a profit motive for investing in the building, and the property became useless. You must also show that you have permanently deserted the building and discontinued trying to rent or sell it.

But note: Just not using the building—or a decline in its value—isn't conclusive evidence that you have abandoned your property. You must show that you have actually forsaken it. For example, the IRS would consider cutting off utilities, boarding up windows, and cancelling insurance as proof of abandonment.

Undertaking—both rental and nonrental operations

Let's say you're a partner in a partnership that owns a hotel. In the hotel lobby are five commercial stores that the partnership leases to tenants. These commercial rentals make up 15 percent of the gross income of the hotel. Are the rental operations of the commercial stores considered a separate rental activity from the operations of the hotel?

The answer is no. The rental operations of the commercial space don't constitute a separate activity from the hotel.

Where an undertaking consists of both rental and nonrental operations and one of the operations is dominant, then that operation constitutes the single activity.

In this case, the hotel operations are dominant— that is, they contribute more than 80 percent of your revenues—and accordingly, the rental operations aren't considered a separate activity.

Installment sales

Say you owned a limited partnership interest in a piece of rental real estate. You sold out in 1985 on an installment-sale basis, so you are still receiving income. Is this income passive?

The answer is yes. Uncle Sam treats the income as passive, even though the passive-loss rules weren't in place when you sold your partnership. However, note that any interest income received would be treated as portfolio and not passive income.

Multiple partnerships

Say you own interests in four partnerships and all are engaged in similar ventures. Your percentage of ownership in the four partnerships is as follows: partnership A, 30 percent; partnership B, 52 percent; partnership C, 15 percent; and partnership D, 8 percent. You are a material participant in partnership B. How many activities are you engaged in?

Since you own a substantial interest (greater than 10 percent) in partnerships A, B, and C, you combine them and treat them as a single activity.

You don't hold a substantial interest in partnership D, so you treat it as a single activity separate from your other partnership interests.

Paired investments

As their name implies, paired investments are limited partnerships with two distinct businesses. One business generates income and, hopefully, cash. The other business generates losses—at least for tax purposes—to offset that income.

Paired investments are just another variation on the tax shelter theme. Our advice? Invest in one of these vehicles only if it makes economic sense.

Material participation

Let's assume you are the sole owner of a small company that provides word processing services. Your business is organized as an S corporation, and it is the only company in which you have an ownership interest. Your son is in charge of the day-to-day operations, but you are actively involved in consulting, arranging financing, and monitoring the corporation's financial success. You spend about 400 hours a year in these efforts. In fact, your financial analysis is used regularly in the actual decision making process of the business. In 1991, your business reported a loss. Do you report this loss as a passive loss?

The answer? It depends. You spend only 400 hours a year on the business—that is, you fail to meet the 500-hour material participation test.

The only material participation test that you might pass is the facts-and-circumstances test. But the IRS has yet to issue guidance on what criteria would allow the losses to be treated as nonpassive for purposes of the facts and circumstances test. However, the IRS is slated to issue further guidance on this test.

Single or multiple undertakings

Say you own an 8 percent interest in one partnership and a 6 percent interest in another. Both partnerships own the same type of business—fast food restaurants. Do you classify these restaurants as a single undertaking or as multiple undertakings?

The answer is that these restaurants are single undertakings and single activities because your ownership isn't direct (that is, it is through a partnership) and it isn't substantial (meaning—in the eyes of the IRS—that it adds up to 10 percent or less).

Single or multiple activities

Say you're a partner in a partnership that owns five convenience stores, each in a different location. The partnership is owned by two unrelated partners. Do you categorize the stores as a single activity or multiple activities?

The stores probably fit into the category of a single activity. Why? They share the same owners and fall into the same SIC code. In this situation, businesses are usually treated as a single activity even though they are located in different places.

10

Does It Still Pay to Invest in Tax Shelters?

Tax sheltering used to be a game almost anyone could play. Now, few of us want to—and for good reason. Tax shelter losses used to offset—or shelter—other income, but they no longer have that capability. Congress took it away a few years ago.

And here's another problem: In the past, when you sold or, in the words of the IRS, "disposed of" a shelter at a profit, you often benefited from lower capital gains rates. The 1986 Tax Act changed this favorable treatment and, for years 1987 through 1990, capital gains were taxed at the same rates as ordinary income.

The 1990 Tax Act changed the rules again. Congress enacted a top 28 percent rate for capital gains beginning in 1991, a rate which is less than the top statutory rate of 31 percent on ordinary income. However, this rate differential alone does not provide nearly as much benefit as the maximum 20 percent long-term capital gains rate that applied before the 1986 Act. (For more on capital gains, see Chapter 4.)

These days, a traditional tax shelter generates what are

known in the tax code as passive income and losses. As we saw in Chapter 9 losses from passive investments offset only gains from passive investments but not income from, for instance, wages or salary, except in the year you dispose of the tax shelter.

So, whereas investments that promised to generate big losses early on in their lives used to make sense, they don't, with few exceptions, under the new rules.

This chapter deals mostly with the exceptions. Had we written this chapter a mere five years ago, the topic of tax shelters could easily have taken up half this book. We would have discussed topics such as solar energy property, cattle breeding and feeding, orchards, and windmill farms—all potential tax shelters.

Now, though, the at-risk and, more importantly, the passive activity rules have all but slammed the door on these investment options. In recent years, tax audits—and subsequent court decisions prompted by those audits—have taken away a great number of shelter benefits.

The courts have ruled, for example, that many "businesses" organized as shelters weren't even operated with the goal of making a profit.

Also, the courts have said, investors often were too aggressive in claiming big deductions on their tax returns. As a result, some taxpayers have, on audit, had to pay back taxes, including interest and, at times, penalty charges, when their shelter deductions were denied.

What's left when it comes to tax shelters? The answers are rental real estate, building rehabilitation, low-income housing, and working interests in oil and gas properties.

You may use losses generated by these investments to offset your regular income—subject, you won't be surprised to learn—to certain limitations. The effect of this dramatic change in the law on investment strategies has been enormous.

In the past, you no doubt decided whether to invest in a tax shelter based on the rate of return—a rate of return that included substantial tax write-offs.

Nowadays, you should look to limited partnerships for solid economic returns, solely in the form of cash flow and appreciation potential.

Today, high cash returns are almost a prerequisite to making these investments worthwhile. Put another way, if an investment doesn't have a reasonably good probability of making a return on your money, tax reasons will provide little, if any, additional incentive.

Investors are also demanding protection from total loss, since Uncle Sam now foots less of the bill. Therefore, many shelters now promote themselves as safe investments and offer risk protection through guarantees of income, protection from losses, and promises of cash returns.

☞ CAUTION You should view these guarantees, however, merely as added benefits, not as reasons to invest in a deal. If times get tough, many guarantors may default. And in good times, you probably won't need the guarantees.

☞ CAUTION Because of the changes in the shelter market, you shouldn't purchase new shelters without carefully considering how they might help or harm you.

WORKING WITH EXISTING TAX SHELTERS

What about those shelters that you purchased in years past? If you acquired them before the 1986 Tax Reform Act and they generated losses, Uncle Sam allowed you to deduct a portion of those losses. However, for 1991 and beyond, you may not deduct any of your passive losses from your regular taxable income. (See Chapter 9 for more information on passive losses.) You also aren't allowed any losses for shelters acquired after October 22, 1986, the Act's enactment date. (Certain exceptions, however, apply to investments in rental real estate. See Chapter 11 for details.)

Don't give up all hope, though. We present some ideas here that may help you use your losses currently and minimize your tax liability.

Passive income generators

If you have substantial passive losses from old tax shelter investments, consider PIGs. And no, we're not talking about farm animals.

PIGs, or passive income generators, are, in effect, reverse tax shelters. A PIG may generate a positive cash flow as well as taxable passive income.

Among the more common types of PIGs are limited partnerships that operate ongoing, profitable businesses such as a ski resort, golf course, or conference center. The benefit of these investments is that the income they generate is passive, and you may use your passive losses to offset this passive income.

But how do you know which PIGs might make sense for your circumstances? First, you should know that many PIGs are syndicated—that is, they're offered to the public through public offerings—and are actively marketed by brokers. However, special rules may limit the benefits from such syndicated offerings. These rules will be covered shortly when Master Limited Partnerships are discussed.

Once you've decided that a passive income generator may help you at tax time, you should compare a specific PIG to other investments and consider the investment merits of the PIG exclusive of any associated tax benefits.

Using the same methods, compare rates of return. Also,

TAX

take a look at how the deal and the promoter stack up against others in the same industry. Make sure to include in your analysis any fees that might be involved in buying or selling both investments.

If you're interested in investing in PIGs, you should have no trouble finding them. Your investment adviser, stockbroker, or financial planner will know the names of some of these partnerships. You may also run across names of PIGs in financial publications.

Other options

Here's a useful strategy if you own a profitable corporation that isn't organized as a personal service corporation or an S corporation. Transfer ownership of investments that generate passive losses to your corporation.

The reason: The law allows a corporation to use passive losses to offset its regular business income. And, it makes no difference if the corporation is closely held.

☞ **CAUTION** This strategy doesn't make sense if your passive investments currently generate income (not losses), or will do so in the not-so-distant future. That's because the income a corporation earns is taxed twice—once at the corporate level, then again when the income is passed along to you in the form of dividends.

Another drawback is that if the shelter has phantom income, such income may be triggered upon transfer. We'll discuss phantom income in a moment.

TIP If you're the owner of a profitable corporation but don't materially participate in business operations, another alternative is to elect S corporation status. Since you don't materially participate, your income from the S corporation is passive. And you can use your passive losses to offset profits from your S corporation.

Remember, you add together income and losses from all

your passive investments. So, if you find yourself locked into some older investments that you expect will generate passive losses, follow the obvious strategy. Invest in vehicles that generate passive income so that you may then use this income to offset your losses.

☞ CAUTION Make sure your investments make economic sense apart from the tax benefits. (*See* Chapter 9 for more on the passive loss rules.)

Phantom income

In the past, tax shelters were structured so that investors could claim tax deductions—accelerated depreciation, say—in the early years of ownership. However, these deductions diminished over time, often leaving the shelter with only paper profits or phantom income.

A shelter that generates no further losses and may produce taxable income but doesn't generate cash is known in investment circles as a "burned-out" shelter.

The phantom income generated by this burned-out shelter usually occurs when you sell or dispose of the shelter. You must report on your return an amount of income on the sale or disposition that exceeds—often by a considerable amount—the sales proceeds you actually receive. In other words, the phantom income represents a "reversal" of those tax shelter deductions you took in prior years.

TIP If you find yourself with a burned-out shelter producing taxable income, consider this strategy: Phantom income is, in fact, passive income. So, you can invest in a new tax shelter that generates passive losses to offset phantom income from your old shelter if you have no other passive losses to offset the phantom income.

TIP Here's another idea to consider. Sell the investment, but be warned that you'll usually have to sell at a deep discount. Besides losing money on the sale, disposing of the investment may create taxable—and phantom—income for you. Selling the shelter, however, may help you minimize the amount of phantom income that you'll have to report on your tax return.

Master limited partnerships

You've heard a lot about publicly-traded partnerships. How do you treat—for tax purposes—income and losses from these partnerships?

Interests in master limited partnerships—that is, MLPs or publicly traded partnerships—are traded on public exchanges, just like shares of stock. So, they're much more marketable and much more liquid than other types of partnerships.

Originally, these publicly traded partnerships were thought to provide passive income to investors with passive activity losses. These investors could then use the losses to offset their income. The partnerships came under congressional scrutiny, not only because they offered this opportunity to save on taxes, but also because they paid no tax (instead, the individual partners paid tax on their share of any profit) while having many common characteristics of publicly traded corporations.

As a result of congressional action, Uncle Sam now treats net income from publicly traded partnerships as portfolio income. That means you may not use this income to offset passive losses from other investments.

What's worse, losses from publicly-traded partnerships are treated as suspended losses. You may subtract these losses only from net income from the same partnerships. But, you may claim any unused suspended losses when you dispose of your interest in the partnership.

Moreover, the IRS taxes publicly traded partnerships

formed after December 17, 1987, as corporations. Therefore, profits and losses no longer flow through to the partners.

There is, however, an exception to the corporate treatment rules. If 90 percent of the partnership's gross income comes from interest, dividends, real-estate rents, gains from the sale of capital assets, income or gains from certain oil and gas activities, and gains from the sale of certain trade or business assets, Uncle Sam will still treat the MLP as a partnership.

Leveraging your passive investments

Given the dramatic changes in the tax-shelter rules, does it still make sense to highly leverage your passive investments? Generally, no.

It used to make sense to leverage your deal to the greatest extent you could; that is, it paid to borrow as much money as possible. The reasons?

You could collect significant deductions with only a minimal cash investment. Also, you could deduct fully the interest you paid on any borrowed funds.

Now, however, you may want to minimize leverage in your passive investments, so you reduce your interest expense. When you do minimize leverage and cut your interest expense, you also may end up creating passive income, perhaps breaking even in operations or at least reducing your passive losses.

It's possible that your investment will produce positive cash flow in excess of the passive income. This can happen as a result of noncash deductions, such as depreciation and depletion, that don't require a cash expenditure.

Other investments

So far we've discussed some options to help you deal with existing investments you may own that are subject to the limitations of the law. But what if you don't have any current investments? Or, what if you want to explore opportunities to currently reduce your tax liability?

We discuss the tax implications of investing in real estate in Chapter 11, so we won't cover that topic here. Instead, let's consider oil and gas.

Oil and gas

There are different ways to invest in oil and gas. One way is through a stake in a limited partnership known as an oil or gas "program." Another may be through a "working interest." You still may reap tax benefits by investing in a working interest in oil and gas properties. Lawmakers made an exception to the tax-shelter rules for working interests in oil and gas properties when you're liability isn't limited, even though you do not materially participate in the venture.

Let's take a look at each of these two alternatives.

The purpose of oil and gas programs is to explore or drill for oil or to purchase producing wells. Usually these programs come in the form of joint ventures or partnerships. And because they are limited in liability, partners in such programs are subject to the normal limitations on losses from passive activities.

Who offers these programs? They're put together and offered to investors either by independent oil companies or by oil investment managers. These programs come in four basic varieties—exploratory, development, balanced, and income.

Exploratory programs try to discover new petroleum reserves. Since exploration usually takes place in untested areas, the success rate is often miserable.

Moreover, an exploratory well must be developed after it's discovered. So, you may be tapped for more money before the partnership even produces positive cash flow.

☞ CAUTION   If everything goes well, your return on capital may be extraordinary. You should know, though, that it may take a long time to collect on your investment.

These deals are risky, too.

Development programs set up wells near existing oil reserves in areas where production is already underway; therefore, chances of success are higher than in exploratory programs.

Also, you can expect a faster return on your investment than with exploratory programs.

As you might expect since the risk is lower, the return on your capital is often less than you'd get with successful exploratory programs.

Balanced programs include both exploratory and development wells in about the same proportion. They try to combine the advantages of high yields produced by successful exploratory wells with the early cash flow and lower risk of development wells.

Unlike either exploratory or development programs, income partnerships purchase producing properties rather than develop drilling sites, so the risks are much less.

Income programs also don't offer the same tax benefits. Most of their tax write-offs come from the depletion of their oil reserves rather than from development costs.

The principal advantage of these programs is that you get income over the life of the oil well, which might be 10 years, or the gas well, which might last 15 years.

As the oil or gas is removed from the well, the income falls until the well is abandoned as commercially unproductive.

If you're thinking about an investment in an oil and gas partnership, make sure you look for a reputable financial adviser who has experience in evaluating these programs. Ask if he or she has performed an in-depth review of the investment.

Now, on to the second way to invest in oil and gas. A working interest or operating interest is one in which the partners pay a share of development and operation expenses.

Your losses in these partnerships aren't subject to the normal limitations on losses from passive activities, so you may deduct them from your regular income. And you don't have to participate in the actual operations yourself to do so.

☞ **CAUTION** The problem: In order to be exempt from the passive activity rules, your working interest cannot limit liability. And this rule holds true even if the investment is made through a partnership or S corporation. For many people, unlimited liability is reason enough to steer clear of these investments.

What's deductible on your tax return if you own a working interest in an oil or gas well? Day-to-day operating costs, for one. Intangible drilling costs, for another.

What are intangible drilling costs? They're all the expenses you incur in drilling and developing a well, except for equipment. They include amounts you spend for core analysis, engineering, management, and geological studies. They also include the costs of drilling a dry hole.

Uncle Sam gives you a choice when it comes to intangible drilling costs. He says you may write them off currently, or you may capitalize them and write them off through depletion.

While intangible drilling costs are deductible for regular tax purposes, they may be limited when it comes to the alternative minimum tax (AMT).

TIP If you're subject to the AMT, you may want to elect to write off intangible drilling costs in equal installments over 60 months.

By doing so you deduct only a portion of the intangible drilling costs in the current year. The rest is deductible in future years. As long as the AMT does not apply in those years you get the benefit of these additional write-offs.

If the AMT does apply, complicated adjustments may limit the benefit of the intangible drilling cost deduction. However, in 1990, Congress enacted AMT relief provisions specifically targeted to oil- and gas-related items that generate AMT adjustments and preferences. These special AMT energy provisions are subject to various limitations and special rules. So you would be wise to consult with your tax advisor if you're in an AMT position and have investments in oil and gas properties.

Depletion is also deductible for regular tax purposes but it may not be when it comes time to calculate your alternative minimum tax liability. The AMT will limit your depletion to the amount of your basis in the property.

You use depletion to write off the cost of obtaining mineral rights. Your depletion deduction is the higher of the amount calculated under the cost method or the percentage method.

Here's how these two methods work.

With the cost method, you determine depletion by comparing production sold during the taxable year with the total available production of your property.

Say you acquire the right to drill for oil in a 10-acre site in Oklahoma. You hire a geologist who estimates that the maximum amount of oil on your site is one million barrels. In the first year, you pump and sell some 100,000 barrels of oil from the property.

What's your depletion deduction? If you use the cost method, you may claim as depletion one-tenth of the amount you paid to acquire the reserves. The percentage method of depletion lets you claim as depletion a fixed percentage of your revenues from the sale of oil or gas. That figure is generally 15 percent.

You may be interested to know that in 1990 Congress enacted a 25 percent depletion rate that will apply to marginally producing wells of independent producers—just the type of folks that typically offer limited partnership interests. However, this provision applies only if crude oil prices fall below $20 per barrel. Again, if you invest in oil and gas, talk with your tax adviser.

If you use the percentage method, Uncle Sam generally won't allow you to claim depletion deductions that add up to more than 65 percent of your taxable income. However, you may carry forward depletion deductions you aren't able to claim in the current year to future years.

Beginning in 1991, if you use the percentage method, Uncle Sam caps your depletion deductions at 100 percent (formerly 50 percent) of the taxable income from the property. Taxable income—in this case, at least—is calculated before you claim your depletion deduction, and the limitation is figured on a property-by-property basis.

Any depletion you take reduces your tax basis in the property; however, unlike cost depletion, you can claim percentage depletion in excess of your tax basis in the property. Moreover, taking percentage depletion in excess of basis doesn't increase the gain you compute at the time of the sale of the property.

Depreciation is another deduction you may claim if you own a working interest in an oil or gas well. To depreciate an expense means to write it off in installments over time.

Depreciation allows you to write off the cost of tangible assets—drilling rigs, and so on—over a period of time, or "life," designated by the IRS. Usually, you write off these costs using what's known as the straight-line method or an accelerated method.

Depreciation—as with depletion and intangible drilling costs—is deductible for regular tax purposes, but different rules apply when it comes to the AMT.

Still another deduction you may claim is for so-called surrendered leases. These are leases you acquire but abandon or forfeit. You write off the remaining cost of acquiring these leases in the year of abandonment.

If you own a working interest in an oil or gas well, report your profit or loss and claim your deductions on Schedule C of your Form 1040.

 CAUTION You may not know it, but you may be liable for self-employment taxes

on your net income from a working interest in an oil or gas well. Sometimes you're liable for the tax even if you own a fractional interest through a partnership—five percent, say—and don't even play an active role in operations.

The reason? The partnership, in the eyes of Uncle Sam, is engaged in the active conduct of a trade or business.

☞ **CAUTION** What happens when you sell a working interest in an oil or gas well? A portion of the gain may be classified as ordinary income, not capital gain income, for example, if you previously wrote off intangible drilling costs (either though current expensing or capitalizing and amortizing), or if you took any depletion deductions that reduced your leasehold basis in the property.

The IRS takes back or recaptures certain deductions you previously took. That is, it requires you to report a portion of your gain as ordinary income, not capital gain income. The amount of your gain that is treated as ordinary income equals the total of certain deductions you previously claimed.

Say, for example, your gain adds up to $5,000, and these deductions come to $4,000; then $4,000 of your gain would be taxed as ordinary income. The excess gain—$1,000—will likely be treated as a gain from the sale of trade or business property and may ultimately be eligible to receive capital gain treatment.

11

The Tax Benefits of Rental Real Estate

Before you get into the real-estate game, you need to know your options. And you need to understand the tax risks and rewards of investing in rental property.

In this chapter, we provide you with the lowdown—tax-wise, at least—on rental real estate that you actively participate in managing.

How does Uncle Sam define active participation? As long as you make significant and bona fide management decisions—*and* own at least a 10 percent stake in the property—you're an active participant. It's as simple as that.

The management decisions that count include deciding on rental terms, approving tenants, and approving major expenditures. And, the rules say that, as long as you make these decisions, it's fine to use a rental agent to execute them for you.

Here's something else you should know. Uncle Sam will allow you to deduct losses from passive investments only from income these passive investments generate. And, alas, rental property *usually* qualifies as a passive investment.

So, if the expenses you pile up when you rent property—mortgage interest, depreciation, utility bills, insurance, repair costs, and so on—exceed your rental income, the net loss is deductible only against your income from other passive investments.

Remember, however, that you may carry forward any passive losses you cannot use currently and deduct them in future years—as long as you have enough passive income in those years. And when you sell your property, you get to deduct any remaining losses.

You may also qualify for a special exception designed to help the "moderate-income" taxpayer get around the passive loss rules.

This exception allows you to deduct rental real estate losses of up to $25,000 from your regular income under two conditions: You meet certain income guidelines, and—you guessed it—you must actively participate in the operation of your rental property.

Let's look at the income guidelines.

As long as your adjusted gross income (AGI) is $100,000 or less—figured before you subtract any rental or passive losses—you may deduct from your ordinary income up to $25,000 in rental losses from residential or commercial rental property.

But, you lose the deduction for part of the loss if your income falls between $100,000 and $150,000, and you're entitled to no deduction if your AGI tops $150,000.

What if your AGI is between $100,000 and $150,000? You must reduce the $25,000 limit by 50 percent of the amount by which your AGI exceeds $100,000. Here's an example to illustrate how to perform this calculation.

Say your AGI comes to $140,000; that is, it tops $100,000 by $40,000. You multiply 50 percent times $40,000, and subtract the result—$20,000—from $25,000.

In your case, you may deduct $5,000 in rental losses from your regular income, as long as you actively participate in managing the property. What if your losses top $5,000? You treat the excess the same as you treat other passive losses, (that is, you may subtract these losses from your passive income to the extent that you have any).

You should know, though, that this $25,000 limit applies cumulatively to all your rental property. No matter how many rental buildings you own, the loss you claim, which offsets the regular income, may not exceed the $25,000 total. Uncle Sam makes no exceptions to this rule.

Something else you need to know tax-wise about rental real estate: the at-risk rules. They apply to investments in real-estate after 1986, and under them, you may write off your losses only to the extent that they don't top your "total at-risk investment."

How does Uncle Sam define your at-risk investment? It's the cash you've contributed to your rental real-estate venture plus any money you've borrowed for the venture (to the extent that you're personally liable for the loan) plus the adjusted basis of any property you've contributed.

Put simply, your losses may not exceed the total amount for which you're at risk. However, the law does carve out an exception for real estate.

So-called nonrecourse financing—financing for which you have no personal liability—qualifies for at-risk purposes, if it meets the following three conditions.

- The financing must be secured only by real property; that is, in IRS jargon, the real estate itself.

- The debt must be true debt—not convertible debt or disguised equity—meaning debt that's in reality an ownership share.

- You must have obtained the financing from a qualified

lender—meaning a bank, a savings and loan, or a related party such as a family member or a corporation or partnership in which you hold a greater than 50 percent interest.

But, if you obtain financing from a related party, the debt must be "commercially reasonable" and "substantially similar" to loans made to unrelated parties.

Our advice? Sign a note that's payable on demand or on a specified date or dates and that carries a market rate of interest. Also, Uncle Sam doesn't include seller financing in the definition of a qualified lender; so, you're subject to the at-risk rules if you use seller financing, unless that financing is recourse financing—that is, a loan in which you assume personal liability for the debt.

For more information on the at-risk rules, ask the IRS for a free copy of its Publication 925, *Passive Activity and At-Risk Rules*.

You report your rental income and expenses on Schedule E of your Form 1040. If you own more than three rental properties, use as many Schedules E as you need.

If you'd like more information about rental real estate, ask the IRS for a free copy of its Publication 527, *Residential Rental Property*.

GETTING THE MOST FROM RENTAL PROPERTY

Now, let's take a look at what rental property is worth to you in the tax department. The answers may surprise you.

Rental income

What counts as income when it comes to your rental real estate? Uncle Sam says you must report any rental payments you receive.

☞ CAUTION   What if a tenant pays his or her rent in advance?

You're required to report that income in the year you receive it.

Say a tenant signs a two-year lease in 1991 that requires her to pay you $5,000 annually in rent. But on the day she signs the lease, she hands you a check for the full amount of $10,000. You must report that $10,000 as income in 1991, even though half of that amount is rent for 1992.

TIP   Security deposits normally don't count as income in the year you receive them if you're required by law to pay interest on those amounts.

But if you maintain the right to refund a security deposit or apply it to a future year's rent, then it generally counts as income in the year it's paid.

One way around this rule is to word your lease agreements so that security deposits are "equal to" one month's rent, not "in lieu of" the last month's rent.

☞ CAUTION   The fair market value of property or services you receive in lieu of rent counts as rental income. How do you calculate fair market value? One of the best ways is to get an appraisal from a qualified real estate appraiser.

☞ CAUTION   What if your tenant wants to pay you to cancel his or her lease?

You report the amount you receive as rental income.

☞ CAUTION   Say you receive payments under an insurance policy that reimburses you not only for damages due to fire or some other casualty, but lost rent as well.

How are these insurance payments treated for tax purposes? Uncle Sam requires you to report these amounts as rental income.

Advertising

When you advertise that your property is available for rent, you may deduct the cost of these advertisements.

Commissions

Say you own a mountain cabin in West Virginia, and you enlist the help of a local real estate agent to keep the property occupied. Each time she signs someone up to rent your cabin, you pay her a commission.

How is this commission treated for tax purposes? It's deductible from your rental income.

☞ CAUTION Uncle Sam says some commissions are deductible, but he requires others to be added to the basis of the property. Here are examples of those to be capitalized.

Commissions you pay when you *sell* rental property are effectively added to your basis—that is, they are subtracted from your proceeds from the sale to calculate your gain or loss. As for commissions you pay when you buy rental property, they're added to the cost basis of the property you purchased and may be depreciated.

Depreciation

What's the biggest break you get from rental property? You guessed it—depreciation.

Uncle Sam allows you to recoup the cost of your investment by deducting a portion of your purchase price each year. This gradual write-off, as you no doubt know, is depreciation and compensates you for the effects of wear and tear and decay on your property.

But, there's one restriction. Since—as far as Uncle Sam is concerned—land doesn't decay, you may write off *only* the cost of buildings, not the underlying land.

You write off the cost of residential rental property on one schedule—27.5 years—and commercial property on another—31.5 years. And you must use the straight-line method of depreciation; that is, you must write off the same amount each year.

The law says you may begin taking depreciation deductions once your property is "placed in service," but not before. This bit of IRS jargon simply means that your building is on the rental market or ready for its intended use.

And the law says you must abide by its so-called mid-month convention. This rule goes for both residential and commercial investments.

It means that you figure your first year's depreciation deduction from the middle of the month in which you place your property in service. The mid-month convention applies even if you place your property in service on the first or last day of the month.

Here's an example of how you would figure your depreciation deductions. Say you and a colleague buy a small office complex on August 1, 1991, in a nearby suburban development. The property costs you $500,000—$400,000 for the building and $100,000 for the land.

You spruce up your property and put it on the rental market on September 1, 1991. How much may you now write off on your 1991 tax return?

Even though the complex was placed in service on September 1, the mid-month convention says the property is placed in service on September 15. In 1991, you and your colleague together may deduct three and one-half months in depreciation write-offs, or $3,704.

Your deduction adds up this way: You take the cost of your building—$400,000—and divide it by 31.5 years, the number of years over which you must depreciate commercial property. Then you divide the result—$12,698—by 12 months and multiply by three and one-half months.

TIP While the mid-month convention may seem unfair, it can actually work to your advantage. The reason: You're entitled to a half of a month's depreciation no matter when during the month you place your property in service, even if, as in the above example, it's September 30.

TIP If you fail to claim a depreciation deduction one year, Uncle Sam says you may not take it in a subsequent year. But all isn't lost. You may file an amended return for the year you failed to claim your depreciation deduction.

TIP You should file Form 4562, "Depreciation and Amortization," to claim your depreciation deductions. If you'd like more information on depreciation, ask the IRS for a copy of its Publication 534, *Depreciation*. It's free for the asking.

Mortgage interest

Uncle Sam allows you to write off mortgage interest on rental real estate. As with other expenses, you claim this deduction on Schedule E of your Form 1040.

Operating expenses

The rules allow you to claim on Schedule E of your Form 1040 deductions for a whole host of expenses associated with your rental property.

For example, you may write off amounts you pay for cleaning, utilities, fire insurance, and liability insurance. And you may even deduct the cost of any supplies—a receipt book, let's say—that are normally deductible for profit-oriented activities.

Travel—whether it be across town or across the country—also is 100 percent deductible on your Schedule E, as long as the trip is strictly for real estate business. Say you own a

house on the Florida coast that you rent, and you
head south to inspect and make repairs to your rental
property; your expenses are deductible. That is, you may write
off the cost of your airplane ticket to Florida, plus your local
transportation expenses.

What if you travel to Florida, spend one day attending to
your rental real estate business, then five days vacationing?
You're not entitled to write off the cost of your plane ticket.

TIP Uncle Sam says you may deduct expenses,
even if your property isn't rented for a peri-
od of time. All that's required is that it be made available for
rent. And the IRS won't disallow your deductions simply because your property is hard to rent.

Say you own a house in a high-crime area of your city. De-
spite your efforts to find a tenant, the house remains empty for
months. Uncle Sam allows you to deduct your expenses, even
though the property languished on the market, because you
were actively trying to rent the property.

Property taxes

You may deduct state and local property taxes on Schedule
E of your Form 1040, but you may write off *only* those real
estate taxes you actually pay.

Let's say you and your spouse jointly own a small apartment building but file separate returns. Each of you may deduct only the taxes that you individually pay.

The one exception to this rule are taxpayers in community
property states—such as Arizona, California, Idaho, Louisiana, Nevada, New Mexico, Texas, and Washington. Uncle
Sam considers that taxes paid from community funds are on a
fifty-fifty basis.

Also, you may not deduct payments for real estate taxes
placed in escrow—in the care of a third party—until they're
actually paid out of the escrow account.

So, if your monthly mortgage payment includes an amount placed in escrow for property taxes, you may not write off those escrow payments. You may deduct only the amount of the tax that the lender actually paid to the taxing authority, such as a city or county.

TIP Most lenders pay taxes out of escrow accounts on the tax due date. However, if the due date is shortly after the end of the calendar year, you may want to ask your lender to speed up the payment so that you may claim the deduction a year earlier. But make sure the assessment date (often called the lien date) falls within the earlier year; otherwise, the law will not allow you an earlier deduction.

TIP You should know that if you buy or sell rental real estate during the tax year, you must divide the property taxes between yourself and the seller or buyer. You split the taxes that each of you may deduct based on the number of days each of you owned the property.

If you're the seller, you pay and deduct the taxes up to the date of the sale. The buyer pays and deducts the taxes after the sale.

Repairs and improvements

Uncle Sam allows you to deduct currently the cost of repairs but not the cost of improvements. What's the difference between a repair and an improvement?

A repair keeps your property in good working order and doesn't add to its value or substantially prolong its life. Plastering and painting qualify as repairs, as well as fixing gutters and floors, repairing leaks, and replacing broken windows.

An improvement adds to the value of your property, prolongs its useful life, or adapts it to new uses. Adding a room is an example. So are putting up a fence, installing new plumbing or wiring, or replacing the roof.

TIP Uncle Sam won't let you claim a deduction for improvements you make to your rental property. But he says you may depreciate them.

Salaries and wages

Amounts you pay to people to help with the upkeep of your rental property are 100 percent deductible on Schedule E of your Form 1040.

TIP Here's an idea worth considering. Why not hire your children to perform duties associated with your rental property? The amount you pay them is tax deductible. And they pay taxes on the income at a rate that's lower than your own.

For example, the year is 1990; you're in the 31 percent bracket, you own a small apartment building, and you pay your son John $4,000 to tend to the yard. Your son, meanwhile, is in the 15 percent bracket, and his only income is the $4,000 you paid him.

His tax bill stacks up like this. He pockets the first $3,400 he earns tax-free—thanks to the standard deduction. Then he pays tax at the rate of 15 percent on his remaining earnings, $600. His tax liability is $90—that is, $600 times 15 percent.

You save $1,150 in taxes—that is, your tax rate of 31 percent times $4,000, or $1,240, minus your son's tax bill of $90. (This example doesn't take into account the impact of a possible itemized deduction disallowance or the personal exemption phase-out.)

CAUTION If you hire your children to help with the upkeep of your rental property, it's important not only that you keep records of the hours they work and the wages you pay them, but that you are also able to demonstrate that they performed legitimate services.

Uncle Sam—on audit—is likely to cast a critical eye on

your employment arrangements with your children. He may disallow your deductions without complete records.

Rehabilitation tax credit

The rehabilitation tax credit dates back to 1976 and is intended to encourage the preservation of historic buildings. The credit totals 10 percent of the amount you spend to fix up a building that was built before 1936. Not bad, you say, and you're right—but it may get even better.

The credit equals 20 percent of the amount you spend rehabilitating—but not purchasing—what's known as a certified historic structure (CHS). Your local historical society or an office of the U.S. Department of the Interior can provide you with the guidelines on certified historic structures.

Let's say you buy a 100-year-old cookie factory, and the building is a CHS. You spend $50,000 converting it into offices to house your law firm. You're entitled to a 20 percent credit, or $10,000—as long as you abide by the rules. What rules?

Congress adopted the credit to encourage people to preserve older buildings, not destroy them. So you must keep at least 50 percent of the building's external walls as external walls; that is, you may not erect new walls around more than half the old external walls.

Two more rules: (1) You're required to preserve at least 75 percent of the existing external walls either as internal or external walls. And, (2) you must keep at least 75 percent of the existing internal structural framework. Therefore, if you gut the inside of your building, you're out of luck.

The tax law specifically exempts certified historic structures—such as our cookie factory—from the external and internal wall retention requirements. But as a practical matter, the government probably won't certify a structure as a CHS unless you keep at least 75 percent of the existing external walls as external walls.

You should know too that you may pocket your credit only if the amount you spend rehabilitating the building tops $5,000 or the "adjusted basis" of the building, whichever is greater.

What's the adjusted basis? It's usually the amount you pay for the structure minus any deductions you take for depreciation.

Say you pay $100,000 for a building and previously claimed $20,000 in depreciation. Your adjusted basis is $80,000, and you must spend at least that amount to renovate the structure, or you're entitled to no credit.

One final wrinkle: When it comes time to figure your future depreciation write-offs, you must subtract the amount of the credit you take from the amount you're depreciating. Let's say you own a non-CHS building built before 1936 with an adjusted basis (not including the cost of the land) of $80,000. You spend $180,000 fixing it up. Since the building isn't a CHS, you may take a credit of $18,000 (10 percent of $180,000). But you have to figure your future depreciation deductions on an adjusted basis of $242,000—that is, $80,000 plus $180,000 minus your credit of $18,000.

☞ **CAUTION** Uncle Sam says you must incur your rehabilitation expenses within a 24 month period before you qualify for the credit. This 24 months becomes 60 months in the case of rehabilitation projects where the work is performed in stages.

☞ **CAUTION** In the old days, Uncle Sam set very few limits on the amount of rehabilitation credits you could claim. But the 1986 Tax Reform Act imposed ceilings.

Each year, you may offset the tax on your passive income and no more than $25,000 of your ordinary income—wages or interest, let's say—with the rehabilitation credit or low-income housing credit, which we explain in the next section. You don't even have to actively participate in managing the property. You could, for instance, be a limited partner.

Before we see how this $25,000 limit works, we need to give a quick definition. A deduction reduces your taxes by the amount of your marginal tax rate. If you're in the 28 percent bracket, for example, a deduction of $100 cuts your taxes by $28. But a credit slashes the taxes you pay dollar-for-dollar; that is, a tax credit of $100 reduces your tax bill by $100. Now, let's return to the $25,000 ceiling.

The law says you may claim up to the rehabilitation or low-income housing "tax-credit equivalent" of a $25,000 deduction without being an active participant in the venture. So you may not, alas, take up to $25,000 off your tax bill.

What you may do is take a credit that reduces the taxes you owe by the same amount as a $25,000 tax deduction would. So if your marginal rate is 28 percent, the credit equivalent of a $25,000 deduction comes to $7,000 ($25,000 times 28 percent).

There's one other important rule you should know about if you invest in older structures or low-income housing. The $25,000 credit equivalent phases out as your income rises, except in the case of low-income housing acquired after 1989.

Here's the good news: the $25,000 credit equivalent doesn't phase out until your adjusted gross income tops $200,000.

After that point, you must reduce the $25,000 by 50 percent of the amount by which your AGI exceeds $200,000. And then you must convert this amount to a credit equivalent. So you get no benefit from the $25,000 credit equivalent once your AGI reaches $250,000.

Finally, it's important to realize that both the rehabilitation and low-income housing credits are classified as general business credits. And you may claim in general business credits no more than $25,000 plus 75 percent of any tax you owe over $25,000. Moreover, if you are in AMT or near it, Uncle Sam may impose additional limitations on the amount of general business credit you may claim.

☞ **CAUTION** You own some rental property that you actively participate in managing. Now you're thinking about investing as a limited partner in a rehab deal.

Can you claim both losses—up to $25,000 from your rental property and the credit equivalent of $25,000 from the rehabilitation partnership? Unfortunately, the answer is no. You may deduct from your ordinary income no more than $25,000 a year in *combined* losses from rental real estate and credit equivalents.

How do you calculate how much you may write off?

Here's an example: say you report a $25,000 loss from an apartment building you manage yourself. You post a loss of $5,000 from an oil and gas limited partnership, but you record $15,000 of income from a research and development limited partnership. The rules require you to first count up all your losses from rental properties in which you actively participate; in your case, the total comes to $25,000.

Then you add up any profits from any such rental activities, and subtract your losses from your profits. You post no profits, so you're left with a $25,000 loss.

Next, you add up your income from passive investments— $15,000 in your case. Then you subtract your losses from passive activities, which is $5,000. The result—$10,000—is your net passive income.

Subtract your $25,000 of rental losses from your $10,000 of passive income and $15,000 is the amount you may write off on your return as a rental loss.

Remember, you may only deduct rental losses up to

$25,000. So, if you also invest in a rehabilitation partnership, you may write off as much as $10,000 in credit equivalents.

Now, what if you're in the situation we just described, but you've exhausted the $25,000 limit and still have losses and credit equivalents left? You may carry these losses and credit equivalents forward for use in future years. But, even then, you're subject to all the limits we described earlier, including the $25,000 ceiling on rental losses.

Low-income housing credit

The low-income housing credit constitutes one of the few tax breaks left after tax reform. Unfortunately, it's due to expire at the end of 1991.

The amount of the credit depends on the type of housing involved in the project and when you place the building or buildings in service. You get a higher credit if you construct new housing or rehabilitate existing structures. You get a lower credit for existing housing that you don't rehabilitate and for new housing that you construct with the help of federal subsidies.

To qualify for the credit, Uncle Sam requires that you spend at least $2,000 per housing unit. And the housing must remain as low-income rental property for 15 years. If it doesn't, the government takes back some of the tax benefits you pocketed.

In addition, the housing must be open to tenants after December 31, 1986, and generally before January 1, 1992 (unless the credit is extended). The tenants must meet stringent requirements—for example, their incomes must not exceed preset limits. And the occupants must not be transients; that is, you don't get the credit for dormitories, nursing homes, hospitals and similar facilities.

How do you calculate your credit? The rate of credit for both categories of property is computed by the Treasury Department and published in the Internal Revenue Bulletin. Your tax adviser or local IRS office will help you determine which credit applies in your situation and which percentages to use when you calculate the credit.

To compute the credit, multiply the percent in effect for the month you place your property in service by the "qualified basis" of the property. The qualified basis is usually the cost of the building, plus any improvements or additions made before the end of the year in which you place the structure in service.

☞ CAUTION   The rules require your state or local housing credit agency to approve the amount of the credit you claim on your tax return. And they mandate that the agency fill out and return to you Form 8609 specifying the appropriate rate of the credit and your maximum qualified basis. You attach Form 8609 to your income-tax return when you claim the housing credit.

☞ CAUTION   You should know that your qualified basis is reduced if your entire building isn't used as low-income housing. How do you calculate your reduced basis?

Multiply the total basis by the smaller of these two fractions. One is the percentage of low-income units in the building to total residential rental units (whether occupied or not). The other is the percentage of floor space of low-income units to total available rental floor space.

Once computed, you subtract one-tenth of the credit from your tax bill each year for 10 years.

☞ CAUTION   As part of the 1990 Tax Act, Uncle Sam allowed individuals to elect to increase the credit they claimed during 1990 by up to

50 percent of the otherwise allowable credit. If you made this election in 1990, you must reduce the credit you take in future years by the amount you accelerated it in 1990. Here's an example. Say you elected to claim an additional $70 of low income housing credit in your 1990 return on low income property that has seven years of remaining credit eligibility after 1990. In this case you must reduce the allowable credit in each of the subsequent seven years by $10 per year.

TIP The credit percentages you use to calculate the credit change each month. So you may want to lock in your percentage before the month in which you place the property in service, especially if you expect the rates to drop.

All you do is elect to the use the credit percentage in effect for the month in which you and the housing credit agency agree to your percentage rate and basis. *Or*, if you're financing your project with tax-exempt bonds, you may elect to use the percentage in effect for the month in which the bonds were issued.

In both cases, you must file the election with the housing-credit agency by the fifth day of the following month.

TIP If the credit exceeds your tax bill in any year, you may carry back the excess three years—but not to a year ending before 1988—or carry it forward 15 years.

12

Getting The Most
From Your
Vacation Home

What do you need to know—tax-wise at least—about your vacation or second home? For starters, the tax treatment of your second home varies with how you use it. Is it strictly for your use? Or do you rent it? And if so, to whom and for how long?

As far as Uncle Sam is concerned, your second home is either a vacation home that you and your family use exclusively, rental property, or some combination of the two. How the government treats the home depends entirely on how it's classified.

We cover the details in the section just ahead, but here's an overview of the tax differences among these three categories.

A *vacation home* that you use personally 100 percent of the time gets the same tax treatment as your primary residence, even if you rent the property to others for as much as 14 days a year. You write off your mortgage interest and property taxes, but don't deduct your other expenses such as repairs.

TIP The other good news about a vacation home is that if you rent out your home for less than 15 days a year, the rental income you collect is totally tax free to you. That's right. You pocket the money, and Uncle Sam doesn't require you to pay taxes on it.

Rental property differs from a vacation home. You get income from renting the property, and you may deduct most of the expenses that you run up from that income. You may also depreciate the property—that is, write off a portion of its cost each year.

Combination property is treated differently than rental property. Its treatment depends on how much rental use and how much personal use your vacation hideaway gets.

☞ CAUTION Just one day—one way or the other—often can make a big difference in your tax bill.

PERSONAL USE VS. RENTAL PROPERTY

We covered rental property in the previous chapter, so here we detail the rules governing vacation homes used as combination property. First, let's define some of the differences between a personal vacation home and rental property.

Defining the difference

Since, for tax purposes, the differences between a personal vacation home and rental property are so great, the tax code is precise about which is which.

If you intend to rent your second home and take advantage of the tax deductions that renting brings you, these distinctions are important to you.

The tax law says that you may classify your second home as rental property as long as you don't use it yourself for more than 14 days in the year or for more than 10 percent of the total number of days that it's rented at fair market value, whichever is greater.

So, if you rent your second home at the going rate for 300

days, you could use it yourself for as many as 30 days, and it would still qualify as rental property.

☞ **CAUTION** What happens if you occupy it for 31 days? You may still claim a write-off for mortgage interest and taxes, but you're limited on the deductions you may take for operating expenses and depreciation.

Uncle Sam is quite strict about what he considers personal use. You have used your home for personal purposes—in his view—if on any part of any day your vacation home is occupied by you or any of the following people:

- A person who has an equity stake in the property;

- A spouse or blood relative (meaning your parents, children, siblings, and grandparents);

- A person with whom you have a barter arrangement that allows you to use another dwelling; or

- A person to whom the vacation home isn't rented at "fair market value"—which, according to the law, is the going rate for similar homes in the area.

What if you charge a relative—or someone with an equity interest in the property—a fair rent? Unfair as it seems, the IRS still considers this use personal.

Say, for instance, you own a vacation home in upstate New York. You rent it to your sister—a relative—for the going rate, $1,500 for 10 days.

Next, as part of a barter agreement, you allow your friend Bob to occupy your vacation home for 11 days. In exchange, you use his home in California for 8 days.

Finally, you rent your vacation home to your spouse's boss for 10 days and charge the man only half the fair market rental.

How many of these days are personal days?

By the IRS rules, all 31 days count as personal use. What, by the way, constitutes a day? When you're counting, do it by the 24-hour period the way hotels do.

Suppose you occupy your vacation home from Saturday afternoon through the following Saturday morning. In the eyes of the IRS, you've used your house for 7 days, even though you were actually on the premises for part of 8 calendar days.

The law does make one exception to the rule on renting to relatives. Let's say you rent your property at fair market value to a relative who uses the house as a principal residence—a condo for your parents, for instance. The IRS doesn't consider this use personal.

TIP You may not know it, but there's a way to reduce the rent you charge relatives. Consider this lesson from one tax court case.

In that case, the court allowed a taxpayer to slash by 20 percent the fair market rent he charged his parents. The court ruled that the reduced rent was fair because it reflected the amount the man saved in maintenance and management fees by renting to such trustworthy tenants.

CAUTION If you donate time in your vacation home to a charity, you may have to claim that time as personal use. The IRS has held that a week's use of a vacation home donated by the owner to a charity auction counted as personal use of the home.

The reason? The owner didn't charge the bidder at the auction—the renter—a fair rent. Instead, the bidder paid the rental to the charity.

To make matters worse, the owner couldn't claim a write-off for a charitable contribution because a gift of the right to use property isn't deductible.

TIP If you donate use of your vacation home to a charity auction, try this tactic: Rent your home out for a week at its fair market value, then donate the rental income to charity. That way, you get a deduction for your contribution and avoid piling up personal use days.

Maintenance and repair visits

Anyone who owns vacation homes knows that they require repairs and maintenance. If you stay at the house while doing the repairs, does the IRS count these days as personal use? Not if your "principal purpose" in staying there is to make repairs or perform maintenance chores.

Say, for example, that you own a mountain cabin that you rent during the winter. You and your spouse arrive at the cabin late Thursday evening.

The point of the trip? To prepare the cabin for the rental season. But you're tired, so the two of you enjoy dinner by the fire, then turn in early to get plenty of rest for the days ahead. You work on the cabin all day Friday and Saturday.

Your spouse helps for a few hours each day but spends most of the time catching up on paperwork. By Saturday evening all your work is done. You spend the rest of the evening relaxing, then head home shortly before noon on Sunday.

Since the principal purpose of your trip was for maintenance, none of these days count as personal days. They're all maintenance days.

☞ **CAUTION** If your tax return is audited, Uncle Sam may ask you to prove that the principal purpose of your visit was to make repairs and perform maintenance. He may look at how often you did chores, the amount of time you spent performing repairs and maintenance, and whether friends accompanied you.

If the auditor sees, for example, that you spend most of your time at your home doing maintenance—but always bring along a few companions—he or she may argue that your activities aren't on the up and up and may count those days as personal use.

As a result, you could lose your deductions.

TIP Here's an idea worth considering. Keep a log of your repair and maintenance days. Write down when you arrive, how much time you spend on various tasks, and what kind of work you perform. That way, you can prove how you spent your time should Uncle Sam question you.

RENTAL PROPERTY

You say you maintain your vacation home strictly as rental property? The same rules that apply to rental real estate apply to your vacation home.

We cover these rules in detail in Chapter 11.

COMBINATION PROPERTY

The rules get especially tricky when it comes to combination property. Uncle Sam divides combination property into two categories. With the first, you may make personal use of your vacation home within the 14-day or 10 percent limits and still claim most of the deductions you would get for rental property.

If your use falls into this category, your property—in the eyes of Uncle Sam—isn't a personal residence. It's a rental property, and the rules won't allow you to write off as mortgage interest any interest allocated to your personal use. Instead, the interest is personal interest, the same as credit card interest, and it's not deductible at all in 1991 and beyond.

Take heart. If your personal use is less than 14 days or 10 percent of total use, chances are most of your expense will be deductible as rental expense.

The property taxes allocated to your personal use are deductible on Schedule A. All remaining expenses allocable to your personal use are nondeductible personal expenditures. But, depending on the number of days you actually rent the property, the expenses allocated to personal use could be insignificant.

The tax treatment of the expenses allocated to the rental use are covered in Chapter 11.

With the second type of combination property, your personal use exceeds 14 days or the 10 percent limit, and the tax treatment of your house is substantially different.

The portion of your interest, taxes, and expenses allocated to rental use are only deductible from your rental income. In other words, if your second home falls into this category and you post a loss from renting the house, too bad.

You may not deduct that loss currently from your other taxable income.

Assuming this type of property qualifies as a second residence, you may write off any mortgage interest allocable to personal use as an itemized deduction on your Form 1040. And, of course, you may deduct the personal portion of the taxes.

One other wrinkle: The rules require you to deduct your "rental" expenses in a specified order. First, you write off advertising and commission charges, then property taxes and mortgage interest, then operating expenses, and, finally, depreciation.

Why's the order important?

Uncle Sam is forcing you to first deduct those expenses—such as property taxes—that you could write off in any case (with the exception of advertising and commissions). Only if you have rental income left over may you write off your other expenses.

You can see that if you have adequate rental income and if the home qualifies as a second residence, your total interest and taxes are deductible—either against rental income or on Schedule A.

TIP The rules allow you to carry forward to future tax years any expenses you aren't able to deduct currently—subject to all the limits we've described, of course.

☞ **CAUTION** What if you own a third home and it qualifies as combination property—that is, your personal use is more than 14 days or 10 percent of the total days it's rented, whichever is greater? In this case, different rules apply.

The portion of your mortgage interest allocated to personal use isn't deductible as mortgage interest. That's because you may count no more than two homes as personal residences for the purpose of deducting interest.

So the interest allocated to personal use is treated as personal interest and is not deductible at all in 1991 and beyond. Interest allocated to the rental use is deductible to the extent of your rental income less advertising, commission charges, and taxes.

If, however, your personal use is within the 14 days or 10 percent of the total rental days, the treatment is identical to the first discussion of combination property.

No matter which category your vacation home falls into, the rules require you to allocate your expenses to personal and rental use.

And this holds true even if you use your home yourself just one day of the year—New Year's Day, say, or the Fourth of July. You now must allocate one day's worth of your vacation home's total expenses to personal use. And Uncle Sam makes no exceptions to this rule.

The allocation formula, though, is simple. Here's how it works. You add up the number of days you actually rented your property at a fair market value. Let's call this number "X."

Then you total the number of days you used the property for any purpose other than as a rental. Don't include any days the property was standing vacant, and don't count any repair or maintenance days. Let's call the resulting number "Y."

You allocate expenses by multiplying your total expenses (including property taxes and mortgage interest) for the year by the fraction—X divided by the sum of X plus Y. The product of that multiplication is the amount that you may allocate to rental use.

Now, let's run through a couple of examples to see how to use this formula to allocate your expenses. The examples also show the big difference just one additional day of personal use can make in the tax cost of your vacation home.

Let's assume these facts: Your principal residence is in Connecticut, and you also own a vacation home in New Mexico, which you actively participate in managing.

You take out a mortgage to buy the home in New Mexico. Your interest totals $4,000; taxes, $2,000; operating expenses, $2,000; and depreciation, $5,000.

Your rental income in 1991 adds up to $7,500, after you subtract commissions for the year. Your adjusted gross income is $80,000.

Now, for our first example.

Say you rent your house at a fair market value for 126 days, use it for family vacations for 14 days, and spend four days there making repairs and performing maintenance.

Uncle Sam figures you used the house for 140 days (126 rental and 14 personal). The four days you spent on repair and maintenance aren't included in your total use days.

The result? You may allocate 90 percent—that is, 126 divided by 140—of the costs associated with the house to rental use.

Your numbers stack up like this:

- Total rental income—$7,500

- 90 percent of taxes—$1,800

- 90 percent of mortgage interest—$3,600

- 90 percent of operating expenses—$1,800

- 90 percent of depreciation—$4,500

The result: a rental loss of $4,200.

Note that the rental loss is fully deductible under the passive loss rules, as the assumed adjusted gross income is $80,000. For more on passive losses, see Chapter 9.

You may also write off the other 10 percent of your property taxes, or $200, as an itemized deduction on Schedule A of your Form 1040.

However, the remaining interest—the part allocated to personal use—is classified as personal interest. In 1991 personal interest is not deductible. So, in total, you have deductions against your normal taxable income of $4,400—$4,200 plus $200.

Now, for our second example. In this case, we'll say you increase your use of the house by just one day, bringing your personal use to 15 days for the year, but all the other facts are the same.

Since 15 days exceeds the maximum 14-day limit and is more than 10 percent of the total rental days (126 days), your vacation home is now classified as a residence.

Therefore, your deductions for costs allocated to rental use— that is, 126 divided by 141, or 89 percent—may not exceed the rental income you received. And you must write off expenses allocated to rental use in the following order:

- Commissions and advertising

- Property taxes and mortgage interest

- Operating expenses

- Depreciation

On the plus side, the IRS counts the portion of mortgage interest you allocate to the personal use of your home as deductible—just like the interest expense on your principal residence. You may write this amount off on your personal return.

Here's how the numbers stack up now:

- Total rental income—$7,500

- 89 percent of taxes and interest—$5,340

- 89 percent of operating expenses—$1,780 (not limited since the $7,500 rental income exceeds the interest and taxes by $2,160)

- 89 percent of depreciation—potentially $4,450, but limited to just $380, since that is the amount by which rental income ($7,500) tops interest, taxes, and operating expenses ($7,120)

The result: You posted a loss of $4,070, but you aren't able to claim it currently. The reason? Your deductible expenses may not exceed your rental income, although you may still deduct the remaining 11 percent of property taxes and interest—or $660—on your Form 1040.

As you can see, using your house more than the maximum days allowed can cause your taxes to rise sharply. That extra day's use in our example costs you $3,740 in deductions (the difference between the $4,400 in deductions you pocketed in our first example and the $660 in the second).

The only good news is the rules allow you to carry forward amounts you may not deduct currently—in this case, $4,070—to future tax years.

What else do you need to know about allocating expenses? There's an alternative method for allocating taxes and mortgage interest—approved by the courts, but not the IRS—that you may use. Sometimes it works to your benefit.

How? It reduces the amount of interest and taxes allocated to the rental portion, giving you room to use more of your other expenses as deductions against rental income. And it increases the amount of interest and taxes allocable to personal use, giving you a bigger itemized deduction.

Under the alternative method, you divide the number of rental days by the total number of days in the year. You use the resulting percentage to determine the portion of mortgage interest and property taxes that you deduct from your rental income.

The percentage you calculate under this alternative method is smaller. That's because the earlier method required you to divide the number of rental days by the number of days the property was actually in use. So the alternative method usually results in greater savings.

But to be certain, you should perform both calculations with your own numbers and compare the results. Here's an example. Assume the same facts as in our second example, but let's allocate interest and taxes using the alternative method.

- Gross rental income—$7,500

- Taxes and interest—$2,071 (allocated based on the ratio of rental days to total days in the year—that is, 126 divided by 365, times $6,000)

- Limit on other deductions—$5,429 ($7,500 minus $2,071)

- Operating expenses—$1,780 (89 percent times $2,000)

- Depreciation—limited to the lesser of $4,450 (89 percent times $5,000) or $3,649 ($5,429 minus $1,780)

- Rental income or loss—zero

- Remaining taxes and interest deductible as an itemized deduction—239/365 times $6,000, or $3,929

Here, the alternative method works better for you. It gives you $3,929 in tax and interest deductions compared to $660 using the other method.

13

Tax Tips for Mutual Fund Investors

Mutual funds are among the most popular investment vehicles around today—and for good reason. You get expert management of your money by people who devote their full time and attention to the task. You also get diversification and convenience.

What do you need to know—tax-wise, at least—when it comes to investing in mutual funds? That's what this chapter is all about.

BASIC TIPS FOR THE INVESTOR

Let's begin with a few basics. Mutual funds are investment companies that raise money from shareholders and invest it in a wide range of securities—domestic and foreign stocks and bonds, government securities, and so on.

Mutual funds are either open-ended or closed-ended.

What's the difference between the two? Open-end funds

have an unlimited number of shares and investors generally purchase their shares directly from the fund sponsor or securities broker. The company constantly sells new shares to investors and redeems—meaning purchases from shareholders—outstanding ones. So the amount of money managed by the fund is always changing.

Closed-end funds, on the other hand, issue a fixed number of shares, which aren't redeemed by the company. Investors generally trade them just like they do any other stock—on the New York or American Stock Exchanges or over the counter. With closed-end mutual funds, the amount of money under management is relatively fixed because it's not affected by sales and redemptions of shares.

Open-end funds are the most common type of mutual fund, although you should know that the tax rules for both types of funds are the same.

Most mutual funds are organized as special kinds of corporations—regulated investment companies. Unlike regular corporations, a regulated investment company, or RIC, doesn't pay taxes on income that it distributes to shareholders.

To receive this preferential tax treatment, however, a fund must meet many stringent requirements. For one, it must distribute practically all its income each year. In this regard, the IRS generally treats mutual funds much as it does partnerships and other so-called pass-through entities. The shareholders, rather than the mutual fund, generally pay taxes on any income the fund generates. Now let's take a look at some of the specifics you need to know.

Return on investment from mutual funds

You should recognize that you'll realize a gain or loss from your mutual fund investment from two sources—amounts

passed to you by the fund and your direct investment in a mutual fund stock. You compute gains or
losses from your direct investment in mutual fund stock—
when you sell your mutual fund shares—much the same way
as for other stocks. (See Chapter 4 for the details.)

Basis

You must know your basis to determine your gain or loss.
The amount you pay when you first buy shares in a mutual
fund is your initial basis. This includes not only the listed
price of the shares but also other costs of acquisition such as
commissions or load fees. If you elect to use a dividend reinvestment program (discussed below) your basis will also be
affected.

It might interest you to know how mutual funds calculate
the price you pay for their shares and the amount you receive
when you sell those shares.

If you look at your newspaper's listing of open-end mutual
funds, you'll see listed under the price the letters NAV, which
stand for net asset value per share.

Net asset value per share is calculated by subtracting a
fund's total liabilities from the market value of its total assets,
then dividing the result by the number of shares outstanding.

Open-end funds usually sell or redeem their shares at NAV
less any applicable redemption fees or deferred sales charges.
By contrast, closed-end funds usually sell for an amount that
is higher (that is, they carry a premium) or lower (they sell at a
discount) than their NAV. It all depends on what the market
thinks of the stock. In other words, the stock price of closed-
end companies—like the stock price of other companies—is
determined by supply and demand.

Different types of income from mutual funds

Mutual funds pass through to their shareholders more than just ordinary taxable dividends. They also pass through tax-exempt interest dividends and capital gains distributions. (See Chapter 3 for more on dividends and Chapter 5 for more on capital gains distributions.)

Uncle Sam requires that mutual funds provide you with Form 1099-DIV to report your share of ordinary taxable dividends and capital gains distributions.

Dividends from mutual funds that are reinvested

Many people like to have their mutual fund automatically reinvest dividends (including capital gains distributions) in additional shares of the fund. How does the tax law treat these reinvestments?

You're required to report the amount of your reinvested dividends as dividend income on your Form 1040. You're also required to adjust your basis. You must add to your original basis the value of the shares you acquired with reinvested dividends.

Here's an example. Say it's January 1991. You invest $1,000 in a mutual fund and elect to have your dividends reinvested. In December 1991, the fund pays you a taxable dividend of $100, but you receive no cash. Instead, you receive additional shares valued at $100.

When you file your 1991 tax return, Uncle Sam requires you to report $100 of dividend income, which is the value of the shares you received. What's your basis in the shares? It's your old basis of $1,000 plus $100.

TIP Remember, before you buy, read the prospectus so you know the timing of the fund's distributions. Most mutual funds declare regular dividend distributions at least annually and often much more frequently. You're entitled to receive dividends only if you're a shareholder as of the so-called record date.

If you are planning to have your dividends reinvested, you may not want to buy into a fund just before a distribution. The reason? You may owe taxes on income that does not represent an actual profit to you.

Since you usually purchase mutual fund shares based on the net asset value (NAV) of the fund, the NAV is higher just before the distribution than it is just after the distribution. So, you pay a higher price.

When the fund makes its distribution, you recognize taxable income, but receive no cash because of your desire to have your dividends reinvested. And the overall value of your shares hasn't changed.

Here's an example: Say, you invest $10,000 in a mutual fund. The next day the fund pays a $500 dividend on your shares. Now, you must recognize $500 of taxable income on your tax return. The value of your original shares falls to $9,500, because the NAV changes to reflect the amount of the dividend. However, you acquire additional shares that represent $500 of NAV with your reinvested dividend, so the value of your investment returns to $10,000. So what's the net result?

You pay $10,000 for your mutual fund investment and it's worth $10,000 based on NAV. Your basis is $10,500 (your $10,000 original investment plus the $500 reinvested), but now you have $500 of income to report. Had you waited until after the fund paid the dividend to make your $10,000 investment, you'd have had mutual fund shares worth $10,000, but would not have had the $500 of dividend income to report. However, your basis in this case would have been $10,000, not $10,500.

TIP Say it's likely that you'll have to pay the AMT. In this case, it may make sense to generate taxable income by investing in a fund just before it declares a dividend. Doing so would give you the opportunity to accelerate your income, which, under the AMT rules, will be taxed at only 24 percent.

Let's look at the example we just gave. You accelerated $500 of taxable income—at a tax rate of 24 percent—in exchange for an increase in basis, which you may use in a future year when you sell your shares to reduce your gain or increase your loss. As we just noted, your basis in the mutual fund shares comes to $10,500 even though the value of those shares is only $10,000.

(See Chapter 8 for more on the AMT.)

TIP Say you're the type of investor who likes to receive a regular check from your mutual fund. If so, you may want to purchase shares in the fund, have your dividends reinvested, then ask the fund company to redeem a set dollar amount periodically—monthly, say.

As with other reinvested dividends, the dividend income you receive is currently taxable. The amount that's reinvested increases your basis in the fund. In this way, you may receive level payments from your mutual fund investment similar to a fixed-income vehicle. But note that your desire to receive periodic payments results in the fund's selling some of your shares, which means you generate a taxable capital gain or loss.

Miscellaneous itemized deductions

TIP Your mutual fund incurs expenses in managing and investing your money. But as the fund subtracts its expenses from its net income before it distributes this income to you, these expenses aren't subject to the two percent of AGI floor on miscellaneous itemized deductions. (See Chapter 7 for more on miscellaneous itemized deductions.)

Sales commissions and loads

Sales commissions and loads (money you pay to buy shares) are capital costs, not expenses. You don't write these costs off in the year you pay them. Instead, you include them in your computation when it comes time to calculate your gain or loss by reducing your taxable gain or increasing your taxable loss by the amount of these costs.

You may want to look at "no-load" or "low-load" funds. Why? So-called load funds impose a sales charge of up to 8.5 percent of the amount you pay for your fund shares to cover the cost of marketing their shares through salesmen or brokers. They usually set sliding scales under which this percentage charge gradually decreases as the size of your investment increases.

No-load funds pay no salesmen or brokers. All of the money you invest in no-load funds goes to work for you. A newer breed of mutual fund, called a low-load fund, carries a smaller sales charge of perhaps 2 to 4 percent.

CAUTION Congress adopted legislation in 1989 that limits the adjustment you can make in your basis for load charges in certain cases.

Say, for example, that you purchase shares in a mutual

fund, sell the shares soon after you buy them, and, in the process, incur load charges.

If the investment company allows you to reinvest the proceeds in another of its funds at a waived or reduced load charge, you may not deduct the load you paid on the first shares in figuring your gain or loss.

The good news? The law only applies when you sell or exchange the first shares within 90 days of when you acquired them.

14

Should You Invest In Life Insurance Or Annuities?

Should you invest in life insurance?

Before you answer "no" to life insurance and skip this chapter, consider this one point. Even people who don't need insurance might want to consider owning some.

Many of us overlook the investment value of life insurance. That's not to argue that everyone ought to invest in it and certainly not to say that all life insurance is an investment. But do take the time to explore the possibilities.

In this chapter, we explain the pros and cons of using insurance for investment purposes, including increasing your rate of return by deferring taxes.

Defining life insurance

Let's start, though, with a few key definitions.

A life insurance policy is a contract that's payable at the death of the person who's insured. An endowment policy, on the other hand, is life insurance that's payable either at the death of the person who's insured or at a specified time during that person's life.

An annuity is a contract sold by an insurance company that promises to make installment payments to you commencing at some future date, usually at retirement.

Annuities come in two forms—fixed and variable. With a fixed annuity, the amount you receive is paid out in regular equal installments. You decide how frequently you want to receive payments. For example, you may decide to receive payments monthly or quarterly. Or you may opt for annual payments.

With a variable annuity, the amount you receive fluctuates with the type of account you have. The reason? You decide how the dollars that you set aside are invested, so the amount you receive depends on the value of your underlying portfolio.

Annuity payments are made to you either over a fixed period—20 years, for example—or over an indefinite period such as the remainder of your life. The terms are spelled out in your annuity contract.

Some annuities—so-called joint and survivor annuities—continue to make payments to your beneficiary after your death.

What are joint and survivor annuities? They're annuities that make regular payments over your life and the life of your spouse. So if you die, your spouse continues to receive annuity payments, although the amount of the payments may change.

Annuities are available from a variety of sources such as insurance companies, financial planners, banks, and brokerage firms.

What if you exchange one type of annuity or life insurance policy for another? You get off easy. If the policyholder remains the same and you receive no cash or other property as a result of the exchange, the transaction isn't taxable to you.

Uncle Sam also exempts from taxation exchanges of life insurance for endowment contracts, life insurance for annuity contracts, endowment contracts for annuity contracts, endowment contracts for endowment contracts, and annuity contracts for annuity contracts. But, he taxes exchanges of annuity contracts for endowment contracts, annuity contracts for life insurance, and endowment contracts for life insurance.

With exchanges for endowment contracts, however, there's a catch. Uncle Sam says the exchange is tax free only if the new policy provides for regular payments to begin no later than payments would have begun under the old contract.

Now, for a few words about death benefits.

Your death benefit—sort of a contradiction in terms—is the amount your insurance company will pay if you die while your policy is in force.

In most cases, your death benefit equals the face value of the policy. If you take out a $500,000 policy on your life and subsequently die, your insurance carrier will pay $500,000 to your beneficiaries—the people you designate to receive your death benefit.

Death benefits paid in a lump sum aren't taxed as income to your beneficiary; Uncle Sam carves out an exception to this rule in the case of a beneficiary who acquired a policy in exchange for payment.

Say you accept as payment for an amount owed to you, an insurance policy covering the life of another person. If you continue to make premium payments and ultimately receive the death benefit, some of the proceeds received may be taxable to you.

Under the rules, you may exclude from your income only the amount of your basis in the contract—that is, the fair market value of the policy on the date it was transferred to you plus any premium payments you made on the contract. Usually, the transfer of a policy by gift isn't subject to this exception and proceeds are free from federal income taxes.

Death benefits may escape federal estate taxes, too, if your beneficiary is your spouse and he or she is a United States citizen. Here's why. You may leave your entire estate—no matter how large—to your spouse tax free, thanks to a device known as the unlimited marital deduction.

What if your spouse isn't your beneficiary? Your life insurance proceeds may still escape federal estate taxes. How? Under another device known as the unified credit, estates and accumulated gifts of U.S. citizens with a total value of $600,000 or less aren't subject to estate taxes at all.

You should know, though, that Uncle Sam requires that the proceeds from life insurance policies that you hold in your name be added to the value of your estate when you die. And this amount may cause your estate to be valued at more than the $600,000 threshold for estate taxes.

If you think your estate may be valued at more than $600,000 with the addition of your life insurance proceeds, you may want to talk to your tax adviser about changing the ownership of your life insurance policy. He or she will help you with this complicated procedure.

Although life insurance proceeds paid in a lump sum aren't taxable as income to the person who receives them, it's a different story if the benefits are paid over time.

The reason is simple. The insurance company invests the proceeds from the policy. A portion of the dollars your beneficiary receives is principal, meaning death benefits, and a portion is investment income such as interest, dividends, and so on.

The death benefits your beneficiary receives aren't taxable as income, but that's not true of investment income on those benefits. It's subject to ordinary income taxes.

If your spouse died before October 23, 1986, and you receive insurance death benefits in installments, Uncle Sam treats you kindly. He says you may exclude from taxation up to $1,000 a year of the interest included in those installment payments.

Let's say your husband passed away in June 1986, and you opt to receive the proceeds of his $75,000 life insurance policy in 10 annual installments of $11,250. Principal payments add up to $7,500 a year, while interest on the installments comes to $3,750. You pay taxes on only $2,750 of your interest income—that is, your interest payments of $3,750 minus the $1,000 annual exclusion.

What if your spouse died after October 22, 1986? Unfair as it seems, you're not entitled to claim the $1,000 annual interest exclusion.

☞ CAUTION You should know that almost every new tax law that's introduced in Congress takes aim at the interest, dividends, and so on that accumulate tax-deferred in life insurance policies. Some lawmakers, it seems, want to tax these dollars.

Our advice? Keep your eyes on Congress. Chances are, the rules governing the tax treatment of investing through life insurance policies will change sooner or later. But there's no way to know if existing policies will retain their current tax treatment.

Term insurance

Term life insurance is what agents refer to as "no-frills" insurance. It provides coverage for a fixed period, usually a year. All your premiums go to pay for your current coverage. In other words, term insurance includes no investment portion.

☞ CAUTION Unfortunately, the cost of term insurance—or any other life insurance policy for that matter—isn't deductible on your personal return. That's because, in the eyes of Uncle Sam, life insurance is a personal expense.

☞ CAUTION You should know that Uncle Sam requires your employer to report as income to you the cost of life insurance it provides, unless the insurance is provided under a group-term policy. But even under group-term plans, the benefit is tax free only up to $50,000 of coverage.

Amounts your company pays for additional coverage is compensation to you. The cost of additional insurance that's reported as income to you isn't what the company actually pays. Rather, it's an amount based on an IRS table of "average" or "uniform" premiums.

Here's the table: employees under the age of 30, 8 cents a month for each $1,000 of life insurance protection; ages 30 to 34, 9 cents; ages 35 to 39, 11 cents; ages 40 to 44, 17 cents; ages 45 to 49, 29 cents; ages 50 to 54, 48 cents; ages 55 to 59, 75 cents; ages 60 to 64, $1.17; ages 65 to 69, $2.10; and ages 70 and older, $3.76.

Whole life insurance

Whole life insurance is simply term insurance with an investment feature built in. It works like this: You hand over to your insurance company or carrier money in the form of premium payments. Then, the company takes a chunk of your cash to pay for the insurance portion of the policy. The remainder of your premium, with the exception of some insurance company administrative expenses, is invested by the insurance company on your behalf.

Here's where Uncle Sam gives you a break. He doesn't tax the interest and other earnings that accumulate on your deposit until those amounts are withdrawn. This deferral is the primary tax reason to use a life insurance policy as an investment.

TIP In most cases, Uncle Sam doesn't treat as taxable income amounts you borrow from your life insurance policy. (We cover the exceptions to this rule later in this chapter.) The interest you pay on these loans is deductible based on how you use the proceeds.

For example, if you borrow $4,000 on your policy and use the money to purchase $4,000 worth of stock, the interest is classified as investment interest and may be deductible under the investment interest expense rules. (See Chapter 6 for the details on how to write off interest.)

☞ **CAUTION** Now, what if you borrow money to pay your insurance premiums? The interest on the loan is treated not as investment interest but as personal interest. Beginning in 1991, personal interest is not deductible.

Also, if you borrow any portion of four or more of the first seven annual premium payments, the interest paid on the amounts borrowed is probably not deductible.

☞ **CAUTION** Here's another scenario. Say you cancel your life insurance policy and receive what's known as its surrender or cash value. Except in the case of modified endowment contracts, which we discuss later, amounts received from surrender of a life insurance policy is first treated as a recovery of your premiums, then as ordinary income after your investment is recovered. However, if the amount you receive on complete surrender is less than your investment, you're not allowed to deduct the loss. The reason? The amount is considered a personal expense of insurance protection.

Because the surrender of a policy may cause an income tax payment, a policyholder should evaluate whether it's more advantageous to borrow from the policy rather than surrendering it.

💵 **TIP** Dividends from your insurance policy are partly a return of the premiums you've paid. Uncle Sam says you don't need to include these dividends in your income until they add up to more than all the premiums you've paid under the policy.

☞ **CAUTION** Say you have a life insurance policy. The policy credits dividends to you annually, and you can choose to withdraw them whenever you like, apply them to your premium payments, or leave them on deposit to earn interest.

You opt to leave the dividends your policy earns on deposit with the insurance company. The interest you earn on these deposits is taxable to you when it's credited to your account.

For some policies, however, the insurance company restricts your ability to receive the interest that it credits on your deposits. In this case, the interest becomes taxable in the year that the restriction no longer applies.

TIP   The Form 1099-INT mailed to you by your insurance carrier lists the interest earned on insurance dividends that were paid in past years and are now accumulating in a savings account. You should ask what rate of interest you're earning; you may want to withdraw your money and invest it elsewhere.

Universal life insurance

Universal life—a variation on whole life—is one of the more popular types of policies. In fact, this type equals about one-third of all policies sold today. With universal life, the investment portion of your premium goes into money-market funds that yield current interest rates.

And, unlike the cash value of a traditional whole life policy, a universal life policy's cash value grows at a variable rate. The rate varies with the money markets, but most insurance companies will notify you annually of the interest rate your policy will earn in the coming year.

One selling point of universal life policies is that they offer life insurance protection along with a competitive yield on the savings portion of the policy.

Another advantage of universal life over traditional whole life is that you may vary your annual death benefit and your annual premium. Whole life premiums are usually fixed, but with universal life you may decide, within limits, what you can afford to pay in premiums each year.

In leaner years, you may skip paying the premium altogether. When you skip payments, the carrier simply deducts the cost of maintaining the life insurance portion of your plan plus administrative expenses from the accumulated cash value.

In good years—financially speaking—you may decide to put more money in the policy and get a faster buildup of your cash value.

☞ **CAUTION** If your premium payments for a universal life policy—or any other life insurance plan—top limits outlined in the law, Uncle Sam may classify your policy as a modified endowment contract. That's bad news for you tax-wise.

With a modified endowment policy, Uncle Sam assumes that the first dollars you borrow or withdraw are your accumulated earnings. And these dollars are subject to income taxes.

Also, if you're under the age of 59½, the IRS slaps you with a 10 percent penalty on the amount of earnings you borrow from such a plan.

Now, what if your policy is classified as a modified endowment plan but you don't borrow or withdraw any of your dollars? Then it's business as usual.

The amounts you contribute to your policy continue to accumulate tax-deferred until you withdraw them or assign or pledge the policy as collateral for a loan. When you assign or pledge a policy, the amount is treated as a distribution to you for tax purposes.

The modified endowment rules apply only to policies entered into or changed after June 20, 1988. And Uncle Sam exempts from these rules policies with death benefits of $25,000 or less that are purchased to cover burial expenses or in connection with prearranged funeral expenses.

Our advice? If you want to avoid the tax trap of the modified endowment policy rules, see your tax adviser before you boost your premium payments. With the help of your insurance agent, he or she will be able to tell you if your plan will be reclassified as a modified endowment policy.

Variable life insurance

As with traditional whole life, a portion of the variable life premium goes to cover the cost of insurance, and the rest is invested. But while whole life premiums are usually invested in long-term bonds and mortgages, such as Ginnie Maes, and universal life premiums usually go into money-market funds, variable life premiums are invested according to your wishes as the policyholder.

The carrier will invest your premiums in an array of investment vehicles, ranging from mutual funds to fixed-income instruments. You should know, though, that carriers manage the specific funds in which your money is invested. So, you can't choose an investment that's not in your carrier's portfolio.

Several times a year, you may—as the terms of your insurance policy allow—switch among investment vehicles without penalty. It's up to you, for instance, to decide when to move funds in or out of a stock or bond mutual fund, and you're the one making the calls on market turns.

If you're comfortable with investment decisions, variable life offers a hands-on alternative to whole life policies while also meeting your basic insurance needs. On the down side, the cash value of variable life policies is uncertain. The cost of the insurance portion of the policy, though, never falls below a certain floor.

☞ **CAUTION** You also should keep in mind that variable life is expensive. The sales commission and service fees cut considerably into the amount available for investment.

Like whole life policies and universal life, variable life policies may not be for those concerned with short-term insurance needs. Rather, variable life is better used by those who can predict their future insurance needs with reasonable certainty.

Flexible-premium variable life insurance

These plans combine features of universal and variable life. As with universal life, you may change the premiums and death benefits.

However, as with variable life policies, you specify how you want the savings portion of the policy invested. With most policies, you may also shift your money from one investment vehicle to another during the year, although the insurance carrier may charge you a fee to make the switch.

Single-premium insurance

Here's how a single-premium life insurance policy works. You put up a large sum—usually no less than $5,000—to pay for your death benefits, and you earn a competitive tax-deferred interest rate.

You may obtain cash from the policy at any time through a policy loan that charges interest of about six to eight percent. Insurance companies offer attractive interest rates, and they may offer guarantees to hold a steady rate over three to five years if you direct them to.

Be aware that the company may impose a back-end load; that is, they may charge you a percentage of your account when you take your money out.

For example, one carrier's early cancellation penalty comes to seven percent of premiums in the first or second year and drops by one percent a year after that time. In other words, you must keep your money in the policy for nine years before you withdraw it without an insurance company penalty.

☞ CAUTION You should know that any single-premium policy that you enter into or materially change after June 20, 1988, falls into the category of a modified endowment policy. So, you may want to think twice before you use such a policy for investment purposes.

☞ CAUTION As a savvy investor, you want to make sure the company offering this type of policy is sound. Single-premium and other investment-oriented policies often attract a fickle pool of policyholders, quick to bail out with changes in market conditions. So a large run on a particular type of policy may seriously undermine your insurance company's ability to return your money.

How do you check out the financial stability of your insurance carrier? One good source of information on insurers is A.M. Best. It publishes a directory, available in most libraries, of insurance carriers and rates them according to their financial strength.

☞ CAUTION A separate rule applies to interest you pay on money borrowed to purchase a single-premium life insurance policy. It says the interest isn't deductible. Under this rule, any contract where substantially all of the premiums are paid within the first four policy years is classified as a single-premium contract.

Borrowing from a single-premium contract to make other investments, such as the purchase of corporate stock, is classified as interest incurred to carry the contract and is therefore not deductible, even under the investment interest rules.

Annuities

When do your investment dollars grow fastest? The answer is in a tax-deferred account such as an annuity. Millions of annuity policies are in place nationwide.

One way to think of an annuity is as the opposite of a life insurance policy. A life insurance policy pays after you die; an annuity, while you're alive. Although annuities come in a variety of types, the two primary ones are immediate annuities and deferred annuities.

With an immediate annuity, you usually begin receiving benefits 30 to 90 days after you purchase your contract, usually with a lump sum.

A deferred annuity, on the other hand, pays you benefits starting at some future date, usually at retirement. You buy your annuity contract either by paying a lump sum, making installment payments, or through some combination of the two.

☞ **CAUTION** You may want to think twice before you borrow money to purchase an annuity contract. Why? It's likely that Uncle Sam will classify interest on loans taken out to buy annuities as investment interest. Although classification as investment interest is certainly better than classification as personal interest, investment interest is only deductible to the extent of your net investment income.

And interest on loans to purchase single-premium annuities isn't deductible at all. In fact, the same interest deductibility rules that apply to single-premium life insurance policies, which we discussed earlier, apply to single-premium annuities.

With an annuity, the interest, dividends, and capital gains you earn accumulate tax-deferred until they're paid to you under the terms of your annuity.

Annuities are long-term investments. Why? Restrictions apply to amounts you take out. For example, Uncle Sam imposes a 10 percent penalty on certain taxable amounts you withdraw from annuities before you reach age 59½.

These amounts are all taxable with the following exceptions: those made on or after the death of the annuityholder; those made after the annuityholder becomes disabled; those that are part of a series of substantially equal periodic payments made for the life of the annuityholder or the joint lives of the annuityholder and his or her beneficiary; or those allocable to investment in the contract before August 14, 1982.

In addition, any amount you receive as a loan against your annuity or the value of an annuity pledged or assigned for a loan is treated as a withdrawal and is treated as taxable income. Also, your insurance company may impose surrender charges if you cash out early.

What happens to you tax-wise when you begin receiving your regular annuity payments? Part of each payment is taxable, and part is not. Which is which?

A portion of the dollars you receive is a return of the amount you paid for the contract—your cost basis, sometimes called your investment in the contract—and a portion is investment income such as interest, dividends, and so on. You pay taxes *only* on your investment income.

How do you calculate the portion of your annuity payments that are taxable? Quite simply, the taxable amount of each annuity payment is your entire payment minus the portion that's treated as nontaxable.

As with distributions from IRAs, the recovery of your nontaxable cost basis is spread over the payments you expect to receive from the annuity.

For instance, with a fixed annuity, the exclusion ratio is applied to each regular payment to determine the nontaxable amount. The exclusion ratio is the relation of your cost basis in the contract at the date annuity payments begin to your total expected payments from the annuity.

With a variable annuity, your nondeductible amount is spread evenly over the number of annuity payments you expect to receive. Since most annuities don't call for a fixed number of payments, the IRS has devised actuarial tables of life expectancies to determine the number of payments you can expect.

And, as with IRAs, the taxable portion of your annuity may be subject to a 10 percent penalty for withdrawals prior to age 59½. However, there are exceptions to the penalty that are similar to those that apply to IRAs.

See Chapter 18 for the details on IRA withdrawals and IRS Publication 575, *Pension and Annuity Income*, for details on determining your cost basis and expected return from an annuity.

☞ **CAUTION** Some annuities allow you to "partially surrender"—that is, partially cash out—your contract before your regular annuity payments are scheduled to begin. You should know that the money you receive is taxable to you but only to the extent of the income on the contract.

Different rules apply, depending on when you made your deposits in your contract. For annuities where the deposits are made after August 13, 1982, any partial withdrawal is treated as a return of your investment income first. So any amount withdrawn is taxable to the extent of the income accumulated in the contract.

Say you deposited $5,000 in a deferred annuity in January 1985 and until now you've made no withdrawals. The cash value of your account has grown to $7,500. Now, you want to get your hands on $2,500. Under the rules, the withdrawal is all taxable as income from the contract. None of it is treated as a nontaxable return of your investment. And, as we pointed out earlier, you may also be faced with the 10 percent penalty tax for withdrawals before age 59½.

Another rule applies to annuity deposits made before August 14, 1982. In this case, you get to withdraw your deposits first and your investment earnings last. Until the point when you've received the full amount of your deposits, you have no taxable income to report.

As you might expect, the rules are a bit more complicated if you own a contract to which you've made contributions both before and after the August 13, 1982, cutoff. Still, you get to pull out your pre-August 14, 1982, deposits first. But after that, you pay taxes on up to the full investment income earned in the contract.

TIP Uncle Sam allows you to switch from one annuity contract to another with no tax consequences to you. This switch is known in IRS parlance as a Section 1035 exchange.

If you plan to make a Section 1035 exchange, consult your tax adviser before you make the transfer. That way, you're sure to make the exchange according to the rules.

CAUTION Think twice before you purchase an annuity to fund your child's college education. Why? The amounts you withdraw to pay tuition bills are subject to a 10 percent early-withdrawal penalty if you're younger than age 59½.

Therefore if your child will enter college before you reach age 59½, you may want to steer clear of annuities.

TIP Are you thinking about making a nondeductible contribution to an IRA? Consider putting your money into an annuity instead.

Why? With an annuity, you aren't subject to the $2,000 ceiling on IRA contributions. Nor do you have to report the amount you sock away to the IRS. For more information on IRAs, see Chapter 17.

15

Your Guide to Employer-Provided Stock Options

It would be hard to imagine better aids to employee recruitment and retention than stock options and stock appreciation rights. Both let employees share in the success of their employer. And, from the company's perspective, both boost employees' incentive to work for that success.

Some companies restrict options to top executives; others spread this benefit down the line. Often, options are a negotiable part of a total compensation package.

You can use stock options and stock appreciation rights to your best advantage if you understand the tax rules that govern them. These rules aren't difficult, and they do provide lots of flexibility, which means that you have choices to make.

This chapter helps you make those choices. We begin with a few words about how options work. (We cover options that aren't employment-related in Chapter 5.)

When your employer grants you a stock option, you've gained the right to buy a specific number of shares of your company's stock at a specific price within a specific period of time. You don't have to buy, but you may—at your option, so to speak.

STOCK OPTION CONSIDERATIONS

One of the beauties of optioned stock—which you purchase through your company, not through your stockbroker—lies in the price you pay.

Say, for instance, that as a result of your outstanding performance last year, your boss gave you a bonus—an option on 2,000 shares of company stock.

The option price is $12 a share. Wait a minute: What do we mean by option price? It's the amount you pay for the stock when you exercise your option and, in most cases, is the fair market value of the stock on the date your option was granted.

Now, a year later, the market price of the stock has soared to $20 a share, and you decide to exercise the options. When you do, you pay $24,000—that is, $12 times 2,000 shares— for stock that is currently worth $40,000. Not a bad deal.

But it's an even better deal if your options are incentive stock options (ISOs). As it happens, options come in two varieties—ISOs and nonqualified stock options (NQOs). The difference lies mainly in the tax benefits that ISOs provide.

There's no regular tax due on an incentive stock option until you eventually sell or exchange the stock, and then only if you sell or exchange it for more than you paid for it. (You should know, however, that you must hold ISOs for a specified amout of time if your profits are to be taxed as capital gains. See "Capital gains" in this chapter for the details.)

Generally, with NQOs, on the other hand, there's an immediate tax bite when you exercise the option, as well as a tax you pay when you sell the stock at a profit.

Let's return to our example.

If your boss had granted you NQOs instead of ISOs, you would have incurred a tax liability when you exercised them. The IRS taxes you on the difference between the option price, $12, and the market price, $20, at the time you exercise the option. So you're taxed on $16,000 when you exercise your NQO, and this income is treated as ordinary income.

If you're able to sell the stock, say, a year later for $30 a share, you're taxed again—this time as capital gains on the difference between $20 and $30. With an ISO, you're taxed just once for regular tax purposes—when you finally sell the stock for $30 a share.

But, with an ISO, the entire amount of your gain—the difference between the $30 a share you receive at the sale and the $12 a share option price that you originally paid—is taxed as a capital gain. (For more information on capital gains, see Chapters 4 and 5.)

You can see the advantage of the ISO. You pay no regular tax until you actually realize a gain when you sell or exchange your stock, and all of that gain is treated as a capital gain.

With the NQO, on the other hand, you pay tax on your paper profit as ordinary income when you exercise the option. That means that you not only must have cash to buy the stock when you exercise an NQO, you also need the money to pay Uncle Sam his due. (An amount normally must be paid to your employer to be remitted as withholding taxes.)

Fortunately, you do get to increase your basis in the stock—that is, the stock's cost to you—by the amount of your reported gain.

You should know, though, that the bargain element—the difference between the price at which you buy your stock and the fair market value—on the exercise of ISOs is a preference item when you compute your alternative minimum tax (AMT).

So, timing is an issue. You may not want to exercise an ISO if it will throw you into an AMT situation. (See Chapter 8 for the details on the AMT.)

Which is the better deal? ISOs? NQOs? The answer is: it depends. You may be better off from a tax perspective with ISOs, but ISOs do come with a set of rules that can make them less desirable for other reasons.

RULES AND RESTRICTIONS

These rules are what define an ISO. If a stock option doesn't conform, it is, by definition, an NQO and is automatically treated as such. Even if an option qualifies as an ISO, you may be able to treat it as an NQO if its terms give you that option, or, if you violate the rules, your ISO will be treated, taxwise, as an NQO. So, let's take a look at these rules and the restrictions they impose.

Employee status

From the day you receive the ISO until three months before you exercise it, you must be employed by the company (or a related company) granting it. So you may—if your employer's plan allows—exercise the option within three months after you leave the company, and still obtain the favorable tax benefits.

But, if you leave a company due to permanent and total disability and your employer's plan allows it, you have up to one year to exercise your ISOs. Sick leave or any other company-approved leave doesn't count, however.

What if you die? Your options go to your beneficiaries—meaning the people you specify as your heirs—and they may, in turn, exercise them.

Option period

You must exercise your ISO within 10 years of the date it's granted, unless you own more than 10 percent of your company's stock. In that case, the option period may not top five years.

Another rule you should know: The company must grant ISOs within 10 years of the date the shareholders formally approve the stock option plan or the plan is adopted, whichever is earlier.

Fair market price

The rules say that the option price must not be less than the fair market price of the stock on the date the option is granted. A special rule applies to individuals who own more than 10 percent of a corporation's stock. In their case only, the option price must at least be equal to 110 percent of the fair market value of the stock on the date the ISO is granted.

$100,000 ceiling

Of all the ISOs you are granted after 1986, no more than $100,000 worth (valued at the time they're granted) may become exercisable for the first time in any one year. If you violate this rule, the first $100,000 of options still qualifies as ISOs, but the remainder falls into the category of NQOs.

You calculate the first $100,000 of options that qualifies for ISO treatment by adding together your options in the order you receive them. Here's an example.

Say your company grants you two options that are first exercisable in 1991. You receive the first, which is to purchase 6,000 shares at $10 a share (or $60,000), on January 15. You receive the second—to purchase 7,000 shares at $10 a share, or $70,000—on July 15.

The first option of $60,000 qualifies as an ISO. So does $40,000 of the second option. The remainder of the second option ($70,000 minus $40,000, or $30,000) falls into the category of an NQO.

Understand, though, that this limit isn't on the value of the options your employer may grant you; your company may grant you any amount in options it sees fit. Rather, the limit is on the value of the stock options that are first exercisable by you in any year. You determine the value of the option by multiplying the number of shares in the option by the fair market value of the stock at the time the option is granted.

Say, for instance, that your employer grants you $300,000 worth of options in 1991. The entire amount would qualify as ISOs—as long as the option states that you could exercise no more than $100,000 in 1991, and the second and third $100,000 worth of options in 1992 and 1993, respectively.

You don't have to exercise them, or you could exercise all three in 1993; however, you may not first exercise more than $100,000 in any one year.

What if your employer grants you $150,000 worth of options in 1991, all of which can be exercised in the same year? In this case, you should instruct your employer at the date of exercise to issue you separate stock certificates for $100,000 of the stock, and identify the certificates as an ISO exercise in the stock transfer records.

Otherwise, each share of stock will be treated as two-thirds acquired by an ISO and one-third acquired by the exercise of an NQO. The separate designation will provide you with greater flexibility in recognizing income in future years.

Order of exercise

You must exercise ISOs granted to you in 1986 and earlier in the order in which they were granted. But you may exercise ISOs granted *after* 1986 in any order you like.

Let's say you hold an option to purchase 2,000 shares of stock at $15 a share, another to buy 1,000 at $10 a share, and still another to purchase 5,000 at $5 each. You received the $15-per-share option in 1985, the $10-per-share option in 1986, and the $5-per-share option in 1987. You may exercise the post-1986 option—the $5-per-share option issued in 1987—before the other two.

But, you must exercise options issued before 1987 in the order in which they were granted. In other words, you must exercise the 1985 option before you exercise the 1986 option.

Capital gains

You may claim long-term capital gain tax treatment from gains on the sale of stock bought with ISOs *only* if you hold the shares for the later of more than two years from the date the option was granted, or more than one year from the date the shares were actually transferred to you.

Otherwise, your gain—the difference between the option price and the amount you collected when you sold your stock—is taxed as ordinary income.

For example, you receive an option on July 3, 1991. You exercise the option six months later on January 3, 1992. Under the law, in order to have your gain considered long-term, you must hold the shares until after July 3, 1993—that is, two years after the option was granted to you.

Transferability

There are a number of other requirements which must be met to make sure that your options will be treated as ISOs rather than NQOs.

You may know that only you and your heirs may exercise ISOs. But did you also know that you may not contribute your options to an IRA or other retirement plan? The IRS doesn't want you deferring gains on options even longer than the options themselves permit.

No one else—not even your spouse—may exercise your ISOs during your lifetime, and you may not assign options in a divorce settlement. Therefore, it's not surprising that options are often an issue during separation or divorce negotiations. Both sides must devise a formula to compensate for the fact that much of an executive's wealth may consist of nontransferable stock options.

This rule also means that you may not sell your right to exercise an option or use the right as collateral for a loan.

With all the restrictions that apply to them, why might you still prefer ISOs to NQOs? Tax deferral is perhaps the best reason. As we pointed out earlier, you report no gain for regular tax purposes until you sell or exchange your ISO stock.

TIP This and the fact that you may use company stock you already own to pay for ISO stock, which is another feature of many plans, allow you to use a powerful strategy.

Say that you join a young company whose shares are selling for $2. At the time you come on board, you buy 1,000 shares of stock and receive ISOs for 5,000 shares at $2 a share. In five years, the stock price hits $10, and you decide to exercise your option.

You do so by paying with the 1,000 shares you bought earlier. Now, you own 5,000 shares worth $50,000 at the current market price, but your investment cost just the $2,000 you paid for that initial stock. This transaction is tax free until you sell the option shares.

Let's say that you use this same strategy but, instead of paying with shares you bought, you pay with shares acquired under an ISO.

The same rules apply—but only if you have held the stock for more than two years after your ISOs were granted or more than one year after the shares were transferred to you, whichever is longer. Otherwise, the shares you exchange no longer qualify for treatment as ISOs.

You have made a so-called disqualifying disposition;

that is, you have disposed of ISO stock before meeting the holding period requirement. Therefore, you must pay tax on your profit, the appreciation, at ordinary income rates when they are exchanged.

TIP The capital gain income that ISOs yield— besides giving you the benefit of the preferential tax rate ceiling on long-term capital gains—may be useful for other tax purposes. For instance, you may use these capital gains to offset your capital losses. (For the details on capital gains and losses, see Chapters 4 and 5.)

NQOs, however, have their place. With NQOs, you don't have to worry about the AMT. Nor do you have to worry about any of the special rules affecting ISOs, including limits on when you can exercise your options or sell the stock you have acquired.

Stock appreciation rights

At the beginning of the chapter we mentioned stock appreciation rights, SARs for short. With SARs you never actually buy your company's stock, but you still profit from the stock's appreciation.

Let's say your company gives you a one-year SAR on 5,000 shares of stock when the market price is $2 a share. A year later the stock price has risen to $3. You could get a check for $5,000 (less any withholding tax, of course). Or, your company could give you $2,000 (again, less any income tax withholding) plus 1,000 shares of stock valued at $3 a share. At any rate, your total compensation comes to $5,000.

The gain is taxed at ordinary rates—just like the gain on an NQO. But, unlike stock options, you never have to put up any cash of your own with a SAR. Because you put up no cash with SARs, companies sometimes use them in tandem with ISOs to provide employees with the dollars they need to exercise their ISOs.

Say, for example, that your company grants you a one-year SAR on 5,000 shares of stock. At the end of the year, it yields $1 a share or a total of $5,000. You receive a check for $4,000—that is, your $5,000 minus 20 percent of the total for federal income-tax withholding taxes.

Say, too, that along with your SAR your company grants you an ISO to purchase 2,000 shares of company stock at an exercise price of $2 a share. You use the dollars you receive from your SAR at year end to exercise your option. You're out of pocket only the additional taxes you pay on income from your SAR.

Insider rules

If you're a corporate insider—generally an officer, a director, or a more-than-10-percent shareholder of a public company—take heed. You must conform to special requirements regarding ISOs and NQOs. Amont these requirements is the so-called ''six-month rule'' imposed by the Securities and Exchange Commission (SEC) under which you may have to forfeit to the company profits realized from the purchase and sale of the company's stock.

☞ **CAUTION** For 1991 you have to watch out for *two* six-month rules. Generally, the old six-month rule applies to options you exercised before May 1, 1991 and the new rule to options exercised on or after May 1.

Under the old six-month rule, you may have to forfeit the profit you realized from the purchase and sale of company stock if you sell any company stock, whether or not acquired by option, either six months before or after you *exercise* your options.

Generally, you will be subject to the new rule only if you exercise or otherwise dispose of options within six months of the date the options were *granted* to you. However, most

stock option plans don't allow you to exercise or
otherwise dispose of your options within six months of the
date they were granted, so the new rule will not apply in the
usual case. If, under your company's stock option plan, you
may exercise options within six months of the date of grant
and you do so, our advice is to contact your attorney to determine whether this new rule applies to you.

The SEC rules thus impose restrictions on when an insider
may sell his or her company stock. Accordingly, Uncle Sam
generally does not require you to recognize your paper gain
from the exercise of a NQO—or your AMT income from the
exercise of an ISO—until the SEC restrictions on sale no longer apply. In the unusual case where the new six-month rule is
applicable which prevents you from selling the stock immediately after you exercise the option, an election is available that
allows you to recognize the income as of the exercise date. If
the situation is right, and you can benefit from this election—
just be sure to make the election within 30 days of the exercise
of your option. See your tax adviser for details on how to
make the election.

☞ **CAUTION** Insider regulations are quite strict
and complex. You need to choose
carefully when you exercise and when you sell your stock. If
you're an insider, our advice is to ask your tax adviser and
attorney to help you evaluate your personal situation. Enlist
their help as soon as you get an option. This way, you won't
unknowingly violate these rules and jeopardize your gain.

16

Retirement Planning Basics

When you invest in a tax-deferred retirement plan, you win in two ways. You slash your current tax bill by deducting—within limits—your contributions.

And the income you earn in the plan—interest, dividends, and so on—escapes taxation until you withdraw it, usually at retirement.

The effect of this tax-deferred compounding is almost magical. In fact, when you work out the numbers, you may be tempted to toss your calculator into the trash. But don't throw it away. It's telling you the truth. Here's an example.

Say you're in the 31 percent bracket and you sock away $7,000 a year for 25 years in a Keogh, a tax-favored retirement plan for someone who's self-employed.

Actually, your out of pocket is only $4,830—your $7,000 contribution minus a tax savings of $2,170 (31 percent times $7,000).

Say, too, that your contributions earn 10 percent annually. At the end of 25 years, when you pull out your money in a lump sum, you pocket—after taxes—$522,518.

Now, what if you'd taken the same $4,830 and invested it

each year in a plan that isn't tax-favored? How much would you have after taxes at the end of 25 years?

If your investment increased in value at the same rate as your Keogh, 10 percent, you'd end up with $321,921—that is, $200,597 *less* than in your Keogh.

Obviously, a tax-deferred plan is an excellent tool for helping you save taxes and achieve your goal of a comfortable retirement.

CHOOSING A RETIREMENT PLAN FOR YOU

In this chapter, we begin with a rundown of the types of tax-deferred plans from which you can choose. We explain how these plans work and who's eligible to participate in them. Then, in the next two chapters, we tell you how to put money into these plans and how to take it out.

With the knowledge we provide, you should be able make intelligent choices among the retirement plans available to you—whether you work for yourself or someone else.

Let's start, though, with a few basics.

You may make contributions to these tax-deferred retirement plans *only* if you have earned income—that is, compensation for services rendered.

This compensation may take the form of wages paid to you as an employee or as income you've earned from running your own business. What if your business is managing your investments? Sorry, but Uncle Sam usually classifies this income as investment income, not earned income.

When it comes to an Individual Retirement Account (IRA)—a type of retirement plan you create and contribute to yourself—alimony also counts as earned income. So you may be able to deduct your IRA contribution even if the only income you receive during the year is alimony.

IRAs

As most of us know, IRAs aren't what they used to be. In the old days, anyone with earned income could contribute to an IRA and pocket a deduction, but no more.

Uncle Sam still caps IRA deductions at the lesser of $2,000 or 100 percent of your earned income; $2,250 if you and your nonworking spouse file jointly.

But nowadays, unless Congress changes the rules, only two types of people may pocket an IRA deduction: those who don't actively participate in an employer's qualified retirement plan, and those whose adjusted gross income (AGI) falls below certain levels.

How do you know if you're an active participant? One quick way is to look at your W-2 form. It provides a box labeled "pension plan" for your employer to check. If this box is blank, though, you've got some work to do. For one, you'll need to familiarize yourself with the active participation rules.

In the case of a defined-benefit plan—that is, a plan that promises to pay you a set amount each year after you retire—you're an active participant if the rules of the plan say you're eligible to participate. In other words, it doesn't matter whether you actually take part in the plan. It matters only that you're eligible to participate.

Say, for example, that you're eligible to participate in your employer's defined-benefit plan. Say, too, that the rules of the plan state that your employer won't make any contributions on your behalf unless you kick in some of your own earnings to the plan.

Are you an active participant? The answer is yes—even if

you opt *not* to contribute any of your own dollars to the plan—because you're eligible to participate.

The rules for a defined-contribution plan—that is, a plan that requires your employer to put aside a set amount for you each year—are different. In this case, you're an active participant if—during the year—you, your company, or both of you contribute money to the plan on your behalf. Uncle Sam says you're not an active participant, however, if the only money added on your behalf during the year are earnings from the investments already in the plan.

Now, what if you're not vested? It makes no difference as far as the active participation rules are concerned.

Say, for example, that your company contributes an amount annually on your behalf to its defined-contribution plan. Say, also, that the rules of the plan state that you aren't vested until you've worked for the company for a full three years.

In the eyes of Uncle Sam, you're an active participant in the plan even if you aren't vested and are a one- or two-year veteran of the company. You're also an active participant as far as the IRS is concerned if you take part in a retirement plan for just a portion of the year.

Here's how this rule can trip you up.

Say you resign your post at Freeze-Dried Inc. on November 15, 1990, to accept a more lucrative position at Meltdown Corp. You're a good guy and give Freeze-Dried a one-month notice. On December 15, 1990, you clean out your desk at Freeze-Dried.

Two weeks later, you report for work at Meltdown. So far, so good, you say; but, wait a minute. Under the rules of Meltdown's pension plan, you aren't eligible to participate in 1991, your first year on the job, although you may take part in 1992.

The news doesn't bother you too much, though. You decide you can at least make an IRA contribution in 1991 and deduct it. Well, you'd better think again. Unbeknownst to you, your former employer's pension plan ends its 1990 tax year on January 31, 1991.

So as far as Uncle Sam is concerned, you were eligible and therefore active in that plan for part of 1991. Therefore, the deductibility of your IRA contribution is limited for 1991.

What counts as a qualified retirement plan when it comes to the active-participation rules? Actually, there are several types of qualified plans. And if you participate in any one of them, you're considered an active participant and not allowed to write off your IRA contribution, unless your AGI falls below certain levels. (We'll get to these amounts shortly.)

These qualified plans include qualified pension, profit-sharing, or stock bonus plans such as Keogh plans, 401(k) plans, and simplified employee pension plans (SEPs); and retirement plans for federal, state, or local government employees.

Other plans that fall into the category of qualified plans are: tax-sheltered annuities for public school teachers and other employees of charitable organizations; and certain union plans—so-called Section 501(c)(18) plans.

So much for the active-participation rules. Now, on to the income requirements you must meet to deduct your IRA contribution. Even if you're an active participant in another qualified plan, Uncle Sam allows you to deduct your IRA contribution if your income falls within certain ranges.

If you're married and file jointly and your joint AGI adds up to no more than $40,000, your IRA contribution is fully deductible on your Form 1040.

If your joint AGI is between $40,000 and $50,000, then you're allowed a partial deduction for your contribution; we'll show you how to calculate this amount in a moment.

But if your joint AGI tops $50,000, you're out of luck. Uncle Sam says not one cent of your IRA contribution is deductible on your federal return.

If you're single, you may deduct your entire IRA contribution if your AGI adds up to less than $25,000. If your AGI is between $25,000 and $35,000, you may take a partial deduction. However, if your AGI totals more than $35,000, none of your contribution is deductible.

You should know that your AGI for this purpose is calculated differently. It's your AGI before you deduct an IRA contribution. But it's *after* you claim investment losses and subtract Keogh contributions. It also includes any taxable Social Security benefits that you or your spouse receive.

Now, what if you're single and your income falls between $25,000 and $35,000 or married and your joint AGI is between $40,000 and $50,000? You're entitled to a partial IRA deduction. It's easy to calculate the amount. Let us demonstrate below.

First, add up your AGI, then subtract this amount from the ceiling—$35,000 if you're single, $50,000 if you're married and file jointly. Next divide the result by $10,000. The result is the percentage of your maximum IRA contribution that you may deduct.

Say you're married, file jointly, and actively participate in your employer-sponsored plan. Your joint AGI totals $44,000, so you subtract $44,000 from the $50,000 ceiling to get $6,000.

Next, you divide $6,000 by $10,000, and the result is 60 percent. Multiply 60 percent times $2,000 ($2,250 if you and your nonworking spouse file jointly). The answer—$1,200 (or $1,350)—is the amount of your IRA contribution that you may deduct.

Now, that's not to say that you may not contribute the full

$2,000. It's perfectly legal, but you won't collect a deduction for that extra $800 (or $650).

☞ **CAUTION** Here's another example to consider.

Say you're an active participant in an employer-sponsored plan, but your spouse isn't. Unfair as it may seem, you're both subject to the limits if you file jointly. You don't even escape this strict rule if you file separately. Uncle Sam phases out your IRA deduction beginning with the first $1 of your AGI if you're married and file separately. When your AGI reaches $10,000, you're entitled to no deduction at all.

Let's say your AGI adds up to $5,000. You subtract $5,000 from the $10,000 to get $5,000. Then you divide $5,000 by $10,000 to get 50 percent. Finally, you multiply 50 percent times the maximum IRA contribution of $2,000 to get the amount you may deduct—$1,000.

You do fall under different rules if you're married, file separately, and live apart from one another for the entire year. Then Uncle Sam treats you as if you're single.

In this case, say it's your spouse who's not covered by a qualified plan. He or she may contribute up to $2,000 to an IRA and deduct the full amount, regardless of how much either of you earn. If you're an active participant in your employer-sponsored retirement plan, you may claim an IRA deduction only if your income falls within the limits set for single people.

What else do you need to know about these phase-out rules? You may contribute at least $200 to an IRA and write off the full amount, as long as your calculation shows that your deductible contribution is limited to no less than $10. Why? Because Uncle Sam says so.

TIP Do you own your own business? Does your spouse help out occasionally? If so, think about paying your spouse for the work he or she does.

The reason?

As an employee, your spouse may—subject to the normal deductibility rules—squirrel away all or part of his or her earnings in an IRA and deduct the contribution.

Here's an example. The year is 1991, and you pay your spouse $2,000 a year for her marketing advice. The $2,000 is her only source of income.

You and your spouse file a joint return and declare AGI of $32,000. So, Uncle Sam lets each of you make a tax-deductible IRA contribution up to $2,000.

You should know, though, that Uncle Sam is fussy about your spouse performing real work and being paid appropriately for it.

Don't simply make a deposit in your joint bank account as payment for services. That won't wash with the IRS. Write out a regular payroll check for your spouse. For the same reason, make sure you can prove that your spouse's employment is genuine.

And here's another wrinkle you should know about. When you pay your spouse a salary, his or her wages are subject to Social Security taxes of 15.30 percent for 1991. That's 7.65 percent paid by the employee and 7.65 percent paid by you, the employer.

Keoghs

You say you're self-employed, and you want to know what type of retirement plan makes sense for you? A Keogh may be your ticket to a comfortable retirement.

Sometimes called HR-10 plans after the number of the House of Representatives tax bill that created them, Keoghs came into being in 1962. The author of HR-10 was Eugene Keogh, the late congressman from New York. His idea was that self-employed people should have the same opportunity to save for retirement as employees who enjoy the benefits of employer-sponsored pensions.

Keoghs—like other qualified retirement plans—pack a one-two punch: You slash your tax bill while building your retirement savings at a faster pace.

When you salt away money in a Keogh, you deduct your contribution on your tax return (within limits, of course) and your earnings accumulate tax-deferred until they're withdrawn. Keoghs come in two basic varieties—defined-benefit plans and defined-contribution plans.

With defined-benefit plans, you receive a specified sum every year after you retire. This amount is defined in the plan document. Each year an amount is contributed based on actuarial tables to fund the specified retirement benefit.

In 1991, the ceiling on payouts from this type of plan is generally the lesser of 100 percent of your average annual earnings for the three consecutive years in which you made the most money or $108,963. (This number is adjusted annually for inflation.)

Uncle Sam also says you may not contribute more than your current annual income. And he requires you to make your retirement plan contributions quarterly—not annually.

With a defined-contribution plan, you put away a specified amount—10 percent of your earnings, let's say—each year until you retire. The contribution is credited to an account in your name. And the amount you receive after you retire is based on two factors—how much was set aside on your behalf, and how well that money was invested.

What if you employ people other than yourself? Uncle Sam

requires you to include them in your Keogh plan and make contributions on their behalf. So before you set up your plan, you may want to weigh the cost of providing this fringe benefit.

Sound simple so far? It does, but it gets more complicated.

The second type of Keogh we mentioned, a defined-contribution plan, also comes in two types—profit-sharing plans and money-purchase plans.

With a profit-sharing plan, you may contribute up to 15 percent of your net self-employment income, but you may (and this feature is important to many people) vary the amount you set aside each year based on how well your business performs. In other words, if your business does poorly one year, you aren't required to make a contribution.

With a money-purchase plan, you're required to contribute a set amount each year, up to a maximum of 25 percent of your net self-employment income. With either of these plans, your total contribution may not top $30,000 in any single year.

To make matters more confusing, the rules also require you to subtract your Keogh contribution *and* your deduction for one-half of your actual self-employment taxes for the year in order to calculate your annual net self-employment income.

Here's a simple formula to make this calculation easier. Multiply 12.12 percent times your self-employment income, before you deduct one-half of your self-employment taxes and your Keogh contribution, to figure the amount you may contribute to a profit-sharing plan; 18.59 percent times your self-employment income calculates the maximum contribution allowed to a money-purchase plan.

These percentages are for self-employment income of less than approximately $58,000. If your earned income exceeds this amount, the percentage varies slightly. So you should contact your tax adviser to determine how much you can contribute.

One strategy worth considering is pairing plans, meaning you combine a money-purchase plan with a profit-sharing plan. That way, you get the best of both worlds.

With a paired program, you may contribute and deduct on your return a full 18.59 percent of your self-employment income—again, before deducting half your self-employment taxes and your Keogh contribution—just as if you had fully funded a money-purchase plan. You're not locked into making a mandatory 18.59 percent contribution each year.

How does pairing work? You set up a money-purchase plan that shelters 8 percent of your income. Under the IRS regulations, you must contribute that 8 percent each year.

At the same time, you also establish a profit-sharing plan to which you may contribute, at your discretion, up to an additional 10.59 percent (for a total of 18.59 percent) of your net self-employment income. That contribution is entirely discretionary.

Again, with a paired approach you can protect from taxation up to $30,000, or 18.59 percent of your income, whichever is less.

What's the bottom line? A paired program makes sense if you want to sock away—and deduct on your tax return—more than 12 percent of your earnings in a retirement plan, but you don't want to tie yourself to squirreling away a hefty percentage of your income each year.

TIP Uncle Sam won't allow you to set up a Keogh unless you report income from self-employment. You may not know it, but fees you receive as a corporate director count as self-employment income even if you're employed full time somewhere else.

SEPs

The best way to prepare for your retirement is to save for it, and one way for people to save is through a SEP—short for simplified employee pension.

It may come as a surprise to you, but a SEP is actually a form of an IRA. Instead of setting up a pension plan, your company may contribute to IRA's in the names of each of its employees, and may claim a deduction for the dollars contributed—within limits.

For each employee, the limits are 15 percent of compensation or $30,000, whichever is less. If the SEP allows it, employees may also make contributions toward this limit, but the most employees may contribute is $8,475 in 1991. This limit is adjusted annually for inflation.

Self-employed individuals may also benefit from SEP's. Your earned income—instead of compensation—tells how much can be put into your account.

401(k)s

If you're like most people, you know the basics of your company-provided fringe benefits package—health insurance, life insurance, and so on. However, you may know little about how your employer-sponsored 401(k) plan works. And that's a mistake because 401(k)s are terrific tax-saving devices.

401(k) plans—or cash or deferred arrangements, as they're sometimes called—take their name from the section of the Internal Revenue Code that describes them.

How do these nifty savings plans work?

When you sign up for a 401(k), you authorize your employer to deduct a set amount from your earnings each pay period and put it in an account in your name.

This deferred salary—plus any interest, dividends, and capital gains that accumulate on it—is excluded from current taxation. Uncle Sam gets his due only when you withdraw your money, usually at retirement. Sound familiar? It should, because 401(k)s are similar to IRAs.

What separates the two plans is the way Uncle Sam treats the money deposited. You don't deduct your 401(k) contribution on your Form 1040. Instead, the money set aside in a 401(k) is treated as tax-deferred compensation; that is, it isn't reported as income to you.

Say the year is 1991, and your earned income—salary and bonus, in your case—adds up to $60,000. Say, too, that at the beginning of the year you instructed your employer to subtract $500 a month from your paycheck and deposit the money in a 401(k) plan.

The year comes to a close. When you receive your W-2 form from your employer, you see that it lists your earned income as $54,000, not $60,000.

The reason? You opted to contribute $500 a month for a total of $6,000 to your 401(k). And the IRS treats the $6,000 as tax-deferred compensation.

The only catch—and it isn't a big one—is that the dollars you contribute to a 401(k) are still considered part of your income when it comes to federal Social Security (FICA) taxes. In other words, you pay FICA taxes on the money you contribute to a 401(k), but only to the extent that it and your other earned income falls within the FICA wage base—$53,400 for the OASDI (old-age, survivors and disability insurance) portion of FICA and $125,000 for the Medicare HI (hospital insurance) portion of FICA.

Another difference between 401(k)s and IRAs is the amount of money you may set aside. The maximum you may contribute to an IRA annually is $2,000.

What's the cap on 401(k) contributions? Actually, there are

two—one applies to how much you may contribute, another to how much you and your employer may jointly contribute.

Both limits are adjusted annually for inflation. When it comes to how much you may contribute to a 401(k), the ceiling for 1991 is $8,475; $9,500, for a tax-sheltered annuity.

A tax-sheltered annuity—as you may know—is a tax-deferred retirement account for teachers, church workers, and employees of other non-profit institutions.

Most annuities are sold by life insurance companies in the form of a contract that guarantees a payment to the owner at some future date, usually at retirement.

When it comes to how much your employer may contribute to your 401(k), the rules are more complicated. Together, the two of you may salt away no more than $30,000 or 25 percent of your after-contribution salary, whichever is less, to a 401(k) and all other defined-contribution plans.

The key phrase here is, "all other defined-contribution plans." Say your salary comes to $100,000 in 1991, and you sock away $8,475 of your salary in a 401(k). How much may your employer contribute?

First, multiply 25 percent times your after-contribution salary—that is, your $100,000 salary minus your $8,475 401(k) contribution or $91,525.

The result is $22,881 (25 percent times $91,525).

Since $22,881 is less than $30,000, $22,881 is the most that you and your employer together may contribute to a 401(k) and all other defined-contribution plans.

You've already salted away $8,475, so your employer's maximum contribution is just $14,406 ($22,881 minus $8,475).

You may be better off if you put less into your 401(k). Here's why. Assume that your employer contributes a set percent of your compensation to your 401(k); it doesn't use a matching formula that ties its contribution to the amount you kick in.

Now, let's go back to our previous example. But this time, you slash your contribution from $8,475 to $5,000. Your after-contribution salary would total $95,000—your $100,000 salary minus your $5,000 401(k) contribution. And 25 percent of that amount is $23,750.

By cutting your contribution, you've raised the maximum ceiling on the total retirement contribution for the year by $869 (the difference between $23,750 and $22,881). What's more, you've allowed your employer to increase its contribution.

The company may now chip in as much as $18,750—$23,750 minus your $5,000 contribution. In this case, at least, less is actually more.

Obviously, one reason to participate in a 401(k) is to take advantage of the favorable tax rules. Another is to capture additional dollars from your employer.

Many companies match the amount their employees set aside in these accounts. So it's worth contributing to the plan to garner these extra dollars from your employer.

You should also check with your employer to see if your participation in a 401(k) plan affects the level of other benefits you might receive. Here's how it might work.

Sometimes companies tie benefits—contributions to profit-sharing plans, say, or life and disability insurance coverage—to your total earnings. What you collect in these benefits can go up or down depending on whether your 401(k) contribution is included in your compensation.

Our advice? Ask your company if it reduces your compensation by the amount you've contributed to a 401(k) or if it adds your contribution back before it calculates the value of your other fringes. Many companies take the latter course, even though Uncle Sam doesn't require them to do so.

Employer-sponsored retirement plans

These are plans created, and for the most part funded, by the company that employs you. As with Keoghs, employer-sponsored plans come in two flavors: defined-contribution plans and defined-benefit plans.

And, as with all retirement plans, any earnings that accumulate in employer-sponsored plans remain untaxed until you begin withdrawing funds at retirement.

17

Putting Money into a Retirement Plan

You know how various sorts of retirement plans work. But how do you make your contributions to them? That's what this chapter is all about.

IRAs

Uncle Sam gives you almost complete freedom when it comes to investing your IRA funds. Almost every investment vehicle is at your disposal. So your IRA could be in the form of money-market funds, certificates of deposit, equity mutual funds, even flexible-premium annuities.

Only a few investments don't make sense for an IRA, and one of them is tax-free municipal bonds or tax-free municipal bond funds. Here's why.

When you invest your IRA dollars in tax-free bonds, the income from these bonds goes to your IRA. But the earnings in your IRA aren't free from taxes. They're only tax-deferred; that is, they're not taxed until they're withdrawn from the account.

So what you're doing when you invest your IRA dollars in tax-free municipal bonds is turn tax-free income into tax-deferred income—not a smart move. And the yield on tax-free bonds is almost always lower than on taxable investments.

Although Uncle Sam gives you enormous freedom in investing your IRA dollars, he does impose a few restrictions. You may not invest in stamps or other collectibles, such as art, antiques, or rugs. (Our lawmakers wanted to keep us from using our IRAs to furnish our homes.)

Nor may you buy gold or silver coins, except gold and silver Eagle coins minted by the United States Treasury and coins issued by a state government.

Uncle Sam also nixes so-called self-dealing. That is, you may not use your IRA dollars to purchase assets from yourself or a company you own. For example, if you're the owner of a corporation, you may not invest your IRA dollars in your company's stock.

What if you borrow money from your IRA, say, for a down payment on a home? It's verboten, says Uncle Sam, although there's a move afoot in Congress to allow people to withdraw money from their IRAs—penalty-free—to help them purchase their first home or pay for college tuition.

And not only is borrowing against the rules, you may not even use the money in your IRAs as collateral for a loan, even a mortgage loan.

What happens if you don't follow Uncle Sam's rules?

He treats the amount borrowed as if you'd withdrawn it. You're required to report the amount as ordinary income on your Form 1040 and pay taxes on it at your regular rates. And if you're younger than fifty-nine and a half, you'll also pay a 10-percent penalty for early withdrawal.

When it comes to setting up an IRA, you may have as many as you wish—at as many different institutions as you like—as long as you qualify. The only problem?

Most institutions levy an annual fee—sometimes as high as $50—for maintaining your IRA. So if you have lots of IRAs, all charging fees, your effective yield drops.

It's true that these fees are deductible, but only if you pay them with dollars not deposited in your IRA. Also, you may write them off only to the extent that, when added to your other miscellaneous itemized deductions, they exceed two percent of your AGI.

You may also move your IRA dollars from one investment vehicle to another—a money-market fund, say, to an equity mutual fund—with no tax consequences whatsoever.

But shifting may present some pitfalls for you. Your financial institution may penalize you for switching investments; a savings and loan, for example, may slap you with an early withdrawal penalty equal to several months interest if you cash out of a CD before it matures.

Then, too, as you switch from one investment vehicle to another, you might pile up commissions and other transaction costs that reduce your effective yield.

Uncle Sam also allows you to withdraw your IRA dollars from one institution and within 60 days transfer them to another—often referred to as a rollover—but you may do so only once every 365 days. Even if you roll over only part of your IRA dollars to another institution, you may not roll over the remainder until 365 days later.

One way to get around the once-every-365-days limit on rollovers is this: Use a "trustee-to-trustee" transfer to switch your funds.

All you do is authorize the trustee of the institution that now holds your IRA to transfer those funds directly to the trustee of another institution.

Since you never touch the money—it goes from one institution to another—it doesn't count as a rollover. So it escapes the once-every-365-days limit.

And here's another rule that can work to your advantage. If you maintain more than one IRA, the 365-day rule applies separately to each account.

Say you maintain two IRA accounts—one at a bank and the other at a brokerage firm. On December 1, 1991, you roll over your IRA dollars from the bank to a mutual fund.

You're so pleased with the mutual fund's performance that you decide three months later to roll over your IRA dollars from the brokerage to the mutual fund. What are the tax consequences? None, because, under the law, the 365-day rule applies separately to each IRA account. Alternatively, you could have had the bank or the brokerage firm transfer your IRA dollars from either one or both of the IRA accounts directly to the mutual fund and you would have accomplished the same result.

TIP You may use the rollover rules to obtain what amounts to a short-term loan from your IRA since the law allows you to withdraw your IRA funds as long as it has been at least one year since your last withdrawal that was rolled over. You pay no taxes and no penalties as long as the money is transferred back into another IRA within 60 days.

So you can cash out of your IRA, use the money any way you choose for 60 days, then, at the end of that time, deposit it in another IRA.

And there are no tax consequences to you.

Here's something else you should know about the 60-day limit on borrowing from your IRA. Up until now, tax practioners have assumed that a rollover of an IRA must be from one IRA to another. But that's not what the IRS told a taxpayer we call Pat in a recent private-letter ruling.

Pat withdrew $1,500 from his IRA in 1986, then redeposited that amount in the same IRA 60 days later. He did that again in 1987.

The IRS says Pat is subject to no tax consequences. In private ruling 9010007, the IRS said that an individual may take out IRA funds for his or her personal use, and do so tax-free as long as he or she redeposits the funds in the same or another IRA in time.

You should know that private rulings apply only to the taxpayers involved, so no other taxpayer can rely on them. However, these rulings do hint at the IRS's position on a given subject.

Now, what if your spouse doesn't work outside the home and wants to contribute to an IRA? He or she may open what's known—appropriately enough—as a spousal IRA.

Uncle Sam requires you to meet just two conditions to open a spousal IRA: One, your spouse's earned income must total less than $250, and, two, you must file jointly.

If you meet these conditions, you're entitled to set up a spousal IRA; that is, you may set up an IRA in your name and one in the name of your spouse. The ceiling on your contribution is $2,250 or your combined earned income, whichever is less.

And no more than $2,000 of this amount may go into an account in any one of your names. What's the best way to decide how to split up your contribution?

Think about your financial goals and objectives.

Say you'd like to keep your savings in an IRA for as long as possible—beyond when one of you reaches age seventy and a half, the age when you're required to begin withdrawals. In your case, it makes sense to contribute more to the younger spouse's IRA. What if you want to dig into your savings sooner? Contribute a greater amount to the older spouse's account.

One big question for most people these days is, should you or should you not make a nondeductible contribution to an IRA? So let's take a look at the pros and cons.

The primary reason to make a nondeductible contribution is that the earnings on the dollars you contribute accumulate tax-deferred. That is, they build up at a much faster rate than they would if you paid taxes on them every year.

The primary reason not to make a nondeductible contribution is a penalty on early withdrawals. If you withdraw your IRA dollars before you reach age fifty-nine and a half, you pay a 10 percent penalty on some or all of the money you withdraw.

For example, you pay a penalty on any earnings that have

accumulated in the account and that you withdraw. You also pay a penalty when you withdraw your deductible contributions, although you may withdraw your nondeductible contributions penalty free. As you will see in the next chapter, if your IRAs are made up of nondeductible contributions and either deductible contributions or tax-deferred earnings or both, a pro rata portion of any withdrawals will be considered to come from deductible contributions and tax-deferred earnings, which will result in that portion of the withdrawal being subject to the 10 percent penalty.

TIP A strategy to follow—if you decide to make a nondeductible contribution to your or your spouse's IRA that you may subsequently wish to widthdraw early—is to deposit this nondeductible amount in the name of the spouse whose account already contains the largest proportion of nondeductible contributions.

This strategy will work for you when it comes time to withdraw your IRA dollars early because the amount subject to the early withdrawal penalty will be minimized.

TIP One alternative to making a nondeductible IRA contribution is to invest in tax-exempt municipal bonds or a tax-exempt municipal bond fund.

The interest you earn on these bonds is free from federal taxes, and you won't pay a penalty if you decide you need your money sooner rather than later. Also, you may invest as much as you like. You're not limited to $2,000—or $2,250 for you and your nonworking spouse.

Another alternative to making a nondeductible IRA contribution is to sock away money in your employer-sponsored 401(k) plan. If you must choose between making a nondeductible IRA contribution—or a deductible one, for that matter—and a 401(k) contribution, it's usually smarter tax-wise to opt for the 401(k). The reason? With a 401(k) you may generally sock away more money each year; often your employer will match some or all of your contribution; distributions from a 401(k) may be eligible for favorable tax treatment when you retire; and the list goes on.

Whether you should make a nondeductible IRA contribution, though, depends on your personal situation. So weigh the pros and cons each year before you make your decision.

When it comes time to make your IRA contribution, you may use your own money or money you've borrowed. But if you borrow, don't count on writing off the interest on the loan.

Uncle Sam isn't clear as to whether this interest is personal interest or investment interest. If it's personal interest, it's not deductible at all in 1991 and beyond. If it's investment interest, it's only deductible from your investment income.

Our advice?

If you borrow to make an IRA contribution, see your tax adviser before you claim an interest deduction on your Form 1040. (See Chapter 6 for more on interest.)

What happens if you contribute too much to your IRA?

Uncle Sam will impose an excise tax equal to six percent of your excess contribution. And he will levy this tax annually until you withdraw the money. You may also be subject to a 10-percent, early-withdrawal penalty (we cover this penalty in detail in the next chapter).

One simple way to escape the excise tax and the early-withdrawal penalty is this: Just withdraw your excess contribution before you file your tax return for the year.

Uncle Sam gives you until April 15, 1992—the due date of your tax return—to make an IRA contribution. You claim your IRA deduction in the "adjustments to income" section of page one of your Form 1040.

If you make a nondeductible IRA contribution, the IRS requires you to report the amount on Form 8606 and attach it to your tax return. The IRS uses this form to keep track of the nontaxable part of your IRA. And you face a $50 penalty if you don't file this form.

Keoghs

If your business is organized as a sole proprietorship, you may set up a Keogh plan in your name. But it's a different story if you do business as a partnership. Then your partnership—not you—must set up the plan.

Uncle Sam gives you until December 31 or the last day of your taxable year to set up your Keogh. But he gives you a break when it comes to making your contribution.

In the case of a defined-contribution plan, he says your contribution isn't due until the due date of your tax return, including extensions. With a defined-benefit plan, you're required to make your contributions in quarterly installments.

One question taxpayers often ask is, am I better off with a defined-benefit plan or a defined-contribution plan. The answer depends, in part, on your age. Chances are, if you're older than 45, you can sock away far more in a defined-benefit plan than a defined-contribution plan.

Say you're 55 years old and your self-employment income for the year comes to $55,000. You could put away a maximum of $10,225 in a defined-contribution money-purchase plan or a paired program (18.59 percent times $55,000).

But let's say you'd like to fund an annual benefit of $59,000—assuming your three consecutive years of highest earnings are at least $59,000—after you retire at age 65. Based on actuarial computations, you could shelter from taxation as much as $41,000 this year in a defined-benefit plan—nearly $31,000 more.

SEPs

What if you're self-employed and missed the December 31 deadline for setting up a Keogh? Then consider establishing a SEP. With a SEP, Uncle Sam gives you until the due date of your tax return—plus extensions—to establish and fund your plan.

401(k)s

When it comes to how to invest your 401(k) dollars, your employer may give you a choice. For example, you may opt for stock and bond mutual funds, guaranteed investment contracts that offer a fixed return on your money, or maybe even your own company's stock.

The choice is yours to make.

Employer-sponsored retirement plans

If your employer contributes money on your behalf to a pension plan, profit-sharing plan or other so-called qualified retirement plan, consider yourself lucky.

Employer contributions to these plans are generally not taxable to you when made and the benefits, which should help provide your retirement security, are taxable to you only when you receive them.

18

Taking Money Out of a Retirement Plan

You say you're nearing retirement?

It's time to think about the best way to minimize taxes on the dollars you've saved. And your first decision is how best to withdraw money from your tax-deferred plans.

Deciding how and when to withdraw money from your tax-favored retirement plans may be simple. In fact, most plans offer you only two options. You may pull your funds out all at once, or you may spread your withdrawals out over time.

WITHDRAWING OPTIONS

In this chapter, we take a look at both of these options and explain the special rules that apply to specific types of plans—IRAs, Keoghs, 401(k)s, and so on.

We start with lump-sum withdrawals.

Lump-sum withdrawal

When you take your money out all at once from a retirement plan, it's called—appropriately enough—a lump-sum withdrawal. You pay no taxes on your nondeductible contributions when you withdraw them. But it's a different story with deductible contributions and tax-deferred earnings in the plan. You're going to face a tax liability in the year you take them out.

The good news, however, is that Uncle Sam wants to ease your pain. He allows you to slash your liability by using what's known as five-year averaging.

What's five-year averaging? It's a device that permits you to calculate your taxes as if you'd taken your retirement dollars out not in a lump sum but evenly over five years. And it applies to lump-sum withdrawals from qualified plans—except those from IRAs and SEPs.

Here's how five-year averaging works.

Add up the taxable amount of your lump-sum withdrawal —$250,000, say. Now, divide this number by five—for five years—to get $50,000. Next, using the tax-rate schedules, determine the tax a single person would pay—even if you're married—on $50,000.

Here's the schedule for 1991.

	Single Tax Rates for 1991	
$ 0 to	20,350	15%
20,351 to	49,300	28
49,301 or more		31

So you'd multiply 15 percent times your first $20,350 to get

$3,053, 28 percent times your next $28,950 to get $8,106, and 31 percent times $700 to get $217.

Your total, then, is $11,376. Once you've calculated this amount, multiply it by five—again, for five years. The result, $56,880, is the total federal tax you owe on your $250,000 lump-sum withdrawal.

Does five-year averaging save you taxes? You bet it does, and here's why. When you calculate the tax due, you do so independent of your other income.

That is, you calculate the tax on your lump-sum withdrawal without adding it to your other income. So a portion of your withdrawal is taxed at 15 percent.

What if Uncle Sam had required you to add your lump-sum withdrawal to all your other income? You'd pay taxes on all of it at your highest marginal rate.

TIP If your lump-sum withdrawal adds up to less than $70,000, Uncle Sam gives you another break when you average. He says a portion of your withdrawal is tax-free to you.

How much? Your maximum tax-free amount—or, in IRS jargon, "excluded" amount—is 50 percent of your lump-sum withdrawal but no more than $10,000. So if you receive a lump-sum distribution of $20,000, you may exclude $10,000 from taxation.

But for every dollar your distribution tops $20,000, your tax-free amount declines by 20 cents. So a person who withdraws $45,000 in a lump-sum from a retirement account may exclude only $5,000 from taxation, and a person who takes out $70,000 may not exclude a cent.

Before you climb on board the five-year averaging bandwagon, though, you should know that Uncle Sam attaches a few strings to his generosity.

First, he says you may use averaging only once in your lifetime. And you may use it only if you're age fifty-nine and a half or older. Also, not all lump-sum distributions are eligible for five-year averaging. What are the rules? Let's take a look.

Uncle Sam says you must have participated in the retirement plan for at least five tax years before the tax year in which you take the lump-sum withdrawal. (He will waive this rule, though, if the withdrawal is made in the case of death.)

He also says the sum you receive must equal the full amount due you from all plans of the same kind—for example, profit-sharing, pension, and stock bonus plans.

And you must receive the distribution in one year.

Another requirement is that the retirement plan from which you're making the withdrawal must specify that you're entitled to a lump-sum distribution because you've reached age fifty-nine and a half, become disabled or died, or terminated your employment.

TIP When our lawmakers enacted the five-year averaging rules in 1986, they gave taxpayers whose birth dates fell on December 31, 1935, or earlier, a choice.

They may use five-year averaging or 10-year averaging, and there's only one catch. People who use 10-year averaging must use the 1986 tax-rate tables.

Uncle Sam also provides another benefit if your birth date was December 31, 1935, or earlier. You may receive a distribution after age 50 and before age 59½ and still use averaging. However, you have to receive your money because of a separation from service.

Say you meet the age requirement. Are you better off *taxwise* with five-year averaging or 10-year averaging? As a rule of thumb, if a 1991 distribution is less than approximately $410,000, ten-year averaging results in the lower tax.

Payments over time

Many people don't withdraw their retirement dollars in a lump sum. Rather, they choose to receive their retirement benefits in the form of an annuity—that is, over time.

Usually, the amount of your annuity payments is based on your life expectancy, or, in some cases, the life expectancy of you and your spouse. Sometimes, you may, if your retirement plan allows, choose to receive your payments over a fixed period of time—10 years, say.

It should come as no surprise that Uncle Sam requires you to pay taxes on the payments you receive. And he carves out only one exception to this rule.

If a portion of your payments is a return of nondeductible contributions you made to the plan, you pay no taxes on that amount.

This nontaxable portion is based on what's known in tax jargon as your "exclusion ratio." Stated simply, this ratio equals the proportion of nondeductible contributions you've made to the total payments you expect to receive from your retirement plan. You multiply the exclusion ratio by each payment you receive to get the amount that's nontaxable.

You may not exclude this portion indefinitely, though.

If the amount of your payment is based on your actuarial life expectancy, you're required to include all your benefit payments in your taxable income once you reach your life expectancy. The way Uncle Sam sees it, you've now withdrawn all your nondeductible contributions from the plan. So any future payments are taxable in full.

As a general rule, if you should die prior to your life expectancy and the annuity ceases, you're allowed a deduction for your unrecovered nondeductible contributions.

Similar rules apply to partial withdrawals which are not part of an annuity. For example, you have an IRA worth $10,000. You have made $2,500 of nondeductible contributions.

If you withdraw $1,000 from the IRA, 25 percent ($2,500 divided by $10,000)—or $250—is considered a withdrawal of your nondeductible contributions and is not taxable to you when you withdraw it. And the rest—$750—is considered taxable.

Excess distributions

Here's something else you may not know but should. Uncle Sam imposes a special tax on what he calls "excess distributions." How do you know if you've received one?

Add together the money you've received this year from all your tax-deferred retirement accounts, but don't include your Social Security benefits or any amount that's a return of your nondeductible contributions to a plan. Now, from this total, subtract $150,000.

The result—unless you've taken a lump-sum payout this year that's eligible for five-year averaging—is your excess distribution. What if you've taken a lump sum distribution? Your excess distribution equals the lump-sum amount that tops $750,000. In both cases, excess distributions are subject to a 15 percent tax.

You should know, too, that some individuals whose total vested benefits as of August 1, 1986, totaled more than $562,500 may have previously elected to apply special rules for determining excess distributions. Distributions of their August 1, 1986, balance will avoid the excise tax, but lower thresholds will apply.

And the excess distributions rules apply no matter when you make your withdrawal, whether it's before or after 59½.

Here's some good news, though. Uncle Sam won't impose

a 10 percent early withdrawal penalty on the excess distribution. (We discuss the 10 percent penalty shortly.)

If you think a portion of your retirement benefits are going to fall into the category of excess distributions, you may want to withdraw some of your money early.

Your tax adviser will help you with this matter.

Early withdrawals

To most of us, retiring early means leaving our jobs before age 65—but not to the authors of the Internal Revenue Code.

They've decreed that retirement begins precisely at age 59½. And only then may you withdraw your money from your tax-deferred retirement accounts—IRAs, Keoghs, 401(k)s, and so on—without paying a penalty.

What if you take out your money sooner? The IRS will slap you with a 10-percent early-withdrawal penalty. Uncle Sam does make a few exceptions to this rule, though.

For example, you pay no penalty if you roll over the money into another tax-sheltered account within 60 days. When else do you escape penalty?

One is when you use the dollars you withdraw to pay deductible medical expenses. Another is if you die or become disabled. And still another is if your retirement plan is an Employee Stock Ownership Plan (ESOP), and you received distributions before January 1, 1990.

You also pay no penalty when you separate from service—that is, leave your present job—after reaching age 55.

Another instance where you're not subject to an early-withdrawal penalty: You separate from service and opt to receive your retirement benefits as annuity payments that are payable

at least once a year and drawn in substantially equal installments over your life or the joint lives of you and your beneficiary.

TIP One alternative to withdrawing money from
your tax-deferred retirement plan is to borrow. Many employer-sponsored 401(k) plans allow you to
borrow or make hardship withdrawals—although there's no
IRS requirement that they do so.

Our advice? Find out if your employer-sponsored 401(k)
plan allows for loans or hardship withdrawals before you take
out money from another plan (more later on hardship withdrawals from 401(k)s).

Special rules governing IRAs

When it comes to withdrawing money from your IRA, Uncle Sam is strict. In fact, he imposes some special restrictions
on IRA withdrawals.

For example, he won't allow you to ease your tax burden by
using five-year averaging when you take out money from your
IRA. Instead, he says, you must pay taxes on the amount you
withdraw—in the year you withdraw—at the same rates as
your ordinary income.

If you find yourself in this situation, here's a strategy to
consider. Why not withdraw the money over a number of
years, rather than all at once?

This tactic makes sense if you don't need the money all at
once—say, you just need a little money to supplement your
income from other sources. You should remember that the
longer your funds stay in your IRA, the more valuable the tax
deferral.

On the other hand, you may need your IRA money all at

once—for a large downpayment on a vacation house, for example. Our advice is to run the numbers so that you understand the tax implications of each of the options available to you.

TIP The rules say you're not required to begin withdrawing IRA dollars until you reach age seventy and one-half. And you may pull out your money—in any amount and at any time—without penalty once you reach age 59½. So take care to plan carefully.

Remember: You must ante up a 15-percent excise tax on so-called excess IRA distributions. And since IRA withdrawals aren't eligible for five-year averaging, the special $750,000 exemption isn't available.

Also, as you recall, if you want your IRA money before you reach age 59½ and you aren't disabled, you'll pay a penalty—10 percent of the taxable amount you withdraw.

Is there any way to avoid this penalty? You may, if you withdraw your money in the form of an annuity, or payments made at least once a year and spread out over your lifetime.

According to Uncle Sam, you must make sure that the payments are of approximately equal amounts. And, you must base the payments on your life expectancy or the joint life expectancies of you and your beneficiaries. The IRS provides tables that outline life expectancies.

Here's an example of how it works. Say you're age 50. According to the IRS tables, you have a life expectancy of 33.1 years. In your IRA, you've accumulated $100,000. So you may withdraw $8,679 annually (assuming an 8 percent interest rate) from the account without paying a penalty.

Once you start these withdrawals, you must continue to receive them for at least five years and at least until you reach age 59½. Otherwise, your distributions don't escape the early withdrawal penalty.

As we've mentioned, the IRS doesn't like late IRA with-drawals any more than early withdrawals. According to the rules, you must begin withdrawing your accumulated IRA funds before April 1 of the year following the year you reach age seventy and one-half.

The amount you're required to take out depends on either your own life expectancy or—if you prefer—the joint life expectancies of you and your beneficiary.

What happens if you fail to pull out the required amount? Your mistake will cost you in the form of a hefty penalty. You'll pay a penalty that comes to 50 percent of the difference between the amount you pulled out and the amount the law said you should take out.

Consider this example. You are age seventy-one and one-half, and the IRS tables say that, based on your life expectancy, you must withdraw at least $6,000 annually from your IRA. But, in 1991, you compute the amount incorrectly and take out only $3,000.

Uncle Sam says you must ante up 50 percent of the difference between the amount you withdrew—$3,000—and the amount you were required to withdraw—$6,000. So, you'll cough up a penalty of $1,500—that is, 50 percent times $3,000.

TIP You may reduce the amount of required withdrawals from your IRA by naming a younger person— your child, for example—as your beneficiary. If you do, your joint life expectancy will be quite long. So you'll be required to withdraw much less from your IRA account than you otherwise would.

But keep in mind that the law allows only a spouse, but not a child, to roll over an IRA he or she inherits from a spouse who dies. And the spouse won't have to withdraw any money from the IRA that received the rollover until he or she reaches age 70½. A child or other beneficiary must include the untaxed portion in his or her income when received.

If you're not a spouse and you inherit an IRA, you have two choices: You must either pull out the money within five years after you inherit it—or you must start collecting annuity payments immediately.

Special rules governing 401(k)s

When it comes to withdrawing money from your 401(k), you must play by two sets of rules. One set is imposed by your employer, the other by Uncle Sam.

As you may expect, your employer's rules may never treat you more generously than Uncle Sam's do. However, your employer's plan may prove less generous. So you should become familiar with the requirements of your employer's 401(k).

Uncle Sam's rules on withdrawing money from a 401(k) plan are very similar to the restrictions that apply to other retirement plans.

What happens if you face a financial hardship; you need money to send your child to college, for example. The IRS says feel free to withdraw money from your 401(k) as long as your employer's plan allows. However, unfair as it seems, you must still pay taxes and fork over a 10-percent penalty if you're younger than age 59½.

If you leave a company (or in other limited circumstances), your employer may distribute the cash in the plan to you, even if you have not yet reached age 59½. But you can escape paying any penalties. Just act fast.

Uncle Sam tells you that you have 60 days to roll over these funds into a qualified retirement plan, such as an IRA. It makes sense to take advantage of this provision in the law. That's because the government taxes any amount you don't roll over as ordinary income, unless the distribution qualifies for five-year averaging. And, to make matters worse, you must pay a 10 percent penalty if you haven't yet reached age 55.

TIP If you take another job and your employer has a qualified plan that accepts rollovers, it's often better to roll your funds into this plan. The reason? The subsequent distribution may qualify for five-year or 10-year averaging. An IRA distribution doesn't.

What about borrowing from your 401(k) plan? While the IRS prohibits your withdrawing money in the form of a loan from most retirement plans, such as IRAs, it's somewhat more lenient when it comes to 401(k)s. You may borrow from these plans if your employer's rules permit loans.

You should know, though, that borrowing from your 401(k) is complicated. And you may not borrow unlimited amounts. The rule?

Your loan, together with any outstanding loans, is limited to the lesser of: $50,000 or the greater of $10,000 or one-half of your vested 401(k) account balance. Moreover, the $50,000 limit is reduced by the excess, if any, of:

- The highest outstanding loan balance during the one-year period before the date of the new or extended loan, over

- The outstanding loan balance on the date you take out the loan.

An example should make this rule clearer. Say on January 1, 1991, the amount you have vested in your 401(k) comes to $100,000, and outstanding loans from your plan total $40,000. Eight months later, on September 1, you want to borrow more money. You've already paid back $15,000 of your loan, so your outstanding loan balance now totals $25,000.

Now you need another loan and want to know how much more you can borrow. The answer is $10,000—$50,000 less the current balance of your outstanding existing loan ($25,000), less the difference between the highest outstanding loan balance during the previous year ($40,000) and the outstanding balance of your existing loan ($25,000), or $15,000. What happens if you pay off the $40,000 balance by September 1? It makes no difference.

There's a simpler way to state the answer: According to the rules, you may borrow $10,000—$50,000 less the highest amount that was outstanding during the previous year ($40,000).

Uncle Sam attaches other conditions to borrowing from a 401(k). He says that you must repay the amount you borrowed within five years. There's an exception to this time period, though: Say you borrow money from your 401(k) and use it for a downpayment on a principal residence. If that's the case, you may take as long as your plan rules allow—usually 15, 20, 25, or 30 years, the terms of typical mortgages.

You must also repay your loan in equal payments; which you make at least quarterly over the loan's term. And you must pay "reasonable" interest on the loan—that is, it may not be too low or too high.

What about deducting the interest you pay on a 401(k) loan? The law says you may not deduct it, even if the law would otherwise allow the deduction—as mortgage interest, say. Here's the reason for this rule: Congress figured you should not be able to write off interest that you are, in effect, paying to yourself.

However, if you took out a loan from your 401(k) plan

before 1987, you're in luck. You may still deduct the interest
you pay under the regular interest rules. For example, you'd
classify interest on a loan you use to buy a bond as investment
interest (see Chapter 6).

If you borrowed money after 1986, you may not deduct a
penny. It doesn't matter how you use the money.

That's not all. When you begin withdrawing money from
your 401(k), the IRS taxes you on the amount of interest you
paid in. Uncle Sam treats it just like any other interest or dividends that accumulate.

☞ **CAUTION**   Say you leave a job and still have
a 401(k) loan outstanding. If your
plan requires repayment at the time you stop being an active
participant in the plan—which in fact most plans do—your
failure to repay the loan when you leave is a default. The
amount of any defaulted loan balance will be treated as a distribution at that time.

In that case, you'll pay taxes on the amount. And, what's
worse, you'll pay the 10 percent early-distribution penalty,
unless you fall under one of the exceptions to the rule; for
example, you're age 55.

19

What Else You Need to Know

What else do you need to know—tax-wise, at least—when it comes to your investments? In this chapter, we take a look—starting with investment clubs.

Investment clubs

You say you belong to an investment club? And you want to know how your club is treated for tax purposes? Let's take a look.

No matter how your club is organized, it's required to have its own employer identification number or EIN for short. What if your club doesn't have one?

Ask the IRS for Form SS-4, "Application for Employer Identification Number." Fill out the form and mail it to the IRS office where your club would file its tax return—in many cases, that's the same IRS office where you file your return.

If your club makes investments in its name, it must give its EIN to any payor of dividends or interest. If your club makes investments in the name of one of its members, it must provide payors with the Social Security number of that person.

Then that individual—as a "nominee" for the club—must file a Form 1099-DIV or 1099-INT listing the EIN of the club and showing that the dividends or interest belong to the club.

Most investment clubs are organized as partnerships and taxed as such. But a few are organized as trusts or corporations and are taxed accordingly.

If your club is organized as a partnership, Uncle Sam requires it to file a Form 1065, "U.S. Partnership Return of Income," each year. It also must provide you and every other member with a Schedule K-1 showing your share of the club's income or loss and deductions for the year.

You report these amounts on your Form 1040.

Here's something else you should know: Uncle Sam allows your unincorporated investment club to choose *not* to be treated as a partnership for tax purposes, but only as long as the club isn't used for the active conduct of a business.

If you elect not to be treated as a partnership, you and other members of the club report your share of income, deductions, and credits on your Form 1040. You deduct your investment expenses as miscellaneous itemized deductions—the same as if you'd paid them yourself.

Why would you want not to be treated as a partnership? Your club avoids a host of paperwork requirements, including the need to file an annual Form 1065.

How do you make this choice? Your club must file a Form 1065 for only its first year of operation by the due date, including extensions, of the return. Also, it must attach to this return a statement containing:

- the names, addresses, and identification numbers of all club members;

- a statement that the club is used solely for investment purposes and that the partnership has no income other than from its investments;

- information about where the terms of the agreement under which the club operates may be obtained (this agreement may be written or oral); and

- a statement that members have chosen unanimously for the club not to be treated as a partnership.

If you'd like more information on how partnerships are taxed, ask the IRS to send you a free copy of its Publication 541, *Tax Information on Partnerships*.

What if your club is a corporation? It must file a Form 1120, "U.S. Corporation Income Tax Return." All income, expenses, and gains or losses are reported by the corporation—not by you personally—although you report any distributions you receive.

For more information on how corporations are taxed, get a copy of IRS Publication 542, *Tax Information on Corporations*. It's free for the asking.

Now, what if your club is an association (that is, an unincorporated organization having certain corporate characteristics)? The IRS may tax the club as a corporation if its found to possess a majority of the following corporate-like characteristics: continuity of life, centralization of management, limited liability, and free transferability of interests.

In most cases, Uncle Sam doesn't classify as an association an investment club that's organized as a general partnership in which each partner has a say in investment decisions and which restricts the rights of a partner to transfer his or her ownership interest.

But watch out if your club is organized as a limited partnership or trust. The IRS may, on examination, deem your club an association.

If you'd like more information on how associations are taxed, ask the IRS for a free copy of its Publication 542, *Tax Information on Corporations*.

Hobby losses

Uncle Sam doesn't mind if you dabble in a little business just for the fun of it. But he doesn't want to help foot the bill if you're genuninely not interested in making a profit—hence, the rules governing hobby losses, or the rules affecting losses from what's known in tax jargon as "activities not engaged in for profit."

You may deduct your hobby expenses up to the amount of your hobby income, but no more. And you're not allowed to use losses from your hobby to slash your overall tax bill.

A number of activities—horse breeding, farming, antique collecting, and coin collecting, to name a few—may not show an annual profit. So the IRS developed two tests to determine if your business is profit-oriented or a hobby.

First, the IRS imposes an objective test. The law presumes that you're operating a for-profit business if you recognize a profit from your business in three out of the most recent five consecutive years. What if you post a loss for three consecutive years? The IRS may challenge your for-profit status.

Uncle Sam carves out an exception for horse breeding and racing. If the sport of kings is your passion, you need to make a profit in only two out of seven consecutive years.

Second, there's a subjective "facts-and-circumstances" test. Under it, the IRS weighs eight factors in determining whether you operate your business for profit. These factors—which apply to sole proprietorships, partnerships, and S corporations alike—are:

1. The manner in which you conduct your business. You should operate your business in a businesslike way. And that includes maintaining a complete set of books.

2. Your finances and other sources of income. If you're a high-bracket taxpayer and claim large losses, the IRS may suspect that you're engaged in an activity solely to capture tax write-offs, especially if the activity is of a recreational nature.

3. Your expertise. If you know little about the activity in which you're engaged and don't seek outside counsel, the IRS may question your profit motive.

4. The time you devote to the business. The more hours you spend on your business, the easier it is to establish your profit motive.

5. The expectation that assets used in your business will appreciate in value. Say you purchase a small apartment building. With interest and depreciation deductions, you report a loss for the year. But the property is appreciating at some 15 percent annually. So you expect to make a killing when you unload it. In this instance, you'd pass this test.

6. Your success in other similar activities. If you've made money in much the same kind of venture in the past, your business is more likely to be viewed as profit-making.

7. Your history of profits and losses. You're inviting trouble from Uncle Sam if you claim business losses year after year. Don't worry if your business is drowning in red ink during its initial phase. Such losses are expected. However, the IRS may question your profit motive if you continue to operate in the red long past the time when similar businesses have turned a profit. If your losses are due to circumstances beyond your control, such as drought, fire, theft, or depressed market conditions, however, your loses would not indicate that your business is not operated for profit.

8. The element of recreation involved. Beware if you devote your off-hours to the activity, and it's of a recreational nature such as fly-fishing.

Say, for example, that you're an attorney and own a large sailboat that you use four months out of the year. During the week and on holiday weekends you enjoy the boat with family and friends. On the remaining weekends, you lease your sailboat for chartered cruises.

You advertise your charter service in several local newspapers and magazines and fully expect to make a profit. You first started operating your sailboat charter service in 1988. Since that time, you've made a profit in two years and shown a loss in the other year.

You also anticipate a loss in 1992.

Under the law, you have to realize a profit in 1991 to meet the statutory test. If you're unable to show a profit in 1991, you must then demonstrate that the charter operation wasn't a hobby under the facts-and-circumstances test.

TIP Here's a way for some cash-basis taxpayers to turn red ink black. Simply delay paying bills from one tax year to the next.

☞ **CAUTION** Hobbyists beware. Uncle Sam restricts your deductions for a hobby to an amount less than your hobby income. How? Let's take a look. Uncle Sam allows you to take hobby deductions only in the following order and only to the following extent:

1. Amounts, such as real estate taxes or mortgage interest, that are deductible regardless of whether the activity qualifies as a hobby or was engaged in for profit.

2. Amounts that are deductible if the activity has been engaged in for profit, but only if the deduction doesn't result in an adjustment to the basis of property used in the activity. These amounts include utilities and maintenance. Such deductions are allowed only to the extent that the gross income of the activity exceeds the deductions under item 1.

3. Amounts, such as depreciation, that result in an adjustment to the basis of the property used in the activity are deductible only to the extent that income tops the deductions under items 1 and 2.

The deductions in items 2 and 3 are classified as miscellaneous itemized deductions. You claim miscellaneous itemized deductions only to the extent that their total exceeds 2 percent of your AGI.

So while you must include the full amount of your hobby earnings in your taxable income, your hobby write-offs offset this income only to the extent that your miscellaneous itemized deductions, when added together, top the 2 percent floor. (And, they may also be affected by the new overall limitation on certain itemized deductions. See Chapter 1 for details.)

What if your combined miscellaneous itemized deductions are less than 2 percent of your AGI? You get no tax deduction for your hobby expenses.

Related parties

Uncle Sam doesn't prohibit you from selling or exchanging property solely for the purpose of locking in a loss. But he won't allow you to claim this loss on your tax return if you sell the property to or exchange it with a related party.

Who's a related party? Anyone in your immediate family such as your spouse, grandparents, parents, brothers, sisters, or children. But your immediate family, in this case, doesn't include uncles, aunts, nieces, nephews, cousins, or dear friends of the family.

Related parties also include corporations, partnerships, certain trusts, in which you or other related parties own more than a 50 percent interest, and corporations that are members of the same "controlled group," to use the language of the IRS.

Don't let the term controlled group confuse you, though. A controlled group is simply a group of corporations that have the same owners. A controlled group may also be groups of corporations that are subsidiaries of the same parent company.

At-risk rules

One way to ease the pain of losing is to share your loss with Uncle Sam. Unfortunately, he caps the losses you may write off on your return with his at-risk rules.

Congress adopted the at-risk rules to prevent people from using inflated losses they piled up in one investment to offset profits they earned in another.

The at-risk rules apply to all investments financed by someone else—meaning those you purchased solely or partly with borrowed money. Under these rules, you may write off your losses only to the extent that they don't exceed your total at-risk investment.

How does Uncle Sam define your at-risk investment? It's the cash you've contributed plus any money you borrowed for the venture (but only those funds for which you're personally liable) plus your depreciated basis in any property or equipment you contributed.

Here's an example. Say you're an investor in a video store. You kick in $5,000 of your own money, plus $20,000 that you borrowed on a nonrecourse note, meaning one for which you're not personally liable. You also work every day in the store.

Are the losses you may claim from the store limited for tax purposes? The answer is yes. Under the at-risk rules, you may claim no more than $5,000 in losses on your return. That's because $5,000 is your total at-risk investment.

You'd be able to claim losses of up to $25,000—your $5,000 investment plus the $20,000 you borrowed—if you borrowed the money on a recourse note, meaning you were personally liable for it.

When it comes to calculating your profit or loss from a venture and the amount you have at risk, Uncle Sam provides a special form for this purpose. It's Form 6198, "At-Risk Limitations." (See Chapter 11 for the rules governing nonrecourse financing in real estate transactions.)

For more information on the at-risk rules, ask the IRS for a copy of its Publication 925, *Passive Activity and At-Risk Rules*. It's free for the asking.

Anything more you need to know?

We've discussed a mixed bag of tax topics in this chapter to generally round out the role of taxes in your investment picture. But, because no two individuals' investment objectives and tax situations are exactly alike, other topics could be relevant to you. Your best bet? Consult your tax adviser who can answer your questions with your particular investment needs and past and present tax history fresh in his or her mind.

20

Looking Ahead

Did you know that your Form 1040 can give you valuable clues to better tax and investment planning? By providing you with a road map to your recent financial past, your return can help point the way to a more prosperous future. How? Here's our line-by-line guide.

Line 7

Take a look at Line 7 where you record your salary. How, you ask, can you lower the amount that's subject to federal income tax?

You may want to consider contributing some of your salary to a 401(k) plan. That way, you may collect three benefits at once: You cut your current taxes, you save for retirement, and, in many cases, you pocket matching dollars from your employer.

The name 401(k) doesn't tell you much. It refers to the portion of the Internal Revenue Code that describes these attractive retirement plans.

The primary selling point of a 401(k) plan is that you contribute money on a pre-tax basis, and the earnings that accumulate grow tax deferred. That means your savings accumulate more rapidly than they would otherwise. How much faster? Let's take a look.

Say you've invested in two plans—one tax deferred and one not. With both plans, you invest in the same mutual fund each year for 20 years. The fund earns 10 percent a year, and you reinvest these earnings, less any taxes due, in the account. Your marginal tax rate is 31 percent.

In order to compare apples to apples, we'll say that you invest $8,475 from your salary (the maximum the law allowed for 1991 tax-deferred plans) in the taxable fund, minus the $2,627 you owe Uncle Sam in taxes, or $5,848 each year.

How much will you have at the end of 20 years? This taxable fund will have grown to more than $253,000. A hefty sum, you say.

But the tax-deferred fund is much larger—it comes to $368,000 after taxes—and here's why. You've been able to invest a full $8,475 each year, since money earmarked for your 401(k) isn't taxed currently, and you've not had to pay federal income tax on the earnings as they accumulated.

Another advantage to a 401(k) is that your employer may match your contribution to the plan; for example, it may put in 50 cents for every $1 you deposit. If your employer matches contributions, and you don't participate in the plan, you're really losing a valuable fringe benefit.

Here's something else you should know: Tax deferred doesn't mean tax free. You pay taxes, usually at retirement, on the money you withdraw from your 401(k).

But Uncle Sam allows you to reduce these taxes using five-year averaging. With this tax-saving strategy, you calculate the tax due on a lump-sum withdrawal as if you received the money evenly over five years instead of all at once.

Some people worry that tax rates may be higher when they

withdraw their money than rates are now, but they
needn't be overly concerned, at least as long as
five-year averaging remains law. Also, many people are in a
lower tax bracket after they retire—a fact that could offset
most tax rate increases.

Lines 8 and 9

You record your interest and dividend income on Lines 8
and 9. Now, take a look at these amounts. Did most of your
investment income come from a single source, such as stock
in the company that employs you? If so, you're losing the protection that diversification can provide.

When you diversify, you reduce risk. Essentially, there are
two ways to diversify. First, you can offset your risk by investing in a number of different areas such as cash equivalents,
fixed-income instruments, equities, and hard assets.

The second way to diversify is to spread out your holdings
in any one area. In other words, don't invest all the dollars
you've allocated for equity investments in a single stock. Buy
a number of stocks or invest in mutual funds, which give you
instant diversification.

Also, check the average dividend yield on your stocks. If
it's high—more than 6–8 percent, say—you probably own
mostly conservative stocks.

In this case, you may want to divert some of your assets to a
more aggressive investment—a growth fund, for example—if
you won't need to cash out for five years or more. Over the
long term, more aggressive investments should, in theory,
achieve higher returns.

One more question you should ask if you're in the 28-per-
cent or 31-percent tax bracket: Are you receiving any tax-exempt interest? If not, tax-free investments may make sense for

you, especially if you live in a high-tax state, such as Massachusetts or New York.

Say you live in New York State and are taxed at a rate of 8 percent. You're also in the 31 percent federal tax bracket and itemize your deductions. That means your combined tax rate—31 percent plus 8 percent—is 39 percent.

But wait a minute. Here's another wrinkle. Although your combined tax rate is 39 percent, you deduct state income taxes on your federal return. So your net federal and state marginal tax rate is 36.5 percent, not 39 percent. How did we get 36.5 percent?

Your net marginal rate is the sum of your federal tax bracket—in your case, 31 percent—plus your true, or "effective," state tax rate, meaning your state tax rate after you calculate the benefit of deducting your state tax on your federal return.

Here's how you figure your true state tax rate. Multiply your actual state tax rate (8 percent in your case) times the sum of one minus your federal rate of 31 percent (0.69). The result—5.5 percent—is your true state tax rate.

So a New York State municipal bond that pays 7 percent is the equivalent of an 11 percent taxable yield. Here's how we arrived at that figure. Divide the yield on the bond, 7 percent, by 0.635—that is, 1 minus 0.365, your federal and state marginal tax rate.

What if you want to defer interest income until next year? One strategy to consider is to buy a certificate of deposit or Treasury bill that matures next year. Unless you receive interest during the current year, Uncle Sam will tax your earnings when you receive them, that is when the CD becomes due.

But this strategy applies only to short-term certificates with a maturity of one year or less. That's because the law requires you to pay taxes on interest from long-term CDs in the year the interest is earned, rather than in the year it's paid.

Line 13

You report your net capital gains or losses, which you determined by using Schedule D, on Line 13 of your Form 1040. Use this figure to calculate your return on your investments. Then compare the returns you received against the Standard & Poor's 500 index.

Also, examine the volume of trades and holding periods detailed on your Schedule D. If you've made frequent trades, you may want to consider holding securities for a longer period. Many savvy investors invest for longer-term performance.

Line 18

You determined your net income (or loss) from rents, royalties, partnerships, estates, and trusts on Schedule E, then reported this amount on Line 18 of your Form 1040.

In the old days, it made sense to invest with heavy emphasis on tax considerations, but no more—thanks to changes in the tax law. Now, it's smart to invest primarily on economic merits. In other words, you should steer clear of investments that make tax sense only.

But what if you still own investments that generate tax losses each year? You may want to consider investments that generate passive income to offset these losses. But, again, make sure the investment is economically sound before you hand over your money.

This year, reducing your AGI becomes increasingly important, thanks to the 1990 tax act. Why? Although the maximum tax rate is 31 percent, your *effective* marginal tax rate may be more because of the impact of the new phase-out of personal exemptions and the new 3 percent floor on itemized deductions. You calculate both the exemption phase-out and the floor on deductions based on your AGI. That means if you reduce your AGI, you can reduce the impact these new items might have on your tax bill. (See Chapter 1 for details.)

Line 34

Check out your deductions, summarized on Line 34 and detailed on Schedule A. Are you paying interest that's no longer fully deductible or that's at a very high rate?

Starting in 1991, Uncle Sam no longer subsidizes your interest payments on your automobile or sound system—on any consumer loans, for that matter.

So you may want to restructure your debt. One tack to take is to tap the equity in your home by applying for a home-equity loan.

The interest on a home-equity loan is 100 percent deductible, as long as the debt doesn't top the lesser of $100,000 ($50,000 if you're married and file separate returns) or the fair market value of your home minus the total acquisition debt.

What's acquisition debt? It's a loan that's secured by your primary or second home and is incurred when you buy, build, or substantially improve your home.

Here's something else to think about.

Uncle Sam allows you to write off miscellaneous itemized deductions only to the extent that they exceed two percent of your adjusted gross income (AGI).

In order to get at least a partial write-off under the rules, you should attempt to bunch as many of these expenses as possible into a single year.

Toward the end of the year, take a hard look at your bills in these miscellaneous categories. If you see that by paying for, say, a continuing education course you took this year, you'll exceed the 2-percent floor, go ahead and write the check by December 31.

But if your calculations show that you'll fall below the floor, wait until January before paying these bills. You may beat the floor next year.

Similarly, your medical expenses must top 7.5 percent of your AGI before you may deduct any of them. So, if these expenses are already high, our advice is to pay as many of them as you can this year in order to exceed the deductibility floor.

Line 48

Do you show an entry on Line 48 for the alternative minimum tax (AMT)? If so, you might consider new tax-planning strategies to avoid the AMT in the future: Note that you may be able to save regular taxes this year as a result of paying AMT last year. How?

In most cases, you get the minimum tax credit, which, in effect, gives you credit for taxes that you prepaid under the AMT system in prior years. (For the details, see Chapter 8.)

If you know you're going to be subject to the AMT again this year, it's not the end of the world, but there are some strategies you should consider.

For example, you may want to accelerate income. It's better to pay tax on that income at the AMT rate of 24 percent than risk paying tax at a higher rate the following year. You may also want to defer deductions to the following year, when they may yield a higher tax benefit.

At a minimum, you should try to defer those expenses, such as state and local income and property taxes, that aren't deductible at all for AMT purposes. Because of the complexities of the AMT, it's always wise to check with your tax adviser before you adopt any game plan.

Line 62

Some people don't know it, but the idea of tax planning isn't to get a big tax refund from Uncle Sam. You want to keep money in your own pocket—not his—for as long as possible. Then you can invest the cash or use it for purchases.

If you've recorded an overpayment on Line 62, that means you've made an interest-free loan to the government. In the future, you want to make sure you pay your taxes no sooner than is legally required, so that you, instead of the government, can earn that interest.

If you're a salaried employee, make sure when you fill out your W-4 or W-4A form that you take all the exemptions to which you're entitled. You should know that the IRS will scrutinize your form W-4 if you take more than ten exemptions. But if you're entitled to them, go ahead and take them.

If you work for yourself, or have substantial income beyond your wages and salaries, plan your estimated taxes. But pay no more than is required.

What if you underpay your estimated taxes? You pay a penalty on the amount your underpayments fall short. The amount of the penalty varies; it rises or falls with current interest rates. As of the third quarter of 1991, it's 10 percent.

You can't deduct the amount you pay in penalties, and that's all the more reason to plan ahead. You can avoid the underpayment penalty for 1991, though, if your equal quarterly payments, along with your withholding, total 100 percent of your 1990 tax liability or 90 percent of the current year's tax liability that will be shown on your 1991 return.

If, as year-end approaches, you realize you've underpaid your tax, increase your payroll withholding to make up the shortfall. Simply file a new W-4, claim fewer allowances, and/or request that additional amounts be withheld.

Index

Thinking About Taxes?

Think about Price Waterhouse. Whatever the level of complexity, Price Waterhouse has very likely dealt with the issues and questions you're facing. Our tax professionals will help you and your company succeed in today's increasingly competitive environment by helping you save taxes and add to your bottom line.

So whether you're in California, New York or somewhere in between, Price Waterhouse is ready to help. If you're thinking about taxes, think about us. Price Waterhouse.

Please consult the following pages for the Price Waterhouse office nearest you.

If you would like more information on personal tax planning or retirement planning, look for our other publications—**The Price Waterhouse Personal Tax Adviser** and **The Price Waterhouse Retirement Planning Adviser.**

Price Waterhouse

Price Waterhouse Offices in the United States

National, New York
(212) 819-5000
Washington National
Tax Services,
Washington, D.C.
(202) 296-0800

Alaska
Anchorage
(907) 563-4444

Arizona
Phoenix
(602) 274-0550

California
Century City
(213) 553-6030
Long Beach
(213) 491-0440
Los Angeles
(213) 236-3000
Oakland
(415) 465-1000
Orange County
(714) 435-8600
Palo Alto
(415) 853-8380
Riverside
(714) 684-9411
Sacramento
(916) 441-2370
San Jose
(408) 282-1200
San Francisco
(415) 393-8500
San Diego
(619) 231-1200
Santa Monica
(213) 396-3844
Woodland Hills
(818) 704-1117

Colorado
Denver
(303) 893-8100

Connecticut
Glastonbury
(203) 657-7300
Hartford
(203) 240-2000
Stamford
(203) 358-0001

Delaware
Wilmington
(302) 656-5300

District of Columbia
Washington
(202) 833-7932

Florida
Fort Lauderdale
(305) 463-6280
Jacksonville
(904) 355-6500
Miami
(305) 381-9400
Orlando
(407) 236-0550
St. Petersburg
(813) 821-8694
Tampa
(813) 223-7577
West Palm Beach
(407) 820-0800

Georgia
Atlanta
(404) 933-9191
Atlanta Galleria
(404) 980-2900
Savannah
(912) 232-0123

Hawaii
Honolulu
(808) 521-0391

Illinois
Chicago
(312) 565-1500

Chicago
Tax Technology Group
(312) 419-1565
Oak Brook
(708) 571-7250
Peoria
(309) 676-8945

Indiana
Indianapolis
(317) 632-8361
South Bend
(219) 233-8261

Kentucky
Florence
(606) 283-1901
Lexington
(606) 224-3337

Louisiana
New Orleans
(504) 529-2000

Maryland
Baltimore
(301) 685-0542
Bethesda
(301) 365-7963
Columbia
(301) 992-6700

Massachusetts
Boston
(617) 439-4390
Cambridge
(617) 439-4390

Michigan
Battle Creek
(616) 965-1351
Detroit
(313) 259-0500
Troy
(313) 259-0500

Minnesota
Minneapolis
(612) 332-7000

Missouri
Kansas City
(816) 474-6590
St. Louis
(314) 425-0500

New Jersey
Hackensack
(201) 646-1550
Morristown
(201) 540-8980
Princeton
(609) 987-9444

New York
Buffalo
(716) 856-4650
Long Island
(516) 681-7114
New York
(212) 371-2000
New York
International
Assignment Tax
Services
(212) 944-9750
Rochester
(716) 232-4000
Syracuse
(315) 474-6571

North Carolina
Charlotte
(704) 372-9020
Durham
(919) 286-9423
Raleigh
(919) 878-5700
Winston-Salem
(919) 725-0691

Ohio
Beachwood (Cleveland
East)
(216) 781-3700

Cincinnati
(513) 621-1900
Cleveland
(216) 781-3700
Columbus
(614) 221-8500
Dayton
(513) 222-2100
Dublin
(614) 764-9555
Toledo
(419) 247-1800

Oklahoma
Oklahoma City
(405) 272-9251

Oregon
Portland
(503) 224-9040

Pennsylvania
Philadelphia
(215) 665-9500
Pittsburgh
(412) 355-6000

Puerto Rico
San Juan
(809) 754-9090

Rhode Island
Providence
(401) 421-0501

South Carolina
Columbia
(803) 779-0930

Tennessee
Johnson City
(615) 929-9121
Memphis
(901) 523-8000
Nashville
(615) 292-5000

Texas
Arlington
(817) 649-1866
Austin
(512) 476-6700
Dallas
(214) 922-8040
Dallas (North)
(214) 386-9922
Fort Worth
(817) 870-5500
Houston
(713) 654-4100
San Antonio
(512) 226-7700

Utah
Salt Lake
(801) 328-2300

Vermont
South Burlington
(802) 864-0671

Virginia
Falls Church
(703) 538-7982
Hampton Roads
(Norfolk)
(804) 622-5005
Richmond
(804) 648-9281

Washington
Bellevue
(206) 462-6550
Seattle
(206) 622-1505

Wisconsin
Milwaukee
(414) 276-9500